Expressing the Heart's Intent

SUNY series in Chinese Philosophy and Culture

Roger T. Ames, editor

Expressing the Heart's Intent

Explorations in Chinese Aesthetics

Marthe Atwater Chandler

SUNY
PRESS

Published by State University of New York Press, Albany

Printed in the United States of America

For information, contact State University of New York Press, Albany, NY
www.sunypress.edu

Production, Eileen Nizer
Marketing, Kate R. Seburyamo

Library of Congress Cataloging-in-Publication Data

Names: Chandler, Marthe, 1941– author.
Title: Expressing the heart's intent : explorations in Chinese aesthetics / Marthe Atwater Chandler.
Description: Albany, NY : State University of New York, 2017. | Series: SUNY series in Chinese philosophy and culture | Includes bibliographical references and index.
Identifiers: LCCN 2016048645 (print) | LCCN 2017032730 (ebook) | ISBN 9781438466590 (ebook) | ISBN 9781438466576 (hardcover : alk. paper) | ISBN 9781438466583 (pbk. : alk. paper)
Subjects: LCSH: Aesthetics, Chinese.
Classification: LCC BH221.C6 (ebook) | LCC BH221.C6 C43128 2017 (print) | DDC 111/.850951—dc23
LC record available at https://lccn.loc.gov/2016048645

10 9 8 7 6 5 4 3 2 1

For Ted

Contents

Illustrations

Acknowledgments

The chapters in this book began as papers presented at the Asian Studies Development Program, the Society for Asian and Comparative Philosophy and the Indiana Philosophical Society. I am grateful for the insightful comments and helpful suggestions from all of my colleagues at those meetings. I am particularly thankful for the advice and encouragement of Faye Beauchamp, Roberta Adams, Howard Giskin, Harriette Grissom, and Mary Bockover. Discussions with Larry Butler in museums in the United States and China have taught me an immense amount about the responsibility of a museum to inform it audience about where its objects were found.

I own incalculable debts to the people who began as my teachers and mentors and became my friends—Henry Rosemont, Jr., Roger Ames and Robert Eno. Henry Rosemont was particularly helpful in reading many drafts, making insightful suggestions, and generally serving as my "Jiminy Cricket."

I have been particularly fortunate to have worked at DePauw University, an institution that values and supports teacher-scholars. My colleagues Martha Rainbolt and Catherine Fruhan read drafts of several chapters and provided invaluable comments. I received very generous financial support from DePauw University's Faculty Development Program thanks to Neal Abraham, Terri Bonebright, Lili Wright, and Terry Bruner. My colleagues Hiroko Chiba and Jinyu Liu have provided translations and advice to smooth my dealings with museums in Japan and China. Brook Cox has been invaluable in helping me navigate the world of digital images, permissions, and copyrights. Lyn Gram has been an unendingly patient and conscientious proofreader and technical advisor.

Last, but not least, I cannot thank my husband, Ted Jelen, enough for listening to me for hours, reading drafts, making kind but pointed comments, putting up with a writing style very different from his own, and leaving me alone for hours at my computer.

Notes on Transcriptions

The modern pinyin system of transcription will be generally used in this book. However, a number of texts use the older Wade-Giles system. In quotations using Wade-Giles the pinyin will be provided in brackets. In a few cases the Wade-Giles transcription will be provided in brackets in order to avoid confusion.

1

Introduction

Expressing the Heart's Intent

"Poetry expresses the heart's intent" (*shi yan zhi* 詩言志) was the earliest definition of poetry in China, and the belief that *zhi* 志—the heart's intent, wishes, desires, ambitions, and emotions—was expressed in poetry and music, and later in calligraphy and painting, became the foundation of Chinese aesthetics. In over two thousand years of history, however, the meaning of "*zhi*" changed. "*Shi yan zhi*" began as a description of a shamanistic religious experience and evolved into a complex and nuanced notion of the creative use of reason and imagination. This book examines several stages in that development.

Considering the roles played by *zhi* in Chinese aesthetic theory will emphasize and help explain the ways the Chinese and Western intellectual traditions tend to conceive of the relationship between art, religion, politics, and morality in very different ways. The difference is intimately connected to assumptions about the nature of reason and order, assumptions we will consider in more detail in the next chapter. Hall and Ames have argued that order can be conceived of as logical or aesthetic.[1] Logical or rational order moves away from unique particulars to find the general form of the relations holding between them. The Western intellectual tradition often assumes that the task of any serious endeavor—philosophy, theology, science—is to find the logical order of the cosmos: in the physical universe, in Plato's Heaven, or in the Mind of God. A logical order is typically quite abstract and may be highly mathematical. The scientific ideal of the "GUT," the Grand Unified Theory of Everything, is one such order. The Grand Unified Theory is, or we hope will be when we discover it, a series of complex but elegant equations describing the laws holding between the fundamental forces and objects that make up the universe. Given the success of science in finding (or imposing) logical order in the world, Western philosophy has often considered science its closest ally, leading Willard Van Orman Quine to famously, or infamously, remark that "philosophy of science is philosophy enough."[2]

In most logical orders, pairs of opposites are generally conceived as a strict dualism; that is, as mutually exclusive categories that cannot overlap: for example appearance and reality, mind and body, objective and subjective, free and determined. This way of conceiving opposites has the benefit of clarity and precision, but faces often insurmountable difficulties when called upon to account for the relationship between the two categories.[3]

Hall and Ames claim that Chinese philosophy conceives of order as aesthetic, in which novelty is constantly being created and each particular makes its own unique contribution to the whole. In an aesthetic order, pairs of opposites are usually thought of as two ends of a continuum which may merge as *yin* becomes *yang*, and day becomes night; or may be balanced in a mutually interdependent and sustaining (but not static) harmony as in well-functioning ecology where human flourishing depends on the health of the natural environment; or the complementary and mutually supportive relationships between members of a family.[4] Hall and Ames write:

> Aesthetic order begins with the uniqueness of one thing and assesses this particular as contributing to the balanced complexity of its context. Because the aesthetic order celebrates the disclosure of the insistent particularity of each detail in tension with the consequent unity of these specific details, plurality must be conceived as prior to unity and disjunction to conjunction. The focus of an aesthetic order is the way in which a concrete, specific detail discloses itself as producing a harmony expressed by a complex of such details in relationship to one another.[5]

For these reasons aesthetics came to play a role in Chinese philosophy analogous to that played by science in Western philosophy. One of the projects of this book is to explore the implications of a tradition motivated to "express the heart's intent" rather than to "search for the truth" and in so doing to understand the claim that Chinese philosophy is "aesthetic."

Classical Understandings of *shi yan zhi*

The Canon of Shun

The phrase *shi yan zhi* first appears in an early section of the *Book of Documents* (*Shujing* 書經) in the section known as the *Canon of Shun*.[6] In this text the sage King Shun instructs Kui, his music master:

> I bid you Kui, the emperor said, to preside over music and educate our sons, [so that they will be] straightforward yet gentle, congenial yet dignified, strong but not ruthless, simple but not arrogant. Poetry expresses the heart's intent (*zhi*); singing prolongs the utterance of that expression. The notes accord with the prolonged utterance, and are harmonized by the pitch tubes. The eight kinds of musical instruments attain to harmony and do not interfere with one another. Spirits and man are brought into harmony.
>
> Oh! Yes, replied Kui. I will strike and tap the stones and a hundred beasts will follow one another to dance.[7]

At first glance, *shi yan zhi* seems to echo the familiar (modern Western) Expressive Theory that art expresses the personal feelings or emotions of the artist. The Expressive Theory, however, relies on certain epistemological assumptions about individualism, in particular that philosophical understanding must begin by considering self-reliant individuals (thinkers, artists, citizens) isolated from their social context.[8] In conjunction with the assumption of strict dualism that pairs of opposites cannot overlap, Western thought often contrasts what is inner, mental, and subjective, with what is outer and objective. Our inner lives are made up of a complex structure of thoughts, feelings, concepts, beliefs, and desires. The outer world is the objective world of physical objects which are, somehow, connected to the inner realm by language.[9] In straightforward factual communication, there is generally a publically accessible "fact of the matter," objectively "out there" which can be stated more or less correctly. Feelings and emotions, on the other hand, are deeply personal and individual. They may be very important to the person experiencing them, but they can be very difficult to communicate, often requiring the language of poetry and art. If "truth" is a property of factual, objective statements, then, if art expresses any "truth" at all, it does so in a very limited and derivative way.[10] Platonists and other lovers of reason are therefore deeply suspicious of works of art which express something ultimately unverifiable about their creator's inner life. Views like this account for the trivialization of aesthetics in much of Western philosophy—in which truth, the objective truths of science and mathematics, are models of the highest kind of human thought.

Not only are there a number of difficulties of the Expressive Theory on its own, it is a very poor candidate for understanding *shi yan zhi*. If poetry simply expresses the poet's inner, personal feelings, it is hard to see how it could it be as important as Shun, and later Confucius, took it to be in the education of the leaders of China.

> The Master said, 'My young friends, why don't any of you study the *Songs*? Reciting the *Songs* can arouse your sensibilities, strengthen your powers of observation, enhance your ability to get on with others, and sharpen your critical skills. Close at hand it enables you to serve your father, and away at court it enables you to serve your lord. It instills in your broad vocabulary for making distinctions in the world around you.' (*Analects* 17.9)[11]

Although in early classical texts *zhi* (志) and *qing* (情) emotions, feelings, were often identified,[12] *shi yan zhi* is also translated as "Poetry is product of earnest thought,"[13] and as "Poetry articulates what is on the mind intently."[14] These translations have been criticized for being too "rationalistic" [15] but they reflect the meaning of *xin* (心), a radical appearing in *zhi* (志) as both the "heart" which feels and the "mind" which thinks. In theories that assume a sharp distinction between thought, which involves reason, and emotions which do not, it is impossible for one thing, *zhi*, to be both a thought and a feeling.

Translations of *zhi* as "intention," or "will" have also been criticized because of the associations these terms have in Western philosophical literature with "free will." Owen notes, however, that if "heart's intent" is taken in the sense of an intense preoccupation, it may be an appropriate translation of *zhi*.[16] Nevertheless, it is important to remember that *zhi* always has both an inner aspect and an outer object which makes translating it as "ambition" often the most appropriate choice. Thus Confucius claimed,

> From fifteen, my heart-and-mind was set upon (*zhi*) learning; from thirty I took my stance; from forty I was no longer doubtful; from fifty I realized the propensities of *tian* (*tianming*

> 天命) from sixty my ear was attuned; from seventy I could give my heart-and-mind free rein without overstepping the boundaries. (*Analects* 2.4)

And Mencius:

> When [a great man] achieves his ambition (*zhi*) he shares with the people; when he fails to do so, he practices the Way alone.[17]

A further difficulty in interpreting *shi yan zhi* involves the question of whose intentions are being expressed: those of the author?[18] of the poem itself? of the person quoting the poem to make a diplomatic point at court? of the community at large? The contemporary Chinese philosopher Li Zehou argues that originally it was the latter; in the earliest texts *zhi* referred to the historical, moral, and philosophical principles of the community, principles which grew out of the primitive religious ceremonies of early humans.[19]

Kui's reply to Shun, "Oh! Yes . . . I will strike and tap the stones and a hundred beasts will follow one another to dance," supports Li's position. Although Kui might believe that his music will entice actual animals to dance, his remark probably refers to ancient, Neolithic totem dances in which dancers, shamans, wore animal headdresses and tails like those depicted in Neolithic pottery.[20]

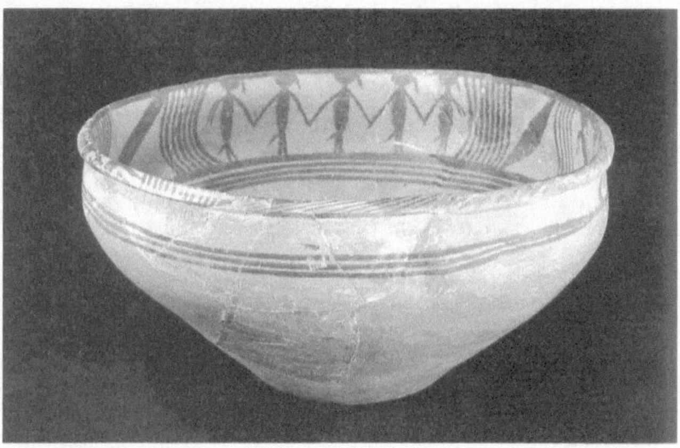

FIGURE I.1. Pottery bowl found in 1972 in Qinghai Province at the site of the Majiayao Neolithic culture. In the collection of the National Museum of China.

Dancing, accompanied by chanting or singing was one of the earliest social activities of primitive humans, a practice that probably predates the appearance of *Homo sapiens*. Our close nonhuman relatives, gorillas and chimpanzees, engage in ritualized rhythmic movements, shifting their weight from foot to foot, waving leaves and branches, and crying out and shouting, or hooting, in excitement.[21]

Shamanistic dances evolved into ecstatic ceremonies with elaborate costumes, ritual objects, drums, flutes, and magical invocations of mysterious spiritual powers and gods. Pre-linguistic humans used these dances to create intense feelings of unity, compassion, and respect leading to the community solidarity and morality necessary for the survival of truly human societies. A community engaging in repeated ritualized movement creates a sense of group identity, in which individual consciousness is merged into a larger group consciousness. One feels part of something almost infinite, controlled by forces and standards outside of oneself.[22] In the dancing and music of these essentially religious ceremonies "spirits and man are brought into harmony."

When the Zhou Dynasty replaced the intensely religious Shang Dynasty, shamanistic dances became formalized into the rituals (*li* 禮) of the Zhou court. Perhaps in part because of Zhou suspicion of the overwhelming feelings roused by shamanistic dances, the focus of importance shifted away from dancing to music, song, and poetry. Moreover, as the remarks by Confucius and Mencius quoted earlier indicate, the early religious concern for harmony with spirits changed to a more secular interest in social and political harmony; but this was only a change in emphasis. In addition to its close association with emotions (*qing* 情), originally the emotions associated with religious ecstasy, *zhi* almost always contains a didactic element intimately connected with political affairs and moral education.

Reformulation in the "Great Preface"

Around the first century CE, several hundred years after the *Canon of Shun* was written,[23] the "Great Preface" to the *Book of Poetry* (*Shijing*) reformulated the definition of poetry.

> Poetry is where the heart's intent goes.[24] What is still in the heart is 'intent'; what is expressed in words is 'poetry.' Emotions (*qing* 情) are stirred inside and manifest themselves in words.

> Emotions move within and take form in words. If words cannot express them adequately, we sigh them out. If sighing is not adequate, we sing them out. If singing is not adequate, we unconsciously move our hands to gesticulate, and stamp our feet to dance.
>
> Emotions are discharged in sounds. As those sounds assume a pattern, they are called 'tones.' The tones of a well governed state are peaceful and joyful; the governance is marked by harmony. The tones of a time of chaos are woeful and filled with anger; the governance is deviate. The tones of a failed state are sorrowful and contemplative; the people are in dire straits.[25]

The "Great Preface" elaborates the process suggested in the *Canon of Shun* by describing poetry as moving between inner and outer. People are born with a pre-linguistic human nature (*xing* 性) which is in a state of "equilibrium and silence" but which possesses certain dispositions.[26] Mencius's theory of the four sprouts describes our innate, inborn dispositions to respond to circumstances in certain ways. The "sprouts" are not full-blown traits (or virtues), but can develop into virtues (benevolence, humanity, *ren* 仁; righteousness, *yi* 義; propriety, *li* 禮; and wisdom, *zhi* 智) only if they are nourished by proper education and favorable circumstances.[27] External objects or situations rouse our emotions, *qing*, which the heart-mind transforms into intent, *zhi*. Taking a linguistic form *zhi* moves outward in the form of poetry. The distinction between "inner" and "outer" is so fluid, however, that Owen argues that there is "one thing": when it is "in" our hearts it is *zhi*; when it is outside it is a poem.[28]

The classical Platonic epistemological metaphor for the relationship between the inner and outer is visual—external objects are mirrored or otherwise represented, by inner, mental forms, concepts, or images. The fundamental Chinese epistemological metaphor is often hearing rather than sight. Like the wind, sound travels invisibly over great distances, passing through barriers impenetrable to sight and causing similarly tuned instruments to resonate with each other across great distances. Relying on the metaphors of sound, waves, wind, and water, a Tang dynasty commentator describes the relationship between *xing* (original human nature) and *qing* (emotions): "*Xing* is to *qing* as a wave is to water. When it's calm it's water, and when it's active, it's waves. Likewise, when it is calm it is *xing*, and when it's active, it's *qing*."[29] A related metaphor, making a political rather than an epistemological point, is found in *Analects* 12.19:

"The excellence (*de* 德) of the exemplary person (*junzi* 君子) is the wind, while that of the petty person is the grass. As the wind blows, the grass is sure to bend."

In both the *Canon of Shun* and the "Great Preface" expressing *zhi* is relatively involuntary. Poetry, music, and dance are natural results of the interaction between human nature (*xing*) and the world. In the *Canon of Shun* the human response is ultimately religious, a shamanistic dance bringing humanity and spirits into harmony. In the "Great Preface" music, which includes poetry and song, has replaced dance as the most important response. Moreover the response has become more secular. The *zhi* of poetry was to produce, or reflect, the political harmony, or lack thereof, present in a particular society. The "Great Preface" emphasizes the Confucian belief that poetry should always be didactic. In the highly political and moralizing Confucian interpretations of the poems in the *Book of Songs* (and events presented in the *Spring and Autumn Annals*) the role of imagination and individual creativity in art seems to be seriously undervalued.

When the Han Dynasty collapsed under pressure from invading nomadic tribes, the Confucian world order began to disintegrate. In the political division and unrest of the Wei-Jin era (220–420 CE) Confucian certainties lost their power as intellectuals turned to the abstract metaphysical speculations of *xuanxue* or Neo-Daoism[30] which focused on individual feelings, thoughts and characters rather than the external realms of religion and politics. As a reflection of this shift, in the Wei-Jin period "poetry originates in emotion" (*shi yuan qing* 詩緣情) was provided as an explanation of "poetry expresses the heart's intent" with "*shi yan zhi*" and "*shi yuan qing*" interpreted as referring to individual aspirations and emotions.[31] Furthermore, by the Wei-Jin era Buddhism had begun to shape Chinese thought, giving it, among other things, a complex psychology and philosophy of mind which contributed to the change in the interpretation of "*shi yan zhi.*" At the same time, as we will see in chapter 3, the growing power of Buddhist monasteries had a profound effect on Chinese economic and political arrangements, while Buddhist sculpture transformed the Chinese tradition.

Six Dynasty Literary Theory: The *Wenxin Diaolong* of Liu Xie

Liu Xie's fifth-century text *Wénxīn Diāolóng* (*The Literary Mind and the Carving of Dragons*) is a comprehensive theory of the origin, nature, function, and epistemology of literature. Liu explained that "[by] literary mind, I mean the mental exertion in writing," and that "[to] carve dragons . . . means to treat the art of writing as a matter of greatest seriousness and to cultivate it meticulously."[32] Liu accepted the *shī yán zhì* tradition that the purpose of literature/poetry was to harmonize, but rejected the strong didactic emphasis of the earlier tradition. Moving away from the classical concerns with religious harmony between humanity and spirits, and political harmony between various parts of society, Liu concentrated on the harmony between creative individuals and the cosmic patterns of the universe or Dao.[33]

Like the "Great Preface," Liu's *Wénxīn Diāolóng* assumes that music, poetry, and song are more significant than dance. However, while the "Great Preface" discusses the sound of poetry and music, Liu explores the role of the visual patterns of writing in achieving harmony between literature, poetry, and the patterns of nature, the Dao.[34]

> It can be inferred that all forms of existence have patterns . . . [T]he sounds produced on the apertures in forest trees resemble music from pipes and lutes; spring water falling on rocks sounds like melodies from jade chimes and bronze bells. Thus with the making of forms, patterns appear; with the making of sounds, writings emerge.[35]

The *Wénxīn Diāolóng* begins with the cosmological claim that *wen* was born from the primeval *taiji* (太極) at the same time as Heaven and Earth.

> Great is the virtue (*de* 德) of patterns (*wen* 文)! It is born together with Heaven and Earth. And how is this? When the blue color parted from the yellow, and the round shape from the square, heaven and earth came into being. Like two interfolding jade mirrors, the sun and the moon reflect the images of heaven, while streams and mountains are interwoven into earthly patterns like gorgeous damask. They are manifestations of Dao. When earthly patterns and heavenly images take shape, inferior and superior places are established, and two primal powers of heaven and earth are born. Yet only when humans join in does the Great Triad form. Endowed with the divine spark of consciousness (*xingling* 性靈), humans are the essence

> of the five elements, the mind of heaven and earth. When mind is born, speech appears. When speech appears, writing comes forth. This is the way of Dao.[36]

Liu understands *wen* quite broadly. It displays/reveals/manifests the cosmic order, appearing in the patterns of the heavens (the sun and the moon), of the earth (mountains and rivers), the brilliant scales of a dragon, the magnificent stripes of the tiger, and the literature of humanity.[37]

Rather than asserting a correlation between human language (*wenren*) and the patterns of heaven and earth, Liu makes the stronger claim that the natural patterns of heaven and earth are only complete when there is something to recognize, know, and understand them. Thus, humans as "the mind of heaven and earth" must be part of the great Triad: Heaven, Earth, and Humanity.[38] "Mind gave birth to speech/language (*yan* 言); when speech appeared, language/writing developed to make the patterns of heaven and earth clear and intelligible."[39]

To make it clear that literature is an essential part of the natural order, not just something humans have "added on" to the cosmos, Liu describes the origin of writing in the markings on the backs of dragons and turtles. These markings were "natural manifestations of the Dao" which the sages clarified to provide moral guidance.[40] Writing became increasingly important when King Shun "composed a song to express his heart felt feelings (*zhì*)."[41] The tradition continued until Confucius

> . . . followed in the steps of earlier sages but outshone them all. By revising and editing the six classics, he brought together the best works up to his time. In the cultivation of human nature and the skillful use of language, his teachings reverberated a thousand *li* like the sound of the wooden bell-clapper. . . . By transmitting the glory of heaven and earth, they opened up the horizons of the people.[42]

Liu continues to praise the *shī yán zhì* tradition, until his critical history of literature comes to the *Songs of the South* (*Chuci* 楚辭). The imaginative flights of fantasy and eroticism in the *Chuci* provoke his disapproval. He complains that it contains

> absurd descriptions such as the dragon-seeds, the cloud-embroidered banners . . . chimerical fantasies, such as the collapse of

> the earth when Kang Hui was enraged, the shooting of the suns by Yi the Archer, the nine-headed monster that pulled up nine thousand trees, and the three-eyed earth god. . . . Licentiousness, as shown in the lines: 'Men and women now sit together, mingling freely without distinction; / Day and night are spent in merry-making and wine.'[43]

Liu is convinced that the *Chuci* began a decline in literature, ushering in an era when literary elaboration, "lavish and inflated descriptions,"[44] expressions of emotional intensity, excess, and sensuous beauty began to overshadow the purity, honesty, and sincerity of the *zhì* of the ancient classics.[45] Nevertheless, Liu insists that "the *Songs of the South* surpasses past and contemporary works in spirit or excellence of language. Its brilliance and exquisite beauty are unsurmountable."[46] Liu praises Qu Yuan, the author of many of the *Chuci*, for his *zhi*; but while, as I have noted, *zhi* usually has a political/moral aspect, Liu's text is lyrical rather than moralistic.

> His startling genius sweeps like the wind,
> His lofty aspirations (*zhì* 志) soar like the clouds.
> Mountains and rivers are endless,
> Feeling and thought are infinite.
> Gold in texture, pure in form,
> His poems exude beauty in every part.[47]

The *Wénxīn Diāolóng* is clearly not consistently critical of deviations from the didactic *zhì* of the classical tradition. Rather than forcing the extravagant and often erotic passages of the *Chuci* into a moralistic straight jacket, the way classical interpretations dealt with similarly troubling poems in the *Shijing* (*Classic of Poetry* or *Book of Songs* 詩經), Liu is delighted with poets who followed the *Chuci* model for their "exuberance and freedom in conjuring new reams of experience."[48]

Liu is generally more concerned with literature as the result of a private, contemplative, and creative process[49] than as part of a public religious or political performance, and the most famous chapter of the *Wenxin Dialong*, chapter 26, *Shensi* (神思), is a psychological study of the role of imagination in literature. *Shensi* is often translated as "Imagination," but it is also translated as "Spirit Thought,"[50] or following A. C. Graham, "Daimonic Thinking."[51] While *shen* (神) originally meant "heavenly spirits," it came to mean also the human spirit, an active and wise force, mysterious beyond reason, concepts, or words. In Liu's work both "*shen*" and "*si*" in *Shensi* are polysemantic. *Shen* retains its meaning as a marvelous, unfathomable, mysterious power, but it is also an ability all humans have to see things with the mind's eye that are not there. Imagining and remembering are normal activities for every one's heart-mind. S*i* (思) can mean thought or reflection:

> The Master said: 'Learning without reflection (思) leads to perplexity, reflection (思) without learning leads to perilous circumstances.' (*Analects* 2.15)

It can also mean "remember with longing" or "think about things that are not present to us now."[52]

The chapter begins with a reference to Zhuangzi and a definition of *Shensi*:

> Long ago someone spoke of 'the physical form's being by the rivers and lakes but the mind's remaining at the foot of the palace towers of Wei.' This is what is meant by spirit thought (*shensi* 神思). And spirit goes far indeed in the thought that occurs in writing. When we silently focus our concerns, thought may reach to a thousand years in the past, and as our countenance stirs ever so gently, our vision may cross ten thousand leagues.[53]

The creative process begins with imagination (*shensi*) wandering outward from its home in the heart-mind,[54] exploring natural phenomenon, colors and sounds, thoughts, memories of the distant past, and the cosmological processes of *yin* and *yang*. In ordinary cases of imagination this may simply result in a fantasy or flight of fancy, but in the process of creating literature the images are infused with emotion and transformed by reason (*si* 思) or concepts (yi 意) into the image-ideas (*yixiang* 意象). The *shensi* then brings this vision, or image-ideas, to the writer's heart-mind. The outward journey is controlled by the writer's *zhì* (intent or purpose) and his *qi* (physiological energy 氣).[55] In the inward journey the writer uses language to reveal what his imagination has seen to others.

> When the basic principle of thought is at its most subtle, the spirit wanders with things. The spirit dwells in the breast; intent

> (*zhi*) and *qi* control the bolt to its gate [to let it out]. Things come in through the ear and eye; in this, language controls the hinge and trigger. When hinge and trigger permit passage, no things have hidden appearance; when the bolt to the gate is closed, then spirit is concealed.[56]

The imagination's journey resembles the spiritual flights of the early shamans, the Daoist immortals, and Zhuangzi's Holy Man of the Ku-she Mountain.[57] It is wide-ranging and completely unfettered—flying off with the wind and the clouds. Describing *shensi*'s journey, Liu writes:

> If at this moment the writer ascends a mountain, his feeling will permeate the mountain. If he surveys the sea, his emotion will overflow the sea. Thus the capacity of his talent will sweep along with winds and clouds.[58]

This experience, however, is only the beginning. In order for *shensi*, imagination, to create literature out of the images and feelings it has gathered in its wanderings, writers must study intensively, experience widely, and cultivate the inner stillness valued in Daoist and Buddhist meditation.

> Thus in shaping and molding literary thinking, what is highly valued is emptiness and tranquility, whereby one dredges clear the inner organs [five viscera] and washes the spirit pure. One must accumulate learning to build a storehouse of treasures, immerse oneself in reason [principle *li*] to enrich talent, investigate experience to exhaust observation, and tame one's inner state to spin out words.[59]

Even when writers are full of energy and concentration, however, they cannot express everything they have experienced in the "exuberant and indistinct vision" their *shensi* has created.[60]

> When he finishes writing, he finds himself only half expressed. Why? Because ideas (*yi* 意), being intangible [empty and formless], rush in like a miracle; words, being concrete [are verified against reality], are hard to make artful. . . . [Thus] instead of racking his brains [working for firm control], a writer should nourish his heart and cultivate his art.[61]

Thus, although the chapter begins with the *shensi* freely wandering and with a number of references to Zhuangzi, it ends with a concern for control of the images by the writer's conscious intent (*zhi*), and by reflection (*si*), study and language.

Although the energy (*qi*), study and cultivation of great writers may be distinctly their own, *shensi* is not an idiosyncratic trait unique to a particular artist. It is the ordinary imagination that allows us to share the vision of writers across the ages. Liu writes

> In reading a work of literature . . . one opens a text and penetrates the feelings [*qing* 情] [of the author]. . . . Although we cannot see the faces of writers of a remote age, we may look into their words and immediately see their minds (*xin* 心).[62]

Thus, literature not only allows us to communicate with people distant from us in time and space, it helps anyone with enough experience and knowledge understand the basic principles of the cosmos or the Dao itself.[63]

> If one's mind is set (*zhi*) on the mountains and rivers . . . a zither can express his feelings. What is more, when the tip of a writing brush brings things into form, where [can] the basic principles remain hidden? [64]

The *Wenxin Diaolong* is a work of literary criticism, but if *zhi* can be expressed in the patterns of writing created by "the tip of a writing brush," it was only a matter of time before scholars recognized that the other arts of the brush, painting and calligraphy, could do so also.

Thus by the sixth century the *shi yan zhi* tradition had evolved into a sophisticated theory about the use of reason or reflection (*si* 思) and imagination that could be extended to include all of the arts.

The *Wenxin Diāolóng* and the Expressive Theory of Art

As I argued earlier, the classical understanding of *shi yan zhi* is very different from the Expressive Theory of Art. On the other hand, the *Wenxin Diaolong* seems to have moved closer to the modern theory. In his classic work on the English and German Romantic critics M. H. Abrams summarizes the Expressive Theory:

> A work of art is essentially the internal made external, and embodying the combined product of the poet's perceptions, thoughts, and feelings. The primary source and subject matter of a poet, therefore, are the attributes and actions of the poet's own mind; or if aspects of the external world, then these only as they are converted from fact to poetry by the feelings and operations of the poet's mind.[65]

Although Liu Xie's theory of poetry and the Expressive Theory require observation, study, and discipline, both theories focus on the emotions of the poet and the creative processes of individual artists rather than on moral content or audience response. Given Liu's conception of *zhi* (expressing the heart-mind's intent) his use of the phrase "*shi yan zhi*" comes very close to Mill's claim that poetry is "the expression or uttering forth of feeling" or Wordsworth's definition of poetry as "spontaneous overflow of powerful feelings."[66]

Of course, emotion (*qing*) has always been part of Chinese aesthetics, beginning as it did in the intense ecstatic feelings roused in shamanistic dances; but in the classical (Zhou Dynasty/Confucian) tradition emotions were controlled and organized by *wen* (文) and *li* (禮). Poetry and music expressed emotions, but wild and unrestrained expressions were not considered appropriate. When Liu praised the *Chuci* (*Songs of the South* 楚辭) without insisting on a didactic, moral interpretation of its eroticism and exuberance, he seemed closer to Wordsworth's view of poetry than to the Confucian admonition that the lewd music of the Zheng should be banned.[67]

The Romantic theorist perhaps most closely resembling Liu is Samuel Taylor Coleridge.[68] Like Liu, Coleridge is concerned with the role of imagination in poetry, and provides a psychological study of imagination. Coleridge makes several important (if not completely perspicuous) distinctions: between Fancy and Imagination, and between primary and secondary imagination. He claims that Fancy and Imagination are disparate mental faculties, and describes Fancy as a passive mechanical ability that takes images from memory and uses "the law of association" to connect images that are close together in time or space, are like or dissimilar, or are logically or causally related.[69] Imagination, on the other hand, is an active, creative agent which may begin with images provided by Fancy, but whose operation is more like the growth of a plant or other living thing, developing along lines set by the organism's inner structure and ultimate form, rather than the association of images for reasons external to the images themselves.

> The rules of the Imagination are themselves the very powers of growth and production. The words to which they are reducible, present only the outlines and external appearance of the fruit.[70]

Coleridge's theory of imagination is deeply influenced by his reading of Kant.[71] He notes that everyone is born with the faculty of imagination and identifies primary imagination as the "living power" that makes perception possible.[72] Coleridge describes secondary imagination as differing from primary imagination only in degree and in its ability to operate by conscious choice, intention, or purpose. Secondary imagination is the "magical power" of poetic creation which

> dissolves, diffuses, dissipates, in order to recreate: or where this process is rendered impossible, yet still at all events it struggles to idealize and to unify. It is essentially vital, even as all objects (as objects) are essentially fixed and dead.[73]

However, while poetic imagination is "organic," in contrast to the mechanical operation of fancy, Imagination is free to develop creatively in ways that natural organisms are not. "Could a rule be given from without, poetry would cease to be poetry, and sink into a mechanical art. It would be *morphosis*, not *poiaesis*."[74] The freedom and mystical creative power of imagination leads Coleridge to assert that human imagination is nothing less than a finite echo of divine creation. "The primary Imagination I hold to be the living power and prime agent of all human perception, and as a repetition in the finite mind of the eternal act of creation in the infinite I AM."[75]

One of the most striking analogies between Liu's *Wenxin Diaolong* and Coleridge's *Biographia Literaria* is the cosmological significance of literature. The power of Imagination and *wen* were both there "in the beginning." Nevertheless, Liu and Coleridge have distinct conceptions of the origin of the universe. Coleridge gives imagination a primary place in the Creation *ex nihilo* by the omnipotent and infinite Judeo-Christian deity (I AM). For Liu the imagination (*shensi*) is associated with mysterious and powerful spirits (*shen* 神), but it is the pattern or form of things in the universe, including literature (*wen*), not the human imagination, that is "born" with Heaven and Earth and out of the primeval substance. In both cases, however, human mental powers (imagination and understanding) are cosmically and religiously meaningful.

The *Wenxin Diaolong* and the Expressive Theory of art also seem to place great importance on the imagination of individual artists. The meaning of "*shensi*" and the ordinary conception of "imagination" seem quite close. They both imply flights of fancy; of remembering or creating images of things not present physically. Both terms are strongly visual and important in poetic creativity.[76] However, "imagination" and "*shensi*" have rather different connotations. "Imagination" has a long and complex history in Western philosophy and literature. Beginning with Plato's association of it with illusions and deception, "imagination" often suggests fictions—fantasies and fairy tales; and is frequently contrasted with "objective facts," "reason" or "intellect."[77] The tendency to think of art (literature, works of imagination) as "not serious" or trivial is grounded in these associations.

Although the first sustained discussion of the role of *shensi* in poetic creation was in the *Wenxin Diāolóng*, Liu's theory of *shensi*, is also rooted in a long intellectual tradition, one that involves shamanistic dances, Daoist mysticism, the evolving conceptions of *shen* as magical and powerful forces, human and otherwise, and of the role of *si* (reflect, deliberate, long for 思) in intellectual, moral and emotional cultivation. Given the Chinese conception of duality as a pair of terms at opposite ends of a continuum that are mutually entailing, that often merge, and must be in harmony with each other, there is no sense of tension between *shensi,* reason and emotion anywhere in the *Wenxin Diāolóng.*[78] The images the *shensi* brings to the poet's mind are always tinged with emotion, but must be controlled and shaped by mind and reason (*li* 理, *zhi* 志 and *si* 思) in order to be put into words.[79]

A particularly striking difference between Liu Xie's theory of poetry and the Expressive Theory demonstrates that although Liu has moved away from the classical *shi yan zhi* tradition, he has not completely abandoned it. In one version of Romantic Expressive Theory, the audience is irrelevant. Wordsworth still believed that poets wrote for other people, but Keats, Shelley, and Mill believed that the poet is writing only for himself. Mill wrote, "All poetry . . . is of the nature of soliloquy." Keats claimed, "I never wrote one single line of Poetry with the least Shadow of public thought," and according to Shelley, "A poet is a nightingale . . . who sits in darkness and sings to cheer its own solitude with sweet sounds; his auditors are as men entranced by the melody of an unseen musician."[80]

To simplify a great deal, proponents of the Expressive Theory believed that the highest level of poetic creativity was the work of a special kind of person, a Genius, whose works could only be appreciated and admired, from a respectful distance, by properly talented readers.

Shensi, however, is not an idiosyncratic trait unique to a particular artist. It shares something with ordinary imagination and allows us to share the vision of writers across the ages. Not everyone has the energy (*qi*), intense dedication (*zhi*) and willingness to work and study that is required to write poetry; but once a poet has written, we can, with a certain amount of effort, share his thoughts and feelings. Liu has widened the scope of the thoughts and feelings that can be shared from community religious and political values, to more personal emotions and beliefs, but he remains in the *shi yan zhi* tradition that the purpose of art is to share the thoughts and feelings, the *zhi* of the artist, to explore the nature of the cosmos and to understand what it means to be part of the human community.

In the Ming Dynasty, however, the *shi yan zhi* tradition faced a serious challenge. Partly in response to the urbanization and commercial prosperity of the age, literature was no longer the exclusive property of an intellectual elite steeped in Confucian proprieties. Vernacular literature took up the topic of desire, particularly sexual desire. Li Zehou argues that literature which openly expresses sexual desire encourages the growth of the kind of individualism that would destroy the ancient aesthetic tradition.

> . . . [D]esire highlights the existence of the individual. The individual here is no longer defined only as a member of an ethically defined relationship or as an element of a cosmic system. Rather the individual is an unrepeatable, irreplaceable, and totally unique sensuous life. This life no longer functions as a stand-in for the significance of life in general, or for a generalized attachment to mortality. Instead, it is a real flesh-and-blood 'self' with desires and needs.[81]

However, rather than celebrating "the triumph of individualism" so highly valued in our society, Li argues that when the community loses value, the value of individuals is also threatened.[82]

Zhi in Contemporary Aesthetics

Li Zehou's aesthetic theory is an attempt to meet these threats by reviving the *shi yan zhi* tradition. Li's theory informs much of the chapters that follow, and his complex and multilayered aesthetic theory draws on the insights of contemporary psychology, sociology, anthropology, and philosophy to deepen and continue the ancient tradition. At the same time Li follows Liu Xie in celebrating both the emotional intensity of poets like Qu Yuan and the role of creative imagination in aesthetic experience. Li describes aesthetic experience as *yue zhi yue shen* 悅志悅神, "pleasures of lofty aspiration (*zhi*) and moral integrity (*shen*)"[83] or "pleasures of the will and spirit."[84] His use of the terms "*shen*" and "*zhi*" signal his intention to build on the ancient association of aesthetic experience with religious ones, and to argue that although philosophers have often understood religious experiences to be the most significant ones a person can have, aesthetic experiences are even more meaningful.

Since the next chapter will explore Li's views in some detail, only a brief sketch of his theory will be presented here. Li claims that aesthetic experience begins when we perceive something—a beautiful sunset, a piece of music, a building, a poem—which provokes a strong emotional response of delight, joy, even ecstasy.[85] As Liu Xie might put it, as our *shensi* roams about the world the images it encounters are infused with emotion. Li Zehou notes that while these feelings are immediate and intuitive, they are usually quite temporary. Occasionally, however, the experience demands a more active response. The work of art forces us to return to it and pay closer attention to its sensory form—the way the parts of a painting are arranged, the sounds and tones of music and poetry. In much the same way the visions (image-ideas) created by a poet's *shensi* are controlled by his mind and intention (*zhi*), this stage of the process intensifies and organizes emotions of joy, sadness, anger, fear, and delight, broadening and structuring our imaginations, teaching us new emotional concepts and ways of looking at the world.[86] While the process is to some degree cognitive, it always involves a great deal of emotion and pleasure and may culminate in an aesthetic experience which includes sensory, intellectual, and spiritual pleasure, but goes beyond all of them. In Li's understanding of aesthetic experience (*yue zhi yue shen* 悅 志悅神), *zhi* (heart's intent, will, or lofty ambition 志) retains all of its historical associations with religious ecstasy, social and political morality. Thus, Li concludes that aesthetics plays the role in Chinese philosophy that religion has played in the West.

If religion and science are seen as completely antithetical, Li's view is inconsistent with my earlier claim that aesthetics plays a role in Chinese philosophy analogous to that played by science in Western philosophy. However, noting that modern science and the Abrahamic religions are equally grounded in the belief that the cosmic order is a logical order may mitigate this conflict. If religious and aesthetic experiences both express an almost universal human "yearning to transcend finiteness in pursuit of the infinite,"[87] the goal of the Grand Unified Theory to provide an abstract and elegant explanation of the entire cosmos, appears to express a similar yearning for transcendence.

Plan of the Book

In a deep sense, this book is modeled on Li Zehou's historical introduction to Chinese Aesthetics, *The Path of Beauty*. This magnificent book presents an historical narrative of the development of Chinese aesthetics from the rituals and magic of Neolithic China to the highly sophisticated art and literature of the Ming and Qing Dynasties. Li's insightful account touches on the social, philosophical, and economic conditions under which art was produced. The book ends with a quotation from the poetry of Mao Zedong referring to the heroes of the past and looking forward to a glorious future.[88]

The present book attempts to fill in some of the details suggested in Li's account. With the exception of the second chapter, each of the following chapters will describe the development of a particular tradition in Chinese aesthetics. These chapters will attempt to mirror and elaborate on the general development of Chinese aesthetics presented in *The Path of Beauty*. Unlike *The Path of Beauty*, however, this book does not present a straightforward historical narrative. Nevertheless, except for the second chapter, the chapters proceed in a roughly chronological order. The introduction focused on ancient classical texts. The third chapter describes the influence of Buddhism on the Chinese sculptural transition from early in the second-century CE through the Northern Wei (386–534). The fourth chapter explores the tradition of Chinese horse painting that began in the Tang Dynasty (618–906). The book ends with a discussion of the poetry of the Song Dynasty poet, politician, farmer, and philosopher,

Su Shi (1037–1101), and the philosophy of Zhu Xi (1130–1200), the architect of the Neo-Confucian synthesis. Throughout the book several themes will be explored: the development of the concept of *zhi* and the relationships between religion, politics, and aesthetics. Chapters 2, 3, and 5 are concerned with the relation between religion and aesthetics. Chapters 4 and 5 consider the connection between politics and Chinese aesthetics.

Chapter 2, "The Aesthetic Theory of Li Zehou," will take up the philosophical aesthetics of Li Zehou, providing the philosophical underpinnings of the work as a whole. (Readers who are impatient with philosophy may skip or skim this chapter.) Li argues that an "aesthetic experience" begins with an emotional response to something that typically strikes us as incredibly beautiful. Sometimes the object inspires us to learn more about it and deepen our appreciation of it. Li identifies this as *aesthetic attention*—"pleasures of mind and mood." The last three chapters of this book may be considered a way to structure the reader's aesthetic attention. Eventually one may experience what Li calls an aesthetic experience which he claims is "higher than" religious experience and can replace it. The notion of a religious experience is highly equivocal and the relationship between religious, spiritual, and mystical experiences is fraught with ambiguity. Thus, in addition to Li's philosophical theory, chapter 2 will explore some traditional views of these experiences in order to become clearer about meaning of Li's claims about aesthetic experiences.

Chapter 3, "Chinese Buddhism: Art and Religion in the Northern Wei," examines a particular episode in the complicated history of the relationship between aesthetics and religion: the evolution of Indian Buddhism into a Chinese religion. This chapter will focus on the sculptural tradition that produced the magnificent Northern Wei Dynasty Buddhas reflecting this transformation. An understanding of this tradition will, as the art historian Steve Goldberg put it, allow us to "see" how Buddhism became Chinese.

Chapter 4, "The Meaning of 'Horse,'" traces the evolution of the Chinese tradition of horse painting from the Tang Dynasty to the end of the twentieth century. Throughout the history of Chinese aesthetics the tradition of *shi yan zhi* continued to contain a didactic element, and in the Chinese Confucian tradition that element was fundamentally political. Although contemporary Chinese horse painting has become highly individualized, these paintings retain their association with political values. This chapter will examine the relationship between art, morality, and politics under changing historical, social, and political conditions.

Chapter 5, "The Red Cliff Odes: Poetry and Philosophy," returns to the relationship of art to religion and politics. The chapter focuses on the work of Su Shi, often known by his literary name Su Dongpo, a philosopher poet who lived and wrote during the time the Neo-Confucian synthesis was being developed. Neo-Confucian philosophy is often presented as a relatively coherent and carefully worked out philosophical system. Su Dongpo's poetry reflects the problems this synthesis was designed to overcome, the ultimate failure of that synthesis, and *a fortiori*, the failure of any abstract philosophical system to resolve the most deeply troubling problems of life. In Su's work these problems were at least as much personal and political as they were logical and metaphysical. Indeed, the separation is artificial. Philosophy worth its name must be personal. The chapter will explore the role of individual creativity in poetry and philosophy, at a time, much like our own, when the political problems of the age are utterly intractable.

2

The Aesthetic Theory of Li Zehou

> The Master said, "Set your sights on the way (*dao* 道), sustain yourself with excellence (*de* 德), lean upon authoritative conduct (*ren* 仁), and sojourn in the arts."
>
> —*Analects* 7.6

In post-Cultural Revolution China the loss of faith in Marxist-Leninist Mao Zedong thought left a vacuum that capitalism seems to be filling. Yet as members of the industrial West have learned, the belief that "to get rich is glorious" is a poor foundation for a meaningful life. Not only is it impossible for everyone to get rich, as more people try, their efforts will have devastating effects on the environment. In the West a loss of faith in traditional religions threatens to divide us between a conservative religious fundamentalism (which often seems to reject modern science and human rights) and the sort of secular humanism that produces isolated individuals, insisting on their freedom and wondering "is this all there is?"[1] Some philosophers are even more disparaging of contemporary life. Rosemont claims that it is "an altogether material life in which many of us are obliged to take jobs we do not like or find satisfying in order to buy things that we do not need and that do not satisfy us either, all the while destroying our natural and social environments as we do so."[2] The contemporary Chinese philosopher, Li Zehou describes "today's capitalist world where people are spiritually empty, moral values are bankrupt and animal-like individualism runs rampant."[3] Sharply critical of both Chinese communism and contemporary capitalism, Li found a response to the problems of meaninglessness and alienation in modern industrial life in the work of Immanuel Kant. On the face of it, Kant seems to be an odd choice for this task, but Li's creative appropriation of Kant's analysis of human cognition, or subjectivity, has implications for the loss of faith in both China and the West.

The aesthetic theory this chapter will present provides the philosophical underpinnings of the rest of the book. This theory owes a great deal to Li Zehou, but Li's work is complex and difficult, and I have relied on a number of different translators, each of whom is working in a unique academic and cultural background, with a distinct set of philosophical assumptions. This variety is fortuitous. Since translations are always interpretations, I have had the advantage of reading several interpretations. However, where the interpretations disagree I am not always sure whether they are reflecting a change in Li's views or a difference in interpretation. Thus, my understanding of Li's work is an interpretation of interpretations, and hence may also be misinterpretation—or at least may take his theory in directions he might not have anticipated. Perhaps, like Li, I am presenting a sympathetic reconstruction of an insightful philosopher.

Kant

As an Enlightenment philosopher Kant assumed that what made humans unique was our rationality and freedom to follow the moral law.[4] He begins his exploration of human rationality with the question "How is scientific knowledge—knowledge about the world that is universal and necessary—possible?"[5] He answers the question in terms of the interaction between human cognitive structures and sensory experience, arguing that human minds impose certain structures on empirical sensory experience.

Kant described this structure in terms of a set of fundamental concepts of thought that he identified as the forms of space and time and the categories of the understanding.[6] Kant's *First Critique* demonstrated that all empirical knowledge involves these categories, which must be a priori, that is, they cannot be learned from sensory experience because they are the prerequisites for any such experience. Since all human sensory experience is filtered through the concepts, Kant claimed they are universal and necessary. Thus Kant explained that science was possible because all such knowledge had to conform to (was filtered through) the rational structure of human consciousness.

Since all knowledge of the world contains a mental element, i.e., the a priori structures of thought, Kant's theory threatened to deteriorate into a subjective idealism that described everything as only, or fundamentally, an idea in my mind. Moreover, because scientific knowledge was structured by universal and necessary categories, Kant's epistemology appeared to imply a scientific determinism in which the cosmos is governed by laws of nature that specify, among other things, that every event necessarily follows from its antecedent causes. If this is so, human freedom, our ability to make choices independent of outside forces, is an illusion and hence, there is no basis for morality. Kant avoided the problems of subjective idealism and determinism by arguing that the empirical phenomenal world we experience must be different from the transcendent realm of things-in-themselves, the supersensible noumenal world. Although we can never be conscious of these things-in-themselves, they somehow authorize or underlie the phenomenal world. Nothing we can know or say about the relationship between the phenomenal and noumenal worlds can be precisely right because human language relies on the logical categories of our cognitive structure, and the things-in-themselves are independent of this structure.

Having established the existence of the noumenal world of things-in-themselves in his *First Critique*, the *Critique of Pure Reason*, in the *Second Critique*, the *Critique of Practical Reason*, Kant provided a logical deduction of the Categorical Imperative (the universal moral law): "So act that the maxim of your will could always hold at the same time as a principle in a giving of a universal law," or in another version: "Act only on that maxim whereby you can at the same time will that it should become a universal law."[7] Since morality requires free will, the *Second Critique* went on to ground human freedom, and hence morality, in the noumenal world.[8] Nevertheless, the relationship between the phenomenal world in which the deterministic laws of science applied, and the noumenal world of human freedom remained more than a little obscure. In the *Third* (and final) *Critique*, the *Critique of Judgment*, Kant returned to this problem which he described as "the great gulf that separates the supersensible from phenomena."[9] He was looking for a way if not to "bridge" this gulf, at least to harmonize the two realms: some way to mediate between them. The *Third Critique* is probably the least satisfactory, and most frustrating, of the three critiques; but it may be the most important. In this *Critique* Kant argued that aesthetic judgments were based on a feeling of disinterested pleasure produced by the "free play of the imagination." The free play of imagination is a particularly difficult notion in Kant,[10] but Kant may have something like the following in mind. In ordinary cognition, imagination and understanding work together. Imagination takes intuitions—particular, immediate sensory information (perceptions)—and combines them into images which fall under (are recognized as examples of) concepts given by understanding, producing a representation that is the basis for a cognitive judgment.[11] Thus, starting with intuitions of redness and heaviness etc. and various appropriate concepts, we come to judge "That heavy red mineral is cinnabar."[12]

While imagination is ordinarily governed by a rule or concept of the understanding, sometimes imagination works freely, without being constrained by concepts, and does not produce a representation (that would require a concept) but instead a feeling of "disinterested pleasure." This feeling of disinterested pleasure is the basis of an aesthetic judgment, for example: "That garden is beautiful." Although in the free play of imagination, the understanding does not provide us with a concept or rule for determining if an object is beautiful, Kant insists that the free play of the imagination is "in harmony" with the understanding because we intuitively feel that a beautiful object is what Kant calls "purposive without purpose."[13] It somehow "fits" our understanding; we feel that it is intelligible, that it was designed intentionally, but yet it has no purpose."[14] The purposiveness without purpose is most obvious in the feeling of pleasure we get from natural beauty. It seems free of what Kant calls "the constraint of arbitrary rules."[15] Science assures us there is no "plan" behind the cosmos, yet a beautiful flower is anything but unstructured chaos. While human artists do in fact work from designs, a beautiful work of art must seem to be natural; its design must not be apparent. If we can see what the artist intended to do, her work isn't beautiful but rather the mechanical satisfaction of some rules or standards; and if it pleases us, it does so because we recognize that it has succeeded in satisfying those rules, not because it is beautiful.

Disinterested pleasure is different from ordinary pleasures—which are "interested" because they are produced by the satisfaction of a desire, and may vary from person to person, and time to time. A cold beer may satisfy a desire on a hot afternoon, but not on a cool morning. On the other hand, Kant argues that everyone should feel disinterested pleasure in the presence of a beautiful object. Judgments of beauty demand universal agreement because they are based on pleasure produced by the cognitive faculties, imagination, and understanding that all people share. We expect everyone to agree with us in our judgments of beauty; when they do not, we may ask for reasons and explanations, but the question ultimately comes down to whether one feels disinterested pleasure. Since a judgment of beauty is not based on concepts, there can be no logical rule, or set of concepts, by which to decide if something is beautiful or not. Nevertheless, when there is disagreement someone is usually "wrong;" someone is making some kind of mistake.[16]

Recall that on Kant's theory, science and morality depend on a "higher transcendent world" (the supersensible world of things in themselves and human freedom) about which we can have no empirical knowledge or experience, but which guaranteed that both our knowledge and values are reliable. In the aesthetic experience of disinterested pleasure, however, we actually have an experience, or intuition, of freedom.[17] In feeling disinterested pleasure we experience the free play of imagination. This fact leads to Kant's claim that beauty is the symbol of morality. Moral behavior,[18] like aesthetic pleasure, must be disinterested, and both involve freedom—imagination in free play, and will freely choose to follow the moral law. But freedom is part of the supersensible, noumenal, ground of morality—about which we can never have any direct knowledge or concepts. In providing an intuition of freedom (a feeling, not a concept) aesthetic pleasure serves as a symbol of morality in which the will freely obeys the moral law. Kant notes that the analogy is supported by number of metaphors; beautiful objects are often described in moral language. "We call buildings or trees majestic and magnificent, landscapes laughing and gay; even colors are called innocent, modest, tender."[19]

Like other writers of his time Kant distinguished beauty from the sublime. The feelings of pleasure produced by something sublime resemble those produced by a beautiful object in being disinterested, universal, and connected to the moral law. The feeling of the sublime is produced by natural scenes whose vastness and power seem to overwhelm our ability to understand them, and yet which lead us to recognize that human reason can grasp universal laws, not just scientific laws, but the moral law itself. On the other hand, the sublime is quite different from the beautiful—there is always a "negative" aspect to a feeling of the sublime—feelings of horror or fear; and it does not involve an experience or intuition of the supersensible world, but rather a recognition of our own cognitive abilities. Nevertheless, since both kinds of aesthetic pleasure connect pleasure with the disinterestedness, universality, and freedom required for morality, they help us cultivate the habits required for moral behavior.

Kant's views have had far-reaching influence. When Western theists argue that the world has an underlying divine purpose, they are using an (oversimplified and often unsophisticated) version of the conclusion of Kant's *Third Critique* that because the world and human rationality seem to have been "designed for each other," moral law and natural law are consistent. Gestalt psychology is founded on Kant's insight that human cognitive structures impose certain patterns on perceptions. Carnap and Wittgenstein transformed Kant's claims that concepts appropriate to the empirical world cannot be used to describe the noumenal world, into claims about language rather than "concepts" and the underlying ("noumenal") structure of language. Thus early analytic philosophers argued that we cannot use human language, which has its own logical structure, to "get behind" and explain that structure. Indeed, in the *Tractatus* Wittgenstein used Kantian language to argue that we cannot talk about aesthetics and ethics because they are "transcendental."

Kant in China

Chinese thought has been expanded and enriched by Western ideas for millennia. Chapter 3 will describe the appropriation and transformation of beliefs brought to China by Buddhist missionaries beginning in the first century CE, and Jesuit missionaries in the sixteenth and seventeenth centuries. The arrival of Marxism in the twentieth century resulted in the development of a uniquely Chinese Marxism. Mou Zongsan (1909–1995) considered Kant to represent the best of the spirit of the Enlightenment and translated the *Critiques* as part of his project to modernize and revitalize Confucian thought. Li Zehou's Marxist interpretation of Kant was particularly central in the post-Cultural Revolution evaluation of Mao's Great Leap Forward and the Cultural Revolution.[20] These highly political debates concerned the definition of human nature or "subjectivity," a topic Marxists of the previous decades seemed to have gotten badly wrong with disastrous consequences for China. Li claims that Marxism has been distorted in at least two ways. First "scientific Marxism" ignored subjective experience entirely, viewing people as passive pawns of their society, completely subject to the laws of economics governing the rise, and eventual destruction, of capitalism, and the ultimate victory of socialism. Scientific Marxism led to the fatalism and determinism of Stalinist Soviet Russia.

Li argues that Mao Zedong's volunteerism was the other extreme, because Mao, like certain Western Marxists, considered human subjectivity capable of changing history practically on its own; but Mao's Marxism differed from that of the West in at least three ways: it reduced human nature or subjectivity to "class nature"; it was based on Mao's experience with Chinese peasants fighting against the Japanese and the Kuomintang; and it was thoroughly sinified. Li claims that Mao merged Marx with traditional Chinese thought, focusing more on the kind of practical reasoning found in classical military texts such as Sunzi's *Art of War* than on Marxist economics.[21]

Moreover, Li claims that while Mao was a brilliant wartime leader, Mao's interpretation of human nature, coupled with his lack of understanding of the technical, material, and educational prerequisites for modern industry, led him to believe that China's economy could be modernized by revolutions in the superstructure, that is, by collective, cooperative ownership, moral appeals to the courage and self-sacrifice of the proletariat, and "thought reform of human hearts and minds."[22] Li concludes that these beliefs led to the Great Leap Forward and the death of six million Chinese by starvation, were used to justify the horrors of the Cultural Revolution, and were disastrous for China as a whole.[23]

Just as Kant's *Critiques* were written to resolve the tensions between scientific determinism of Newtonian science and the free will required for morality, Li believes Kant can be used to resolve the tension between the extremes of scientific Marxism and Mao's subjective volunteerism. In Li's view, Kant's theory of human consciousness provides the resources for a more realistic view of human nature and human consciousness (subjectivity) that can rescue and renew Marxism, allowing it to avoid the political and philosophical disasters of recent Chinese history and continue its mission of changing the world.[24] Li's interpretation of Kant (like Mao's of Marx), however, was thoroughly Chinese.

Kant and Confucian Practical Reasoning

Li argues that "Confucianism" is a "cultural-psychological structure" that has permeated Chinese philosophy for millennia and has become synonymous with Chinese culture.[25] He identifies an "ethics of *ren* (benevolence 仁)" and practical rationality as two of the fundamental characteristics of Confucian thought, describes practical rationality as an attitude that avoids abstract speculation in favor of drawing conclusions from experience, and encourages us to use reasoning only as a guide to action. Practical rationality pays close attention to actual contexts, and considers actions to be appropriate only when they are tailored to particular circumstances.[26]

This sense of practical rationality is quite distinct from Aristotle's conception of practical reasoning which relies on a syllogism of the form:

(1) If I want X, I should do Y.
(2) I want X.
(3) Therefore, I should do Y.

The first premise is a highly abstract generalization resembling a universal law. The actual situation and particular individual natures of "X" and "Y," and of the agent identified as "I" are irrelevant to the application of this law.[27]

What Li describes as Confucian practical rationality appears to a case of the "correlative thinking" identified by A. C. Graham, David Hall, and Roger Ames. Hall and Ames develop Graham's distinction between "correlative" and "analytic" thinking in a discussion of causal cosmologies and correlative cosmologies, or acosmologies.[28] A causal cosmology assumes that the world has a rational order which is expressed in the abstract patterns and rules of logic, in mathematics and in scientific laws. Individual elements in these patterns are interchangeable and can be substituted for each other. It does not matter what actual objects one is considering, two of them added to two others makes four. In both practical and theoretical syllogisms the qualities of the particular objects and agents involved are irrelevant.[29] Historically this cosmology is grounded in Plato's distinction between two realms: the empirical, phenomenal world of appearance and the ideal world of eternal and unchanging forms. Since the phenomenal world is constantly changing, emotionally charged, and sensually pleasing (or terrifying or disgusting), Plato considers it less reliable than the ideal world of universals and mathematics. Although various philosophers in the history of Western thought have valued one realm over the other, the distinction was sharply drawn between the two realms: the "subjective" which was phenomenal, sensual, and emotional, and the "objective" which was intellectual, eternal, and impersonal. In philosophy and theology the phenomenal world was often called "immanent"; while the other realm was transcendent and noumenal. Much of the history of Western philosophy has been devoted to explaining the relationship between the two realms and attempting to overcome their apparent isolation from each other.[30] This task has been difficult, if not impossible, however, because the immanent is often defined as "not transcendent;" and "noumenal" as "not phenomenal."

While Western philosophy began with the works of the ancient Greeks, Chinese correlative cosmology has its roots in the *Yijing* and the *yin-yang* system.[31] Although originally *yin* and *yang* referred to the shady and sunny sides of a hill, they came to represent any pair of polar opposites, opposites which are not contradictories but are interdependent, mutually entailing and complimentary. Not only is each term incomplete without its opposite or complement, but Hall and Ames note that the relationship between terms is dynamic: the shady side of a hill becomes sunny as the sun moves across the sky; *yin* is always becoming-*yang*; *yang* is always becoming-*yin*.[32] Hall and Ames argue that "*yin*" and "*yang*" apply to actual objects, in particular changing contexts and perspectives. At one time, from one perspective, one element dominates; at another time the other dominates. Thus they write: "'[a]s different as night and day' becomes 'as different as night-becoming-day from day-becoming-night.' Precisely where does the difference lie?"[33] Things rise and fall; emerge and collapse—not in a repetitive cycle but rather "a continuing spiral that is always coming back upon itself and yet is ever new."[34]

Li Zehou notes that the concepts of ancient Chinese philosophy (*yin* and *yang*, the five elements, reason, and heart) are generally functional, not substantial, and that opposites are dynamically coordinated and balanced. He writes:

> Dialectics in ancient China dealt with the inter-infiltration, inter-dependence and mutual supplementation ofYin and Yang, the opposites of a contradiction, and the feeding-back function and self-adjustment of the system, which keep the whole organic body and structure dynamically balanced and stable. The keynote of the five elements is that there is Yang in Yin and Yin in Yang functioning together and that, therefore, neither of them alone can generate new things . . . [Confucian practical rationality therefore] attached much importance to "flexibility," "timely changes," "the mean," "peace with difference," "too much as wrong as too little."[35]

As Li understands Confucianism, it rejects both the dualism implied by the claim that there is a "non-sensuous, purely noumenal, reality" radically distinct from the world we experience, and the reductive claims of scientific materialists. Scientific materialists deny the existence of non-material mental structures, a priori concepts and "noumenal causes," and hence deny the both the reality and importance of subjective experience, including emotional and what might be called spiritual experiences. The scientific materialism of Stalinist Marxism reduces subjective experience to epiphenomena of the economic base; reductive physicalists often reduce it to the biochemistry of the brain or the machinations of "selfish genes." Many materialists tend to ridicule talk about "noumenal" or "spiritual" reality, assuming that it comes down to a belief in ghosts, dismissing references to the importance of inner conscious experience as an illusion, rooted in self-deception or superstition.

As a Marxist, Li believes that the phenomenal, empirical, material world is the fundamental reality. However, rather than dismissing the noumenal realm as an illusion, Li, like many contemporary New Confucians, attempts to merge the noumenal and phenomenal, the transcendent and the immanent.[36] From the point of view the casual cosmology underlying much of Western philosophy logical consistency is a necessary condition of any respectable philosophical position, and this merger may not be possible; indeed it may be incoherent in a philosophical vocabulary where the noumenal is defined as what is *not* phenomenal. Something is transcendent or immanent; noumenal or phenomenal, it cannot be both.[37] From this point of view talk of "transcendent immanence" or "immanent transcendence" either undermines this distinction or is simply incoherent.

In a tradition grounded in a correlative cosmology, opposites like transcendence and immanence; noumena and phenomena, may merge or turn into each other, suggesting that the meaning of terms are different in the new context. Given Li Zehou's view of practical rationality, his description of Chinese dialectics and his discussion of a "transcendence [that] does not depart from sensuosity,"[38] his thought is grounded in a correlative cosmology rather than a causal one.

What then are we to make of Li's use of the Kantian vocabulary of "transcendence" and "noumenon"? Li's discussion of the term he uses for "noumenon" indicates that he is aware of the potential objections to his use of Kant's vocabulary. Li translates "noumenon" as *benti* (本體), a "word coined from *ben* (root, origin) and *ti* (stem body)."[39] *Benti* is intimately associated with the physical in that the character for *ti* 體 "substance" contains the character for bones *gu* 骨. Li uses "*benti*" in order to emphasize the historical and biological aspects of the noumenon and to avoid any suggestion of a dualistic ontology. Moreover while some English translations of Li's work translate "*benti*" as "noumenon" without any comment, *benti* is also translated as "historical ontology" and "philosophical anthropology," suggesting that no sharp distinction between noumenon and phenomenon is being made.[40] One might therefore distinguish between two senses of "noumenon": one that entails "not phenomenon" and the other a misleading translation of "*benti*." This distinction would be in accord with the suggestion that we distinguish between two senses of "transcendence": the first of which, *strict transcendence*, would entail "not immanent," while the other sense would be more allied with the less philosophical use of the term to mean "going beyond" or "exceptional." While there are advantages to this strategy, it raises certain questions.

Has Li's "Kantian" vocabulary been transformed so radically that any meaningful relationship to Kant's thought has been lost? If any legitimate interpretation of Kant must use Kant's terms the way he used them and must share most, if not all, of his fundamental assumptions, then Li's philosophy cannot be considered Kantian. But this restriction on interpretations would be impossibly limiting and would make Kantian scholarship a dry and lifeless endeavor. Would we still be able to discuss the Kantian aspects of Gestalt psychology or Wittgenstein's *Tractatus*? One might wonder if every legitimate interpretation of Kant would have to be written in eighteenth-century German.

By interpreting Kant through the lens of Confucian practical rationality and a correlative cosmology, Li is committing what Hall and Ames have identified in another context as a "cross cultural anachronism"—using the thinking of a philosopher from one tradition to understand issues raised in another.[41] As generations of Chinese thinkers "reanimated the old" to understand their own times, Li is reanimating Kant to understand the twenty-first century.

Kant and Marx

Combining Confucian practical rationality and Marxist materialism Li provides an evolutionary explanation of Kant's forms of space and time, categories of understanding and the categorical imperative.[42] Li rejects Kant's claim that these structures are a priori, static and eternal, arguing instead that human psychological (cognitive, moral, emotional) structures have been produced by a long process of biological, cultural, and social evolution by a process he calls sedimentation, a continuing process that produces human nature.[43] Thus, Li rephrases Kant's question—How is human knowledge possible?—as a question about how human nature or subjectivity came about.[44]

Li credits Kant for addressing subjectivity (human nature) in a particularly comprehensive way by considering knowledge, morality, and aesthetics in each of his three *Critiques*,[45] but he faults Kant for focusing exclusively on the intellectual aspect of human nature, and ignoring the contributions of our physical nature, emotions, and daily practices. Li provides Kant's theory of subjectivity with a material basis by turning to Marx's insight about the humanization of our senses.

In the *Economic and Philosophical Manuscripts of 1844*, Marx wrote "The forming of the five senses is a labor of the entire history of the world down to the present."[46] The way people acquire sensory information, our basic senses, is different from that of other animals, giving us a number of unique abilities—the senses that allow us to enjoy beauty, the agency to make our own history, the capacity to feel love. Human senses and abilities developed, and are continuing to develop, in the context of human societies.[47] Marx believes that people became different from animals when we started to produce the things we need to live, but he says little more than this about primitive human beings.[48] Li fills in this lacuna, describing the process of the "humanization of nature" which began when our early ancestors began making and using tools. While the humanization of nature involves an external transformation of the environment that made it more hospitable to human life, the process had profound effects on the psychological nature of humanity, creating a truly human nature. Li describes this inner process of the humanization of nature as making us more human, less animal, more cultivated and "adapted to live in organized society."[49]

Other animals use tools, but only humans make them.[50] On the generally accepted theory of human evolution, about two and a half million years ago *Homo habilis* made stone tools for chopping, pounding, and scraping. Like all our primate relatives, these early humans were social animals, but their linguistic abilities were probably no better than those of today's great apes. About a million years after *Homo habilis* began to make tools, *Homo erectus* produced relatively sophisticated hand axes for killing and skinning animals, digging in soil, and cutting wood.[51] These hand axes were manufactured and used for more than a million years until *Homo sapiens* appeared about 200,000 years ago.[52] The evolution of *Homo sapiens* required complex social organizations which co-evolved with the physical changes in skull and thumb size, and the development of the brain and central nervous systems that distinguish *Homo sapiens* from earlier members of the species.[53] Although the process of biological, and social, evolution of *Homo sapiens* took millions of years to accomplish, within 150,000 years the species became "behaviorally modern," making specialized tools out of stone, bone, antler, and ivory; constructing dwellings with well-designed fireplaces; conducting burial rituals; and creating art for decoration and personal adornment.[54] Since these changes were far too rapid to be the result of biological evolution, they must have been produced by social-cultural evolution.

What sort of animal were we before these changes took place? Cognitive psychologist Michael Tomasello notes that all mammals have some sense of space and time. We all live in a world of permanent objects and can recognize certain categories of objects based on perceptual similarities. Mammals also live in a social world, recognizing conspecifics and members of our social group, communicating in a number of ways, and forming relationships on the basis of kinship, friendship, and location on the social hierarchy of dominance.[55]

Many primates discover innovative ways to use tools and pass their new skills on to each other. Tomasello identifies two kinds of social learning. In the first, other primates see the innovative behavior and imitate it, but unless the new behavior happens to be observed, it does not become part of the community's knowledge and the innovations are lost. Tomasello claims that intelligent innovation is not as important as the ability to pass innovations on to future generations. In the second kind of learning, active learning or genuine teaching, the more knowledgeable individual *intends* to communicate the skill, the less knowledgeable learners understand why the innovator did what she did and continue to engage in the improved behavior, ensuring that innovations become a permanent part of the community's set of skills. Few, if any, nonhuman primates engage in this sort of learning; people do it all the time. Moreover, while genuine teaching could have taken place among pre-linguistic humans, language clearly accelerates the process.

Tomasello argues that the ability to empathize, that is, to understand other humans as intentional beings *like me*. with the same desires, feelings, beliefs that I have, is a necessary condition for the active learning which leads to the development of human languages and the dramatic increase in the store of community skills and knowledge.[56] Assuming that the ability to recognize others as intentional beings has a biological basis, Tomasello notes that once humans had that skill, cultural-social evolution advanced rapidly and dramatically, and concludes: "Genes are an essential part of the story of human cognitive evolution, perhaps even from some points of view the most important part of the story since they are what got the ball rolling. But they are not the whole story, and the ball has rolled a long way since it got started."[57]

Like Tomasello, Li believes that the practice of tool-making had a profound and long reaching impact, and that, roughly 50,000 years ago, *Homo sapiens* possessed the elaborate cognitive, psychological, and social systems necessary for everything we have done and become since. Li would object, however, to the claim that the fundamental part of that evolution was either its biological-genetic basis, or the appearance of an internal psychological state of empathy in individual teachers and learners.[58] The cognitive and individualistic emphasis of the tradition in which Tomasello is working ignores the importance of the sensual and emotional evolution of social groups. Although Li and Tomasello are both concerned with the evolution of human nature, subjectivity, Li distinguishes between two aspects of human nature, individual subjectivity and the subjectivity, or collective consciousness, of humanity as a whole, and insists that the appearance of individual subjectivity depended on the presence of collective human nature. Li writes: "The latter preceded and is a presupposition of the former."[59]

Li argues that in the practice of tool-making a new kind of animal began to appear, one that has a "suprabiological existence" that makes it "more than" an animal.[60] Claiming that the "something more" that distinguishes human nature from animals transcends empirical psychological structures and genetic makeup, Li uses Kantian vocabulary to describe human nature as a noumenal existence. On the other hand, operating out of what we have called a correlative cosmology, Li, unlike Kant, has a monistic ontology.[61] Thus Li's claim that human beings are more than animals distinguishes him from both reductive materialists (physicalists and scientific Marxists) who deny that there is any significant difference between human primates and other animals, and from dualists who believe that the "something more" is a mysterious soul, or "ghost stuff," a noumenal object existing independently of the material world. Li grounds the existence of what he calls the human noumenon on the historical development of human nature, subjectivity—the cognitive, emotional, social, and sensual structures that grew out of the practice of making and using tools. These structures do not exist independently of each other. Li argues that "the rational melds with the sensuous, the social with the individual, and the historical with the psychological."[62]

Li describes human nature (or subjectivity) as social-rationality and animal sensuality "dissolved together in a single whole."[63] In a dualistic ontology social-rationality (Descartes's "thinking thing") is separated from sensuality and emotion, and appears to be supernatural or purely noumenal. Li argues that the "dissolution" of the two parts of human nature is more than a "mixing of two contrary parts, 'half angel, half devil'"[64] which can be considered independently of each other. Human reason, our inner lives and "spiritual existence" are inseparable from human sensuality, emotions, and physiology, and both originated in the phenomena of collective human nature. But how did collective human nature evolve and how could such a "dissolution" have happened? Li addresses these questions in his theory of sedimentation.

Sedimentation (*jidian* 積淀)

Li describes *sedimentation* as "the accumulations and deposits of the social, rational, and historical in the individual through the process of humanizing nature."[65] Sedimentation is a dynamic process, punctuated by breaks and dislocations, followed by re-sedimentation.[66] The process took place, and continues to take place, over the whole history of humanity. Li's conception of sedimentation uses a metaphor of the geological stratification of layers of rock and soil that are deposited over time. The advance and retreat of glaciers, erosion by wind or water and the movement of earth's crust by continental drift means that layers are formed, wear away and change at different rates. Nevertheless, the surface is more variable than the bedrock, which seems relatively invariable and immoveable.

Wittgenstein uses a metaphor quite similar to that of sedimentation to describe the distinction between a priori judgments, which are necessary and universal, and contingent ones, which change with time and place. In *On Certainty* he writes:

> 96. It might be imagined that some propositions, of the form of empirical propositions, were hardened and functioned as

> channels for such empirical postpositions as were not hardened but fluid; and that this relation altered with time, in that fluid propositions hardened, and hard ones became fluid.
>
> 97. The [structure][67] may change back into a state of flux; the river-bed of thoughts may shift. But I distinguish between the movement of the waters on the river-bed and the shift of the bed itself; though there is not a sharp division of the one from the other.
>
> 98. But if someone were to say "So logic too is an empirical science" he would be wrong. Yet this is right: the same proposition may get treated at one time as something to test by experience, at another as a rule of testing.
>
> 99. And the bank of that river consists partly of hard rock, subject to no alternation or only to an imperceptible one, partly of sand, which now in one place now in another gets washed away or deposited.[68]

On Li's theory of sedimentation, the psychological structures Kant identified as the a priori forms of space and time and the categories of understanding correspond to the earliest, most enduring parts of the riverbed whose rocks were created by millions of years of sedimentation, accumulation, and pressure. These structures are the result of our biological, psychological, social evolution into human beings.[69] From the point of view of a particular individual, or even a group of people, these constructions seem necessary, non-contingent, and independent of particular situations, but from the point of view of humanity as a whole they have been formed by millions of years of experience in making and using tools. Since the process of sedimentation is dynamic and continues to occur, the cultural-psychological formations created by primitive sedimentation are more flexible and subject to variation than the a priori structures described by Kant.

Li describes *primitive sedimentation* as "the most fundamental sedimentation, formed from the process of material labor."[70] It began two and a half million years ago when individual humans, the pre-linguistic *Homo habilis*, began to develop strong intergenerational social bonds by teaching each other how to make and use tools. Over long periods of history our biology and our psychology changed. Li argues that our hands changed first becoming specialized tool-using organs.[71] Then our senses, particularly our ears and eyes, became humanized. Animal senses are more focused, more specialized, and more directly utilitarian than human senses. Although human hearing and sight are useful for individual survival, they are also products of culture. As Marx noted, the most beautiful music means nothing to a non-musical ear.[72] Li and Cauvel describe how spatial representations (drawings and maps) feel "right" or "wrong" to members of different cultures, and refer to Gombrich's analysis of the way Renaissance artists taught Europeans to "see" in linear perspective.[73] Chinese landscape painters had their own way of treating space centuries before they encountered European ideas about perspective.[74]

Early humans chipped and ground tools and weapons; they threw pottery, hoed soil, planted seed, and harvested grain. Li notes that the work is repetitious and rhythmic and follows natural patterns of order and linear sequences. In producing and using tools primitive humans recognized the relationship between the form and function of an object: "pointed objects were useful for piercing and round ones for rolling."[75] According to Li, discovering and sharing new uses for natural objects illuminated the patterns and regularities of the objective world. These patterns and regularities became concepts of order, natural law, causality, and mathematics.[76] As human communities became increasingly skilled and sophisticated, rhythmic movement, chanting, and singing made it easier to coordinate human labor. While chants and songs have clear advantages in organizing the work of groups of people, however, Li argues that the emotional power of music and dance in shamanistic rituals was far more important in transforming, humanizing, our emotions and desires.[77]

Just as human tool using was founded on the abilities of our nonhuman primate relatives, shamanistic dances originated in primate behavior. Primatologists report that the great apes, gorillas and chimpanzees in particular, engage in behavior very much like human dancing. In play and courtship, as well as responding to thunderstorms or appearance of a stranger, these apes engage in ritualized movements—excited hooting, rhythmic foot movements, waving branches, slapping the ground, jumping and kicking sideways. Playful young chimpanzees clap, twirl with their hands outstretched, and perform handstands and summersaults. These complex, patterned activities are an enjoyable way to discharge energy and to interact with other primates by attracting attention and expressing emotions and intentions.[78]

In human communities dancing served all of these purposes and more. Li claims that primitive shamanistic dances involved ecstatic mystical ceremonies. Dancing, singing, and shouting in joy or rage were instinctive expressions which transformed human emotional formations, built community solidarity, and created means of communication necessary for human survival. Language itself almost certainly evolved along with music, and there are a number of speculative theories that language and music both began in totemic dances and magic rituals.[79] Dancing was often accompanied by cries and shouts whose repetitive rhythm made them easy to remember. Dances also may have involved symbolic reenactment of dramatic events in the life of the community—an attack by a bear, the capture of an enemy. After much repetition, rhythmic gestures and sounds would have taken on symbolic meaning in the collective practice and consciousness of the community. Li notes Wittgenstein's theory of language games in support of his theory of the collective origin of language: "Wittgenstein put it clearly: language is determined by social life and the activities of social practice and the language of a society determines an individual's perception."[80]

Like tools, rituals and magic were attempts to manipulate nature, controlling the environment to make it more suitable for human thriving and, in the case of funerary rituals, to subject even death to human control. Although magic and shamanistic rituals cannot actually control nature, it is not at all clear that only the immediately effective forms were sedimented into our cognitive structure. Science was a response to those parts of nature we could control, while religion and art developed in response to the things that remained out of control—including the fact that all life comes to an end. Li writes "From primitive times to the present, funeral rites and music humanize the animal terror of death. They mold and change it from an instinctive fear to deep and sad feelings, thereby enriching life and enhancing its value."[81]

In Li's view shamanistic rituals and totemic dances blended many elements: animalistic emotions and impulses to play, religious symbols and imagery, efforts to control nature and communicate with the spirits. Li argues that rituals and dance had a powerful effect on early humans, creating intense feelings of respect, love, and loyalty which sedimented into the emotional, moral, and aesthetic psychological structures necessary for truly human communities to evolve.[82]

Li distinguishes two aspects of these structures: the collective social consciousness, or "big self" (*da wo* 大我), and individual self (*xiao wo* 小

我).[83] The former is primary and created the human cultural-psychology which distinguishes us from animals.[84]

Émile Durkheim also distinguished two forms of consciousness—one in which individual minds are relatively isolated and independent; the other in which individual minds are part of the social whole. In this latter state, people's behavior is regulated by a standard outside of themselves. They forget their individual interests and are willing to perform heroic sacrifices or engage in horrifically destructive violence—often, but not always, in defense of the common good. This state is vividly intense and Durkheim describes it as "in a sense a luxurious activity since it is extremely rich . . . qualitatively different to the everyday life of the individual, as the superior to the inferior, the ideal to the real."[85]

Although this sense of collective unity may have been particularly intense in primitive rituals, it is not entirely absent today. The historian William McNeil described the "muscular bonding" that took place in basic training during months of marching in close formation with dozens of other men:

> Words are inadequate to describe the emotion aroused by the prolonged movement in unison that drilling involved. A sense of pervasive well-being is what I recall; more specifically, a strange sense of personal enlargement; a sort of swelling out, becoming bigger than life, thanks to participation in collective ritual.[86]

This sense of losing one's individual identity, the "I," in a collective "we," is instrumental in making the self-sacrifice demanded of men in combat not only possible but "relatively easy."[87]

Li and Durkheim both believe that this "collective consciousness" is the source of the sense of moral obligation that transcends personal self-interest and is necessary for truly human societies. Durkheim argues that "moral obligation" requires something outside of myself to which I am obliged. This "something" has its roots in the "collective consciousness."[88] Li grounds his own version of the categorical imperative, the highest principle of morality, that of "maintaining and developing the human species" in the *da wo*, big self or collective social consciousness, calling it "the 'noumenon' of morality," something that both "transcends the immediate interests of any particular time-limited individual, group, class or society" and yet depends on the actual interests of humanity as a whole.[89]

Primitive sedimentation transformed human biology and psychology, emotions and desires, until we became radically different from animals, becoming what Li calls "supra-biological" beings.[90] Human life always takes place in the context of our instincts and natural environment, but, unlike that of other animals, human behavior is no longer completely determined by instinct and environment. Like animals we eat when we are hungry, but we also satisfy sophisticated delicate tastes and engage in the social rituals of dining. Like animals we have sexual desires, but in human beings these have been transformed into love.[91] Animals may sacrifice individuals for the group; but they do so by instinct. Human beings do so out of the "noumenal" morality of the categorical imperative (to contribute to the thriving of the human species), recognizing that we are part of a larger transcendent whole, humanity itself.

Although primitive sedimentation formed the psychological—cognitive, emotional, aesthetic—structures all humans share, these structures are remarkably flexible. When humans spread over the globe *cultural sedimentation* continued to create the ways of thinking and feeling shared by members of a particular culture. Once primitive and cultural sedimentation have humanized nature to a certain extent, *individual sedimentation*, which Cauvel describes as "those ways of looking at the world accumulated through our individual life experiences," becomes increasingly important.[92]

Every human being has a predisposition to learn a language, but what language we learn depends on the social and cultural environment. All human beings have some sense of time and space, but there are wide variations in particular details.[93] We all make logical inferences (as long as the scope of logic is not limited to formal deductions), but the rules of inference and standards of proof differ widely.[94] Human morality had its beginning in the emotional bonds and community loyalties rooted in shamanistic dances, but emotional responses and moral standards vary from community to community.

In the West shamanistic rituals became religions, and Greek philosophy, touting "free inquiry" contributed to the habits of mind that sedimented into the causal cosmology and analytical way of thinking discussed in "Kant and Confucian Practical Reasoning." Li notes that in China the process of cultural sedimentation went in another direction, eschewing systematic theology devoted to an independent "transcendent" reality. Shamanistic rituals were transformed into the *shi yan zhi* tradition discussed in chapter 1 and sedimented into the "one-world" ontology, practical rationality, and correlative cosmology of Chinese thought.[95]

Thus, as humans began to live in social groups we gained the ability to transform nature, to think in terms of scientific causality and mathematics, and to engage in the supra-biological social behavior involved in morality and aesthetics. Moreover, Li claims, we learned to recognize social conditioning and develop a morality distinct from it. When sedimented patterns and constructions become fixed and conventional, new forms of social life, new views of life, interrupt them—renovating, refreshing and renewing our habits of life and thought. Creative human beings can question and change the collective behavior and psychological structures of the group.[96] Finally, as a result of the humanization of our senses, emotions, and desires we developed a sense of beauty, something only people living in human communities could have.[97]

The Sense of Beauty

Although Li Zehou identified the "sense of beauty" with Kant's "aesthetic judgment," Li's conception of "beauty" is much broader than Kant's. Kant distinguished the beautiful from the good, the useful, and the agreeable, and argued that while good, useful, or agreeable objects may be "dependently beautiful," only objects which please us in a disinterested way possess pure beauty.[98] Li denies that there can be any totally disinterested beauty, claiming that there has never been any "truly pure art, only art permeated with more or less worldly emotions."[99]

While Kant's discussion involves some complex and abstract logic, Li is specific and historical. He begins with the traditional explanation of the character for beauty (*mei* 美), as "a big fat ram." This immediately associates beauty with food; but Li also notes that *mei* appeared in early discussions of totemic dances in which the dancers wore goat masks, and concludes that "beauty had something to do with rituals and hence had important social implications."[100] Li claims that a great many things may be considered beautiful: pleasures of the eyes and ears, food when you are hungry, a cold drink on a hot day, satisfying a sexual desire. An action that is admirable and honorable may provide moral pleasure; a particularly complicated mathematical proof maybe intellectually pleasing; and both may be considered beautiful.[101] Li argues, however, that aesthetic pleasure, the enjoyment and appreciation of artistic and natural beauty, is unique because the person feeling it must be sufficiently distant from the aesthetic object to see it in a non-utilitarian way. Moreover, while aesthetic pleasure always has a strong sensuous element, aesthetic pleasure is more complex than other kinds of pleasure and is always a complex blend of sensation, understanding, imagination, *and* emotion.[102]

Although to an individual experiencing it, aesthetic pleasure feels subjective and intuitive, Li argues that beauty is neither a purely subjective response on the part of a particular person, nor is it a property a beautiful object possesses.[103] Like our scientific rationality, our sense of beauty has its roots in the primitive sedimentation created by tool-making and using, shamanistic rituals and totemic dancing. In a process Li identifies as *primitive aesthetic sedimentation* humans developed new forms of sensual pleasure; the earliest aesthetic pleasure came from the recognition that human labor could transform nature in ways that made the life of the community easier and safer.[104] Li claims that over thousands of years humans developed a sense of form and order that went beyond an appreciation of the tools and rituals that could be used to manipulate nature. Concepts of formal beauty evolved from the balance, proportion, rhythm, and symmetry that made tools useful, and the human community more productive and secure.[105] Eventually formal structures that originally satisfied purely practical needs began to have an independent function as forms of beauty.[106] Once biological survival had been secured and human life was relatively safe, objects and activities took on symbolic meanings, satisfying social rather than purely biological needs. Nature can only be seen as beautiful, an object can only be considered in harmony with nature, after nature has been transformed to the point that it is no longer immediately dangerous and people are no longer driven by immediate utilitarian concerns—Can I use it? Can I eat it? Can I escape it? Only after human society reached the level of organization and safety required for leisure, could people experience aesthetic pleasure.

Rhythms in song and dance regulate communal labor and shamanistic rituals, but they can also give us pleasure without regard to their practical function. Several thousands of years after people began producing tools, they started to make decorative objects and ornaments for shamanistic rituals and totemic dances, adding to the sensual pleasures of music and dancing. People found they could enjoy poetry, music, and dance independently of their pragmatic value in creating the communities that ensured our survival and comfort. The ability to imagine possible but not actual situations was first useful in developing tools and later in creating hypotheses and theories to manipulate nature. Given leisure and security we can enjoy imaginative constructions for their own sakes, to break out of routines, enjoy fantasies, and experience and delight in the uniquely human aesthetic experiences known as the sense of beauty.[107]

Li argues that individuals learn to have a sense of beauty in a fairly complex process involving three levels or states: (1) an aesthetic attitude; (2) aesthetic attention; and (3) aesthetic experience or sense of beauty.[108] Wang Keping describes these stages in less abstract language. The first stage pleases the ear and eye, *yue er yue mu* 悦耳悦目; the second stage is pleasing to the heart-mind and mood, *yue xin yue yi* 悦 心悦意; and the final stage pleases the will and spirit, *yue zhi yue shen* 悦 志悦神.[109]

Aesthetic Attitude *(Pleasing the Ear and Eye)*

The process begins with a strongly sensuous, emotional experience. We are pleased by something beautiful, or disturbed by something ugly.[110] We may also be startled by a work with the reputation for being great art and wonder why other people value it so highly. The Northern Wei Buddhas, who are the focus of chapter 3, strike many people as strange and not particularly attractive. Li claims these statues are a high point in Chinese sculpture, a claim that is initially quite puzzling.[111] Chapter 4 discusses the painting of *Night Shining White*, a painting I found delightful the first time I saw it. Finally, readers accustomed to the drama and complexity of classical and modern Western poetry may initially find the poetry of Tao Qian and Su Shi discussed in chapter 5 "charming" but almost childishly naïve. In any event, although an individual's first experience of a work of art or natural beauty is immediate, intuitive, and sensual, the experience is generally passive and often quite transitory.

Aesthetic Attention *(Pleasing the Heart-Mind and Mood)*

Sometimes, however, a work of art demands an active response. The work forces us to return to it, pay closer attention to it, and ask certain questions about it. Aesthetic attention focuses on the structure or form of an aesthetic object—the arrangements of the parts of a painting, the sounds and tones of the words in poetry. Li contrasts aesthetic attention with scientific attention in which the formal properties of objects direct us to the logical relationships between them.[112] Scientific attention demands that we measure and classify things, investigating their history and causal powers. Where did it come from? What can it do? Our logical, cognitive skills are all called into play to answer these questions. Close attention to a work of art might make us want to know how it was produced. What materials and technique were used? What was its original setting? Did it have a ritual function? We may have to discover, or be reminded of, the meaning of a cross for a Christian; the symbolism of monks' robes, large ear lobes, and the lotus in Buddhist art. We may have to learn folk tales about Cinderella or White Snake, the story of Adam and Eve, and the Jataka stories about the Buddha's past lives. Moreover, as Larry Butler and others have argued, when a work of art is displayed in a museum, isolated from its original setting, the museum has a responsibility to inform its audience about where the object was found. In many cases, however, because of the exigencies of wars, looting, and thefts of various kinds, this information has been lost. This fact in itself is informative.

Aesthetic attention, on the other hand, is not primarily cognitive. Li and Cauvel explain that it focuses on the sensory form of the actual object, rather than its abstract conceptual properties. It involves our emotions, imagination and expectations, heightening and organizing emotions of joy, sadness, anger, fear, and delight.[113] Aesthetic attention requires imagination and emotion to identify with the artists and their intended audience, as well as with the figures in a painting or the characters in a play or a novel. Knowing that an object is in some sense "not real" frees the imagination from the utilitarian requirement to respond in a practical way. We don't have to comfort the crying heroine, run from the charging tiger, clean up the pooled blood and rotting fruit. A natural object can only become an aesthetic object when we have no reason or obligation to *do* anything about it. Looking at a painting, we are not required to milk the cows, prune the trees, or study the stars to find our direction on a nighttime walk. Aesthetic objects neither threaten us nor demand any practical action. When we consider a work of art that was, or still is, part of a religious ritual, such as the Northern Wei Buddhas or Chartres Cathedral, aesthetic attention frees us from the necessity of examining the truth claims made by the religion, or of responding with outrage at the frequently oppressive function of religion. One of the values of art is that it is not identical to practical life. Our imaginations and expectations are free to play with the ways in which art is like, and unlike, life, and the possibilities and emotional responses these suggest.

Aesthetic Experience *(Pleasing the Will and Spirit)*

Li's conception of an "aesthetic experience" should not be confused with the transitory sensory and emotional responses of an "aesthetic attitude."

On Li's theory the insistence that we enjoy art only for art's sake and avoid consideration of the historical, philosophical, and moral context of a work of art, would limit us to the pleasures of eye and ear of aesthetic attitude and to the emotional pleasure of aesthetic attention. The broader historical and cultural contexts of an artwork are a prerequisite for an aesthetic experience of them, but even understanding the cognitive aspects of an art object is not sufficient for a genuine aesthetic experience. If it were we would be satisfied with scientific or historical understanding, which, valuable as it is, is not enough.

Moreover, focusing on the cognitive dimension of aesthetic attention may tempt us to over intellectualize aesthetic experience, and Li criticizes Kant for being misled in precisely this way into emphasizing the disinterestedness of art over its ability to satisfy sensual desires and provide intense pleasure.[114] Aesthetic experiences are ones of "disinterested pleasure" only in the sense that aesthetic objects are not immediately useful. Our emotional responses to aesthetic objects, pleasure and pain, delight and frustration, cannot be entirely divorced from the sedimentation of thousands of years of productive, social, sensuous life in the world.

In the final state in the aesthetic process all the elements of aesthetic attention: sensation, emotion, imagination, and understanding come together in a complex harmony—with different elements predominating in different experiences. Thus Li claims "[a]esthetic comprehension is richer and broader than strictly logical comprehension because it attracts people to try to understand its implications and to pursue its true worth in a spirit of endless pleasure."[115] Finally, aesthetic experience (pleasure of the will and spirit *yue zhi yue shen*: 悦志悦神) includes the moral, social and religious associations of *zhi* (the heart's intent 志) discussed in chapter 1, and of *shen* (the mysterious spirit 神). Li describes the experience as incomprehensible, illusionary, isolated, and ultimately impossible to express in any ordinary vocabulary. "It can be sensed, but not expressed in words."[116]

Thus, it is important to distinguish Li's conception of aesthetic experience from the highly personal experiences valued by the "aesthetes" of nineteenth-century Europe. These experiences were often highly charged emotionally, but the people who had them were careful to remain aloof from all social and political involvement. Given the individualistic nature of these experiences, Terry Eagleton claims that nineteenth-century aesthetes have evolved into postmodern intellectuals for whom morality and politics have been completely "aestheticized" into matters of "style, pleasure and intuition."[117] Nothing could be further from Li's conception of aesthetics.

Because Li considers social sedimentation to predate and underlie cultural and individual sedimentation, he argues that aesthetic experience cannot be a purely individual experience and his aesthetics is a highly moral project. His Confucian optimism and Marxist historical materialism commit him to a view of human progress in which aesthetic experience helps humanity in "pushing ourselves ahead yet further,"[118] or in Li's version of the categorical imperative, to do whatever helps humanity to thrive.

Li's discussion of morality and aesthetics begins with Kant's claim that beauty is the symbol of morality. Li writes that the fusion of the emotional force of primitive rituals and Confucian moralizing in the moral analogies of Qu Yuan (339–278 BCE) illustrates Kant's thesis.[119] However, Li argues that beauty has to be more than a symbol and claims that "beauty is the practice of freedom."[120] Kant saw the question of freedom in terms of the tension between scientific determinism and the free will required for morality claiming that we can freely obey the moral law, embodied in the categorical imperative. For Li freedom also means following the categorical imperative, making life better for the human species. Li's Marxism commits him to the value of human liberation, but he is clear that freedom does not mean "individual self-will," to be able to get what I want. The desires of an individual are determined by animal passions, prejudices, and social conventions. The presence of this sort of individualism in capitalist societies reduces human nature to animal nature.

Freedom as Li understands it begins with the recognition that we are part of the human species and that we have the ability to work with scientific laws to actively transform nature. Using scientific laws to create something useful does not mean we are constrained by those laws, but that we can operate in partnership with them to make life better for the species.[121] Li argues that this transformation is "beauty as the practice of freedom" which includes the power of modern industry to improve human life, to free us from debilitating labor, and to ensure material prosperity and security for everyone.

While Li's faith in science and technology may be overly sanguine, he calls for an increasing attention to beauty in practical productive life, to harmonize the rhythms of nature and human body "to avoid or at least diminish the alienation found in modern industrialized civilizations."[122] Despite his optimism Li is aware that human life is, and will continue to be, full of struggle, cruelty, bitterness, and despair. His discussion of the value of the sublime highlights the importance of this fact for aesthetics.

While Kant's argument for the claim that beauty is a symbol of morality depends to some extent on the distinction between the beautiful and the sublime, Li tends to blur the distinction between the beautiful and the sublime. Kant's paradigm examples of the sublime are natural scenes—violent storms, mountain peaks, earthquakes, volcanoes. Li's examples of the sublime are the grand monuments of primitive religions: the Egyptian pyramids, Mayan totem poles, and the *taotie* on the massive bronze vessels of Shang Dynasty China. Li reminds us that these structures were created by slaves who suffered horribly in their production; but while the monuments were constructed by the oppression of individuals, Li claims they represent the great strength of collective humanity as a whole and make us conscious of something, "spirits or gods," or collective humanity, that transcends our own finitude.[123] Thus while Kant's examples of the sublime leads to a celebration of the power of science and technology to conquer or humanize nature, and to reverence for the god who created them and us, Li's examples recall how much we owe to the generations of the past and of our obligation to struggle against present oppression, reinforcing the commitment to his version of the categorical imperative.

Li's view of the sublime and his transformation of the view that beauty is a symbol of morality into the claim that beauty is the practice of freedom support his argument that genuine aesthetic experiences are the highest, most meaningful, and liberating experiences a person can have.[124] This view reverses the priorities of a number of philosophers, including Kant, who argue that religious experiences are more significant, i.e., "higher" than aesthetic experiences because a religious experience establishes a relationship with a higher reality that is transcendent in Kant's sense of the word.[125] Not only does Li doubt that there is any such a reality, he notes that belief in such a reality has often justified extremely oppressive social arrangements. On the other hand, despite his general view of religion, the early association of aesthetic experience with the shamanistic dances of primitive religions is sedimented into Li's understanding of aesthetic experience. Therefore, a discussion of the relationship between aesthetics and religion is helpful to evaluate his claim that aesthetic experience is more meaningful than religious experience.

Aesthetics and Religion

The phenomena called "religion" or "religious" are so complex and varied it is difficult to see what, if anything, many of them have in common. It is perplexing why international institutions like the Catholic Church, the esoteric teachings of Tantric Buddhism, the practices associated with the poison oracle of Azande witchcraft, and the new age "Shielism" described by Robert Bella in *Habits of the Heart*, to name just a few, are all called "religion."[126] There is so little agreement on the nature of religion that there is not even a consensus about whether Confucianism is, or is not, a world religion.[127] It will be helpful to narrow our focus considerably and compare Li's description of "aesthetic experiences" with some general understandings of religious, spiritual, and mystical experiences. Like "religion," however, many things have been called religious, spiritual, and mystical experiences.[128] Thus, the discussion will begin with the phenomena John Dewey identified as a "religious attitude" and Henry Rosemont calls "spiritual experiences."

Religious and Spiritual Experiences

Dewey distinguishes "the religious elements of experience" from the beliefs, institutions, and practices associated with particular religions. He describes these elements as a deeply emotional attitude toward one's life that can "carry one through periods of darkness and despair" by changing ones orientation toward life, a change that brings "a sense of security and peace."[129] Dewey argues that if we consider these experiences independently of their associations with any particular religion, they are not all that unusual and are often part of the lives of a great many people: artists, scientists, our fellow citizens, and friends.[130]

Rosemont describes a religious or spiritual experience as one of "wholeness," "timelessness" and benevolence; "a sense of belonging, of safety, of at-one-ment, or attunement."[131] The experience is accompanied by a degree of ego reduction: the belief that not only am I not the most important thing in the universe, but that my family, my nation, my culture, even perhaps my species, are part of something infinite. Rosemont claims that this experience is the goal of all the great religions of the world. For a Christian the experience is the feeling of being secure in the hands of God. The Buddhist experience of enlightenment and the recognition of "no self" (emptiness) are similar in that one is completely present in the present and moved to compassion for all beings.[132]

Rosemont claims that the world's religious traditions identify many paths leading to this experience: *faith*—accepting the views of a particular religious tradition and following its rituals; *scholarship*—dedicating oneself to the study of sacred texts; *a moral life*—devoted to the relief of suffering and promotion of justice; and *meditation*—a contemplative life of mental and physical discipline.

Rosemont argues that making a commitment to the rigorous objectivity of science may also be path to spiritual experience.[133] A number of writers have written about this aspect of science; for example, Kant wrote:

> Two things fill the mind with ever new and increasing admiration and awe, the oftener and more steadily we reflect on them: the starry heavens above me and the moral law within me.[134]

Even Steven Weinberg's reflection suggests a spiritual aspect of science, echoing Kant's sense of the sublime, although without the comfort of a belief in the Christian god. Weinberg writes:

> But if there is no solace in the fruits of our research, there is at least some consolation in the research itself. Men and women are not content to comfort themselves with tales of gods and giants, or to confine their thoughts to the daily affairs of life; they also build telescopes and satellites and accelerators, and sit at their desks for endless hours working out the meaning of the data they gather. The effort to understand the universe is one of the very few things that lifts human life a little above the level of farce, and gives it some of the grace of tragedy.[135]

Although Dewey and Rosemont understand religious and spiritual experiences independently of the beliefs, practices, and institutions of any particular religion, it is often argued that a genuinely religious experience is an experience *of* something, an experience of a transcendent reality, something that Huston Smith writes "slip[s] through the net of science,"[136] for example, the personal God of Christianity, or the Void (emptiness or *sunyata*) of Buddhism.[137] Smith is concerned that experiences which are not *of* anything are "merely psychological." In that case, we might explain them as the result of extreme emotional distress or physical abnormality, and be tempted to accept Bertrand Russell's view of them:

> From a scientific point of view, we can make no distinction between the man who eats little and sees heaven and the man who drinks much and sees snakes. Each is in an abnormal physical condition, and therefore has abnormal perceptions. Normal perceptions, since they have to be useful in the struggle for life, must have some correspondence with fact; but in abnormal perceptions there is no reason to expect such correspondence,

and their testimony, therefore, cannot outweigh that of normal perception.[138]

Russell's claim begs the question. Abnormal (transcendental) objects might require abnormal perceptions. On the other hand, describing religious experiences as experiences of a transcendent other, the Sacred, a reality beyond the empirical, appears to entail an ontological commitment to the existence of two "realms" or worlds: the immanent, sensuous, world and a transcendent reality that is non-sensuous and timeless. While it is fairly certain that people have had spiritual or religious experiences, this fact is not sufficient to commit us either to the belief that a transcendent reality exists, or that everyone who has had such an experience is deluded. One possibility is to distinguish between spiritual experiences and religious experiences in a narrow sense. We can then stipulate that the most significant, perhaps the only, difference between spiritual experiences and religious experiences in the narrow sense, is that the religious experiences purport to be experiences of a transcendental object, transcendental understood in the strict or Kantian sense, and thus make ontological claims that such objects exist. Spiritual experiences, on the other hand, are ontologically neutral and make no assertions about the existence of a nonphenomenal, transcendent object. Convenient as this stipulation might be, many writers, including Dewey and Rosemont, often use the terms "religious" and "spiritual" as if they were synonymous. I will follow this usage unless it becomes important to distinguish ontologically neutral spiritual experiences from religious experiences which make an ontological commitment.

Clearly there is much about Confucian thought that is "spiritual," but does it have a transcendent object? Rosemont describes Confucian spirituality as "a sense of belonging, fully belonging . . . to those who have preceded us, those in whose midst we live, and those who will follow us."[139] Although the human community is less abstract than the spiritual goals of the Abrahamic and Buddhist traditions, it has been claimed that it too is a transcendent reality.[140] On the other hand, while the human community transcends individual lives and particular communities, the human community is not part of Kant's noumenal realm. It is a very large group of actual people, living in specific places at specific times, and therefore, in Kant's terms, decidedly immanent. Nevertheless, as we noted in section 3, "Kant and Confucian Practical Reasoning," in traditions other than the Kantian one, there may be a sense of "transcendence" where the notion of immanent-transcendence, transcendence with a phenomenal element is, or can be made to be, coherent.[141]

The philosophical implications of claims to have an experience of a transcendent reality, including the difficulty of describing the object of such experiences, have contributed to the troubled history of the relationship between philosophy and religion in the West and made it seem important to distinguish philosophy from religion, and both from aesthetics. The crudest form of the distinction is made by philosophers unsympathetic to religion—and theists unsympathetic to philosophy—who distinguish beliefs founded on reason from faith-based claims requiring no support other than revelation. While many thinkers note that religion appears to make truth claims that are completely irrational, it is not hard to interpret these claims as metaphors which are literally false but deeply meaningful.[142] Perhaps even more troublesome is the fact that manifestations of religion have a tendency to divide people, authorizing crusades and jihads, burnings and bombings of sacred sites (and abortion clinics), and massacres of nonbelievers.[143]

Of course, a claim to have experienced a transcendent other does not specifically authorize any bad behavior, nor does it entail any particular truth claims other than that such a reality somehow "exists," but the difficultly of interpreting these claims has produced a growing body of philosophical literature focusing on mystical experiences which seem to be a dramatically intense form of religious or spiritual experience.

Mystical Experiences

Like discussions of religious and spiritual experiences, the literature on mystical experiences distinguishes the experiences themselves from their ontological or metaphysical commitments. The phenomenological aspect of a mystical experience is described as having the following characteristics:

1. it cannot be adequately expressed in words;
2. it "feels" like knowledge of a deep truth;
3. once the experience begins the subject no longer feels in control of it;
4. it appears "timeless," out of time and space;
5. it includes a sense of unity, completion, or wholeness which may be felt as a loss of ego or personal identity;

6. it is accompanied by feelings of peace, happiness, blessedness, joy, etc.; and
7. the experience can have a profoundly transforming effect on the person experiencing it.[144]

Religious and spiritual experiences share many of these features.

The first characteristic, however, raises a problem suggested by Wittgenstein: "Whereof one cannot speak, thereof one must be silent."[145] If mystical experiences cannot be described, how can we talk about them? Even simply saying that they cannot be described, may be a self-contradiction, but few mystics have taken Wittgenstein's advice; as Bai Juyi (772–846) writes:

> *After reading Lao Tzu*
> "One who speaks does not know; one who knows does not speak."
> Thus I have been instructed by the Old Master.
> If you tell me the Old Master was one who knew, I ask,
> Why did he write five thousand words to explain it?[146]

There are many suggestions about how to describe an indescribable mystical experience. One might, for example, describe the circumstances in which the experience occurred, or narrate the events that led to up to it. There is also the strategy of "unsaying" or negative descriptions, i.e., that one cannot say what the experience is; only what it is not.[147] The easiest and perhaps most plausible move may be to say that while mystical experiences cannot be described in literal, factual language, one can use metaphor, analogies, and the language of poetry.

There is also an intimate relationship between the first and second characteristics. Although spiritual, religious, and mystical experiences may "feel like" knowledge, the knowledge in question is an "emotional attitude" (Dewey) and a "sense of safety" (Rosemont), neither of which can be expressed as cognitive, propositional knowledge.

With respect to the third and fourth characteristics of mystical experiences, each of the paths Rosemont describes as leading to a spiritual experience may also induce a mystical experience; but there is no guarantee that any particular discipline will actually induce a spiritual or mystical experience. The experience may, in fact, happen spontaneously.

Thus, these experiences are in some sense out of our conscious control.[148] Finally, the sense of timelessness is probably familiar to many people who have engaged in any of Rosemont's spiritual disciplines. One can become so engrossed in something that you suddenly "come out of it" with no idea of how much time has passed. Scholars have reported becoming so interested in studying something they forget to eat. A devoted gardener may go out to weed after breakfast and "suddenly notice" that the sun is setting.

The last two characteristics of a mystical experience: "a sense of unity, completion, or wholeness which may be experienced as a loss of ego or personal identity" and "feelings of peace, happiness, blessedness, joy, etc." are, except for the reference to "ego loss," completely in accord with Rosemont and Dewey's description of spiritual experiences and a religious attitude. The "ego-reduction" included in Rosemont's account of spiritual experiences may be thought of as a gradual dissolving of ego, a process that could ultimately become a complete loss of ego.

In his classic work on mysticism W. T. Stace argues for a hierarchy of spiritual and mystical states beginning with what he identifies as the *nature mysticism* Wordsworth describes in "Tintern Abbey":

> And I have felt
> A presence that disturbs me with the joy
> Of elevated thoughts; a sense sublime
> Of something far more deeply interfused,
> Whose dwelling is the light of setting suns,
> And the round oceans and the living air,
> And the blue sky and in the mind of man;
> A motion and a spirit which impels
> All thinking things, all objects of all thought,
> And rolls through all things.[149]

Making broad and generous allowances for the differences between the Christianity with which Wordsworth was familiar, and the Confucian, Buddhist, and Daoist literature the Song Dynasty poet Su Shi studied, many of Su's poems seem to be infused with what might be called Daoist nature mysticism. Su's work will be discussed in some detail in chapter 5.

There seems to be a continuum involving an increasing reduction of ego from nature mysticism and Rosemont's spiritual experiences to a state sometimes described as a complete loss of ego in union with the infinite One. The continuum, moreover, is not linear but more like a set of family resemblances.[150]

There are, for example, experiences sharing many of the characteristics of spiritual, religious, and mystical experiences. Zhuangzi's description of various Daoist meditation practices describe a gradual process of "sitting and forgetting" that seems to result in a loss of self.[151] A loss of ego, however, might not result in a feeling of peace, wholeness, and safety. Loss of ego may be quite terrifying.[152] The feeling that one is a "sinner in the hands of an angry god" would provoke fear rather than a sense of blessedness and joy. Kant's description of the feeling of the sublime includes an unpleasant sense of horror. Weinberg's description of the spiritual aspect of scientific understanding concluded that it gives life "the grace of tragedy" rather than a sense of wholeness and peace. These last two examples and the poetry of nature mystics like Wordsworth, Annie Dillard, Wendell Barry, and the Daoist philosophers, suggest what Stace has identified as the "underground connections between the mystical and the aesthetic."[153] For Li Zehou the relationship is anything but "underground."

Aesthetic Experiences

Like spiritual, religious, and mystical experiences, aesthetic experience, the "pleasures of *zhi* and *shen*," are life transforming and characterized by inexpressibility, a sense of completeness and of being part of an integrated whole. The experience that Christians describe as being in the hands of God, and Rosemont calls at-one-ment, or attunement, Li Zehou identifies with a sense of the integration of humanity and the universe expressed in the traditional Chinese belief in the unity of heaven and humanity (*tian ren he yi* 天人合一).[154] The inadequacy of discursive language to express these experiences is reflected in the fact that many of them are described in poetry; and even then many artists are aware, as Liu Xie noted in chapter 1, that their works cannot do justice to the experience.

> When he finishes writing, he finds himself only half expressed. Why? Because ideas (*yi* 意), being intangible [empty and formless], rush in like a miracle; words, being concrete [are verified against reality], are hard to make artful.[155]

Li suggests that contemporary analytic and deconstructive philosophy are disintegrating and that we would do well to stop thinking of language in its scientific and technological use (clear references, unambiguous semantics) and consider language in terms of an aesthetics of poetic metaphor, acknowledging the insight of the Chinese saying "*yan wai zhi yi* (more implications beyond what is referred to by speech)."[156]

Aesthetic experiences are clearly different from religious experiences in the narrow sense in that they do not claim to be an experience of a transcendent supernatural reality. On the other hand, like religious experiences in the narrow sense, aesthetic experiences require an object. Aesthetic experiences have a spiritual, super-sensual dimension, but they are always grounded in the experience of a particular object—a piece of music, a painting, a work of literature or architecture.[157] Moreover the super-sensual dimension of an aesthetic experience is not an experience of a transcendent object in the strict sense, but rather the collective social consciousness, or "big self" (*da wo* 大我), which Rosemont claims is the goal of Confucian spirituality and has described as "those who have preceded us, those in whose midst we live, and those who will follow us."[158]

Religious experiences may begin with sensuous objects (cult objects and religious art) but as Eliot Deutsch argues, in a religious experience one moves beyond the particular to "dispense with artworks entirely" and come into a relationship with Reality itself.[159] Li, like Deutsch and Huston Smith, understands religious experiences in the narrow sense (requiring a transcendent object in the strict sense), but Li is skeptical that such an object exists and thus believes that religious experiences are based on a delusion. Moreover, he argues that religions based on experiences purporting to be of a transcendent God frequently focus more attention on death, the attainment of an other-worldly joy, to the detriment of a goal that was "merely realistic, namely to preserve or obtain a mundane kind of happiness and enjoyment."[160] Li believes that religions attempt to negate or overcome the particular pleasures and pains of actual life, encouraging life denying behavior—asceticism, repression, feelings of misery, a need to purge the soul, and other things Li characterizes as "devastations of natural physiology."[161]

Unlike religious experience, aesthetic experience, pleasure of the will and spirit (*yue zhi yue shen* 悦志悦神), is one of great pleasure.[162] It is not merely the sensual pleasures of the eye and ear, but those of a Daoist sage freely wandering, of Zhuangzi by the River Hao, or of Confucius and Zengxi. When Confucius asked several of his students what they would do if their worth were recognized, all of them except Zengxi described how they would use their power to improve the lives of people they governed. Zengxi, already "sojourning in the arts" with his zither, described an afternoon of artistic, sensual, and social pleasure—bathing, enjoying cool breezes, singing and dancing, in good company.

> Zengxi plucked a final note on his zither to bring the piece to an end, and setting the instrument aside, he rose to his feet. "I would choose to do something somewhat different from the rest," he said.
>
> "No harm in that," said the Master "each of you can speak your mind."
>
> "At the end of spring, with the spring clothes having already been finished, I would like, in the company of five or six young men and six or seven children, to cleanse ourselves in the Yi River, to revel in the cool breezes at the Altar for Rain, and then return home singing."
>
> The Master heaved a deep sight, and said, "I am with Zengxi!" (*Analects* 11.26)

Not only is an aesthetic experience a spiritual experience in Rosemont's sense, it is much like nature mysticism, except that in an aesthetic experience the natural world of which one feels a part includes the human social world. Unlike a religious experience in the narrow sense which focusses on an "other world" outside of sense experience, aesthetic experience returns us to the phenomenal world, the world in which we live and are obliged to follow Li's categorical imperative to make life better for our fellow human beings.

Given Li's views that the sublime is often found in objects whose construction involved tremendous human suffering, aesthetic attention can lead us to understand the often horrific conditions under which great art is produced. Aesthetic experience embraces the whole universe, including its sensual, emotional, and intellectual pleasures as well as its pain, cruelty, and bitterness.[163]

Because the object of aesthetic experience remains in the phenomenal world in which it finds great pleasure, Li claims that aesthetic experiences are the highest and most meaningful ones a person can have.[164] Thus, Li subverts the hierarchy of traditional philosophical theology which has held that when the ultimate goal of every spiritual path, and the most significant experience a person can have, is a religious experience in the narrow sense when such an experience includes a sense of union with a nonphenomenal transcendent One.

Li's argument that aesthetic experiences are the highest ones a person can have historicizes the experience of *tian ren he yi*, the union of heaven and humanity. He traces the common origin of religious, spiritual, and aesthetic experiences to the ecstatic totemic dances that brought humans into a sense of harmony with the numinous spirits or gods and a feeling union with something greater than oneself.

As cultural sedimentation in the West produced the mental habits, orientations, and attitudes of causal cosmology, religious experience became an experience of a transcendent divinity, isolated from the rest of human life, demanding a sacrifice of sensual and emotional pleasure. When parts of the West lost faith in traditional religion and the often comforting belief in a personal god, the goal of reaching a transcendent, eternal realm became the search for the eternal, abstract laws of science. For reflective scientists like Weinberg, the goal of discovering these laws made human life appear tragic, echoing the question asked by citizens not committed to discovering scientific truth: "Is that all there is?"

Li claims that in classical Chinese culture sedimentation took place in an economy of small-scale agricultural production. Although people in this situation were seldom deluded into searching for a transcendental or spiritual "heavenly kingdom," Li argues that the belief in *tian ren he yi* encouraged a passive obedience to the will of heaven—people were completely dependent on the seasons and the whims of their rulers.[165]

The following chapters will describe in some detail a few of the stages of the cultural and aesthetic sedimentation of Chinese culture since classical times. Eventually, however, material progress brought modernization in both China and the West.[166] The humanization of nature has made material well-being for everyone seem possible, although not everyone is as optimistic as Li Zehou is about the unalloyed benefits of science and technology. Moreover, modern industrial society produces isolated and alienated individuals, raising serious questions about the nature of human subjectivity, which in modernity is bound up with the question of freedom.

Aesthetic experiences transform us, teaching us that an individual human life is not only meaningful, but can be supremely pleasurable *because* it is part of a network of interpersonal relations that forms the human community. Aesthetic experience reminds us that the whole of which we feel a part embraces the entire human community, across time and space, and includes the struggle, sacrifice, and hardship so often reflected in religious art. Thus an individual life may be both significant and free when it contributes to the thriving of that community. Such a life was described by Confucius when he said "Set your sights on the way (*dao* 道), sustain yourself with excellence (*de* 德) lean upon authoritative conduct (*ren* 仁), and sojourn in the arts" (*Analects*, 7.6).

Of course, the particular emotions and content of an aesthetic experience will be different for different groups of people at different times, but Li is writing for a global culture: one that honors Confucius, Kant and Marx. The process of sedimentation that has created, and continues to create, human nature and humanized nature, has produced a supra-biological being. We are capable of understanding and changing our environment and ourselves; but much remains to be done to ensure human thriving. As the means and the result of this goal, aesthetic experience is both a delight and a responsibility for all of us.

3

Chinese Buddhism

Art and Religion in the Northern Wei

> . . . [E]normous numbers of our feelings and attitudes towards the most basic issues are based on some more-or-less traditional Christian outlook. But we are no longer living in a Christian society, in any serious sense, and most of us are not Christians. Our general view of the world is not at all like Christ's. And yet we depend for much of our emotional and spiritual succor on art and teaching that not only presupposed the truth of Christianity, but actively propagates it. Many an atheist thinks that the *B minor Mass* is one of the greatest works of art; that is what I feel. But I am not at all clear that I should. The brevity with which I have mentioned this matter means not that it is an after-thought, or tangential to the subject-matter of this paper, but that I am too disconcerted by it to know what to say.
>
> —Michael Tanner[1]

A great many of us share Tanner's unease when we find ourselves standing in temples, looking at statues or paintings; hearing music written for a Mass or listening to the poetry of the *Daodejing* or the *Book of Common Prayer.* Knowing that these things play significant roles in a religious tradition whose faith we do not share, we nervously remember the things we used to believe, things our family and friends still believe. Sometimes when we are guests in a foreign culture, observing the objects, buildings, and rituals of an alien tradition, we attempt to distance ourselves, with a certain contemptuous superiority from "primitive superstition." When we feel we are in the presence of great art we try to appreciate the object "for its own sake," dismissing its context as irrelevant to the "real," i.e., "purely aesthetic" meaning. Sometimes it occurs to us to wonder why so much of the world's great art began as part of a religious ceremony. Other times the distance is so great and we ask ourselves, "How could *this* be part of any human faith?" Experiencing the tension between what something means to me as an aesthetic object and its significance to other people whose beliefs I do not share is disconcerting and Tanner's question is natural—what *should* I feel?

In what follows I will explore the relationship between religious and aesthetic experiences and attempt to answer Tanner's question by considering some powerful and beautiful religious objects: the Northern Wei Dynasty Buddhas.

Northern Wei Buddhas

A first impression of the Northern Wei Dynasties Buddhas is that they are strange and stiff rather than particularly beautiful. Their bodies are emaciated. Their heads are almost square, their waists thin, their necks elongated. Although their robes technically follow Buddhist prescriptions for monk's dress, they are remarkably unlike the thin garments clinging to the rounded bodies typical of Indian and Central Asian Buddhist art.[2] While the robes of Indian and Central Asian Buddhist statues usually leave the right shoulder uncovered, Northern Wei Buddhas and bodhisattvas are quite modest. Their outer robes fall symmetrically over both shoulders covering an inner robe tied with ribbons or a sash at the chest. Frequently a long scarf crosses the front and is held in place by a circular ring.[3] The thick robes and heavy pleats present a unified image revealing very little of the body underneath.

Although this style is named after the Northern Wei Dynasty, it appeared almost simultaneously in both the north and south.[4] Not only do the incredibly thin bodies of these Buddhas and bodhisattvas reflect an ideal of physical beauty common in the Southern Dynasties, their robes look remarkably like the dress of Chinese court officials or traditional Confucian scholars. While the Northern Wei style is decidedly Chinese rather than Indian or even Central Asian, it owes much to the many cultures contributing to the development of Chinese Buddhism. The pleated robes reflect the Greco-Indian style of Gandharan Buddhist

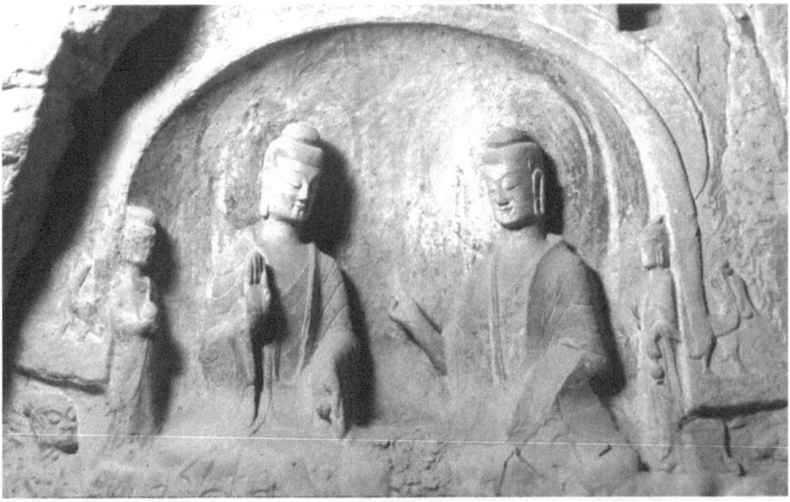

FIGURE 3.1. Shakyanumi and Phrabutarana, Northern Wei Dynasty, Binglinsi Caves, Gansu Province, PRC.

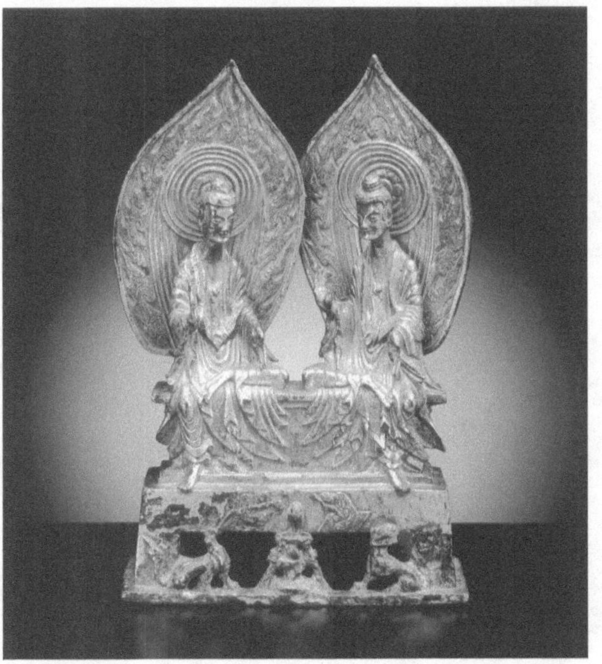

FIGURE 3.2. The Buddhas Shakyamuni and Prabhutaratna. Dated 518. Gilt bronze. From Heibei (Northern China). Northern Wei Dynasty. Photo Thierry Olivier. Musée des Arts Asiatiques-Guimet © RMN-Grand Palais/Art Resource, New York.

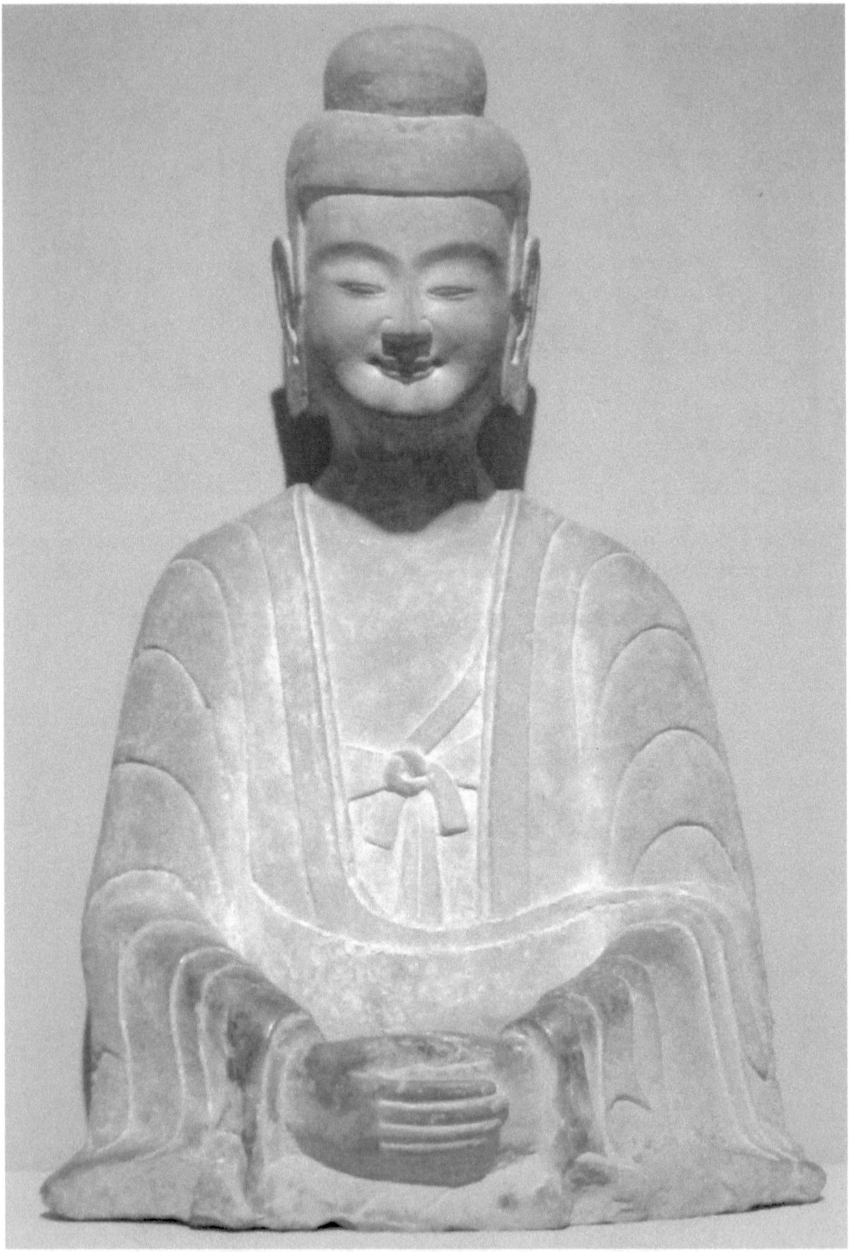

FIGURE 3.3. Buddha China, Northern Wei Dynasty, 6th century Limestone. Honolulu Academy of Arts. Gift of Mrs. Charles M. Cooke, 1930. Photo from http://commons.wikimedia.org/wiki/File:WLA_haa_Wei_limestone_Buddha.jpg.

art. The flowing folds at the feet of many of these Buddhas associate them with the Daoist immortals who, like the Buddha, were thought to be able to fly.

The most striking feature of these statues, however, is their expressions. Buddhas of Central Asian and Indian origin gaze downward, looking inward in meditation, or stare above our heads at some distant vision, but Buddhas in the early Northern Wei style look directly at us, while later Northern Wei Dynasty Buddhas smile gently, returning our gaze through half downcast eyes. Li Zehou describes them as

> solemn and dignified . . . graceful and elegant with their thin faces, small necks, flowing robes in many folds, and a mood that suggests ease, vitality, and complacency, as if all the smoke in the world had been cleared away . . .

Li continues to note that their faint smiles hint at

> a hidden meaning that could not be divulged, the wise look of a philosopher who had found the truth, the carefree manner of one above secular interests.[5]

Li accuses these gently smiling faces of lacking "any love, kindness, or concern for the world," and of expressing contempt for those of us who do not know, or do not believe in, a transcendent reality above the concerns and suffering of the secular world.[6] But must compassion—a sympathetic expression of concern and sadness for the fate of suffering beings—always be tainted with contempt? Tanner's question returns: How should we feel about these thin bodies, flowing yet modest robes, and haunting smiles? What is the relationship between artworks that touch the emotions of people of many times and places and religious works that play a part in a particular faith tradition?

Art and Religion

The anthropologist Alfred Gell believes that "art lovers" have substituted aesthetic experience for the religion whose outward forms they are no longer able to accept. Arguing that during the Enlightenment, the rise of modern science precipitated a religious crisis in which the cult objects of pre-Enlightenment or nonscientific people were replaced by cultural icons "worshiped" in museums, Gell claims he cannot distinguish the experience of premodern people worshiping images in temples and churches from the "aesthetic awe" experienced by people in a museum.

> I cannot tell the difference between religious and aesthetic exaltation; art-lovers, it seems to me, actually do worship images in most of the relevant senses, and explain away their de facto idolatry by rationalizing it as aesthetic awe. Thus, to write about art at all is, in fact to write about either religion, or the substitute for religion which those who have abandoned the outward forms of received religions content themselves with.[7]

If museums are temples, might both places simply be storage areas for things that are no longer part of ordinary life, historical curiosities we have outgrown? Rather than probing these questions, Gell's detached "scientific" point of view seems to preclude asking, much less trying to answer, questions like Tanner's. Nevertheless, the discussion draws our attention to some interesting similarities between religious and aesthetic experiences.

Eliot Deutsch argues that while aesthetic and mystical religious experiences are alike in certain ways, there are significant differences. Both experiences involve a sense of wholeness and integrity and may be transformative, leading to some kind of personal development.[8] On the other hand, Deutsch claims that while an aesthetic experience is an experience of something new, a religious experience feels like a "recovery" of a timeless relationship to a transcendent other. Moreover, Deutsch argues, while an aesthetic experience involves an artwork created by an individual genius, a religious experience requires the participation of a group of people. Deutsch defines a "religion-work" as "a specific rite, hymn, dance, or other symbolic form whose primary function is to lead the participant to a distinctive religious state of being, as this state may be defined in a particular religious tradition."[9] A religion-work may be beautiful (or not), but it must have a ritual function in bringing participants into a relationship with the sacred. Religion-works are created by the people who participate in the rituals that give them meaning. Without such a group, Deutsch claims a religion-work is a lifeless empty form. Finally, since the purpose of religious experience is to establish a relationship with the sacred, a religious experience can dispense with the religion-work entirely and be an encounter with Reality itself.[10] Artists are always concerned with unique particulars that suggest life and change. Religious experience is ultimately an experience of a timeless realm of Being itself. Thus Deutsch concludes, "*The artist and the saint cannot do each other's work*."[11]

Deutsch's distinction between religious and aesthetic experiences hinges on his claim that aesthetic experiences require a sensuous object of some kind while religious experiences are ultimately of a nonsensuous, transcendent Reality. Moreover, on his theory the Northern Wei Buddhas are "empty lifeless forms" since they are no longer part of a religious ritual. The early Chinese Buddhists who performed the rituals in which the Buddhas were a part are long dead. In their original sites the Buddhas were in groups surrounded by colorful murals many of which have been destroyed by time, by farmers who believed their paint made good fertilizer, by Islamic invaders bent on destroying idols, by periodic anti-Buddhist movements, by the ravages of the Cultural Revolution, and by looters and archeologist-adventurers from Germany, France, Britain, Russia, Japan, and the United States. Now the statues can be seen in isolated and ruined cave temples in China and in art museums all over the world.[12]

When I first saw Northern Wei Buddhas on the Silk Road in China, I thought they were quite strange and not particularly attractive. Several years later I read Li Zehou praise their solemn and dignified beauty, noting that he "would recommend Wei sculpture, in which the special property of sculpture art—expressing a highly generalized subject or ideal that commands respect and admiration by means of a human body at rest—appears to be fully utilized."[13] I was puzzled. Why should I like them? But I remembered being haunted by their smiles. Li's remarks suggest that I should like them. His aesthetic theory explains why.

Li Zehou: Confucius, Kant, and Marx

As we saw in chapter 2, Li Zehou argues that genuine aesthetic experiences are the highest, most meaningful, and liberating experiences a person can have. As a Confucian, Li is not committed to the dualism implied by the claim that there is a "higher, nonsensuous reality" radically distinct from the world we experience.[14] As a Marxist, he interprets the religious insistence that there is a "better life" in another world as, at best, an anesthetic in harsh and terrible times; at worst, it is a cruel trick to rationalize the inequities and cruelties of unjust society.[15] Hence he understands Northern Wei Buddhism at least in part as a device to keep the Chinese population submissive under the oppressive rule of their non-Han Tuoba Wei conquerors. Li's view reminds us not to neglect the historical and material circumstances of the Northern Wei. These Buddhas were part of a particular set of historical and social conditions, one we must understand in order to appreciate their eerie beauty. Thus, despite the hint of a Marxist sneer at some "primitive superstitions," Li rejects Mao Zedong's Marxist aesthetic which judges art solely in terms of whether it furthers the communist revolution or supports a reactionary class of aristocrats.[16]

Li's aesthetic theory explains my puzzlement over the smiles of the Wei Dynasty Buddhas as the beginning of a fairly complex process involving three levels or states: (1) an *aesthetic attitude* is the initial emotional response to the art object; (2) *aesthetic attention* is prompted by the aesthetic attitude and involves more serious consideration of the object; and (3) an *aesthetic experience* or sense of beauty combines and heightens (1) and (2) and transcends them. The rest of this section and section 4, "History of Buddhism in Northern China," will examine one possible set of aesthetic attitudes and attention toward the Northern Wei Buddhas. "Aesthetic Experience and Religion," will suggest a particular aesthetic experience of these marvelous objects.

Aesthetic attitude: The Northern Wei Dynasty Buddhas initially seem awkward and strange rather than particularly beautiful, and Li's praise is puzzling. Nevertheless their gentle smiles are haunting and made me return to them and consider them more carefully.

Aesthetic attention begins by focusing on the structure and form of the object, in this case the thin, emaciated bodies of the Wei Dynasty Buddhas, their square heads and the thick folds of their flowing robes. The modesty of the robes identifies these Buddhas as distinctly Chinese rather than Indian or Central Asian, while the rhythmic pattern of the flowing robes and heavy pleats conveys a sense of energy and strength. The thin bodies and gentle expressions suggest an other-worldly ideal of love and compassion.

Aesthetic attention involves our emotions and imaginations allowing us to identify with the artists and their intended audiences. One way to avoid dismissing people whose beliefs are different from ours as superstitious primitives is to empathize with them. Hearing their stories and imagining their lives helps us do this. Imagination also frees us from having to take any practical action. The Wei dynasty was founded by a series of brutal conquests and sustained by the forced labor of conquered peoples; but we have no obligation to help the masses of fifth-century Han Chinese resist their Tuoba Wei rulers, or to try to convince them of the advantages of modern medicine.

When we consider an artwork that once played a role in a religion-work, aesthetic attention frees us from the necessity of examining the truth claims made by the religion, or of responding with outrage at the frequently oppressive function of religion.[17] One of the values of art is that it is not identical with practical life. Our imaginations and expectations are free to play with the ways in which art is like, and unlike, life, and the possibilities and emotional responses these suggest. Thus we might consider a "foreign religion" with the same attitude that we take toward *Macbeth*. We know it is "not real" so we don't have an obligation in one case to prevent the murders, and in the other case we need not worship, believe or protest—"That is NOT true!" The cases are different, but there are important similarities. Without the ability to suspend disbelief, the play doesn't work. People who view foreign religions as "superstitions" are allowing their preconceptions to interfere with the experience of something beautiful and new. In this they resemble people who refuse to read novels because they "don't have time for fiction," completely oblivious to the emotional pleasures and psychological insights found in great literature.

Aesthetic attention to the Northern Wei Buddhas finds us asking a number of questions about them. Since many of them are found in museums displaying "Buddhist Art," one of the first questions might be, what was their original setting? Because of the exigencies of war, looting, and thefts of various kinds, this information has often been lost, but sometimes it can be reconstructed or imagined from archeological sites. Once one has seen the headless Buddhist statues in cave temples in China, the experience of seeing the heads of Buddhas and bodhisattvas in Western museums takes on a new and particularly poignant dimension. Looking at objects in a museum and asking "How did *that* get here?" leads us into complex questions about the relationship between museums, archeologists, and the looting that often follows various kinds of conquests.[18] Another set of questions involves the objects in their original setting. Did they have a ritual function? For whom were they produced and why?

The Northern Wei Buddhas were usually situated in cave temples whose walls were painted in colorful murals representing bloody and tragic events. The scenes remind us of the terrible and horrible aspects of real life, provoking emotions of fear and compassion. In the Dunhuang temple caves the murals surrounding Wei Dynasty Buddhas depicted Jātaka stories, stories of the Buddha's life, including the tale of the prince who killed himself in order to feed a starving tiger and her cubs. Although the mural depicts the story of this sacrifice in fairly bloody detail, Indian pictures of the story are generally much gorier. In the Chinese murals the prince's arms and legs are shown carefully laid out rather than torn and scattered.[19] How did these serene figures in Chinese court robes come to be surrounded by dramatic paintings of horrific stories from India? We want to know more.

Aesthetic attention to the Northern Wei Buddhas will lead us into an examination of a great many things: the journey of Buddhist philosophy and religion from northeastern India to China, linguistic theories of translation, the history of the tribes and kingdoms of Central Asia through which Buddhism traveled, and finally the rise and fall of the Northern Wei dynasty itself. The story is long and complicated and aesthetic attention can lead in many directions, including a serious philosophic study of Indian and Chinese Buddhism, but such a study would almost certainly over-intellectualize the aesthetic experience of the Northern Wei Buddhas.[20] Thus, rather than focusing on philosophical abstractions, the next section will examine the development of Chinese Buddhist institutions and art. The purpose of this exercise in Chinese history is to develop an imaginative understanding of the experiences and emotional responses of the people who commissioned and created the Northern Wei Buddhas, and the Tuoba Wei aristocrats, the generals and foot soldiers, the Han elite, the peasants, craftsmen, slaves, and farmers who worshiped in the temples and grottos where these magnificent statues were placed.

History of Buddhism in Northern China

These temples and grottos were created during the transformation of Indian Buddhism into a distinctly Chinese religion; a transformation that is embedded in many sedimented layers of changing culture, religion and philosophy, violent ethnic hostility, and some particularly brutal military campaigns. The transformation began in the early centuries of the first millennia when Buddhism first entered China and encountered an already ancient Chinese civilization. Chinese and Buddhist sculptural traditions, Central Asian languages and classical Chinese, Confucian and Daoist philosophies and Buddhist thought interacted with and changed each other profoundly. The transformation of Buddhism into a Chinese religion, however, could not have taken place in a peaceful and unified China, secure in its ancient Confucian certainties. Buddhism became Chinese in the centuries before and during the Northern Wei Dynasty, after China had disintegrated into the Sixteen Kingdoms (304–439) and the Northern and Southern Dynasties (420–589). South of the Yangtze River a defeated and demoralized Confucian civilization was ruled by the remnants of the Jin dynasty and by states formed by émigrés and refugees from the north who struggled to fend off northern armies and to dominate the local population.

North of the river the nomadic steppe tribes who had forced the Han out of their ancient homeland established a series of kingdoms that turned on each other in almost unmatched ferocity. The incessant warfare uprooted and slaughtered local populations and devastated the land. Horrific massacres were followed by famine and disease. Many of the tribal military leaders were ignorant, treacherous, and cruel; many of them were intelligent, compassionate, and forward thinking. Some of them were all of these things at the same time. The Buddhist clergy—missionaries from Central Asia and Chinese converts—were often courageous, caring, and talented scholars, many of whom were also politically manipulative and corrupt, also sometimes all at the same time. The northern Chinese peasants and farmers were killed in vast numbers. Those who survived were made to join the nomad armies or enslaved and driven away from their homes into alien lands, losing everything familiar and being forced to work for people who despised them. At the same time, as the nomadic tribes became more powerful and settled they began to absorb Chinese civilization from the peoples they conquered, changing both themselves and China irrevocably. The process of sinicization, however, often made the nomads vulnerable to attack by other tribes who moved in, continuing the slaughter and conquest.

The Northern Wei Dynasty provided a few centuries of relative peace and prosperity in a horrifyingly bleak period. The relative security, the extreme ethnic diversity of the Wei Empire, and the advent of a new faith provided the catalyst for the appearance of a new and astonishing artistic development.[21] The following sections will present an abbreviated version of the complex interaction between Indian Buddhism, Central Asian steppe tribes, and Chinese traditions involved in this development.

The Sculptural Tradition of China

In ancient China sculpture was primarily used to produce funerary objects.[22] Han Dynasty sculpture represented the remarkably cheerful, artless figures of the dancers and musicians, dogs and farm buildings that the deceased

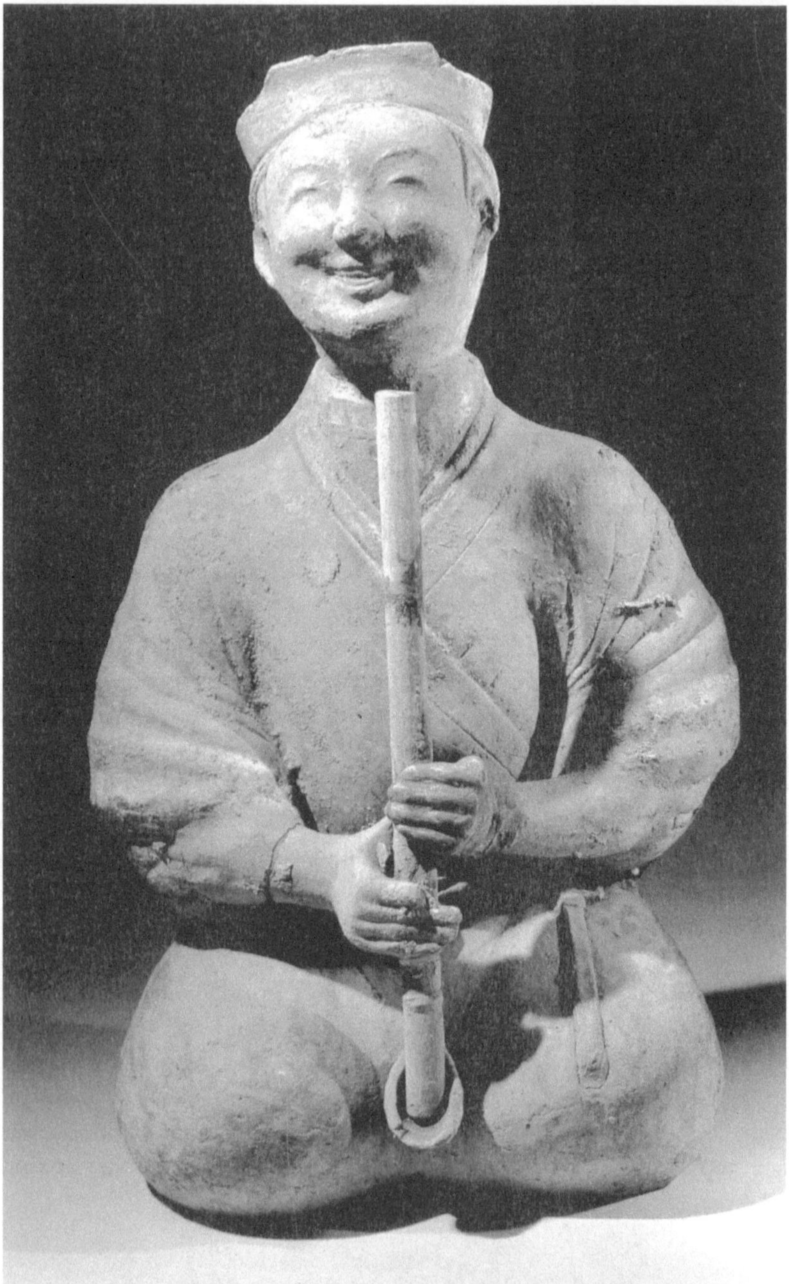

FIGURE 3.4. Flute Player, Sichuan Province, Han Dynasty, second century CE. Pottery, Leshan Museum. Photograph courtesy of Kenneth J. DeWoskin.

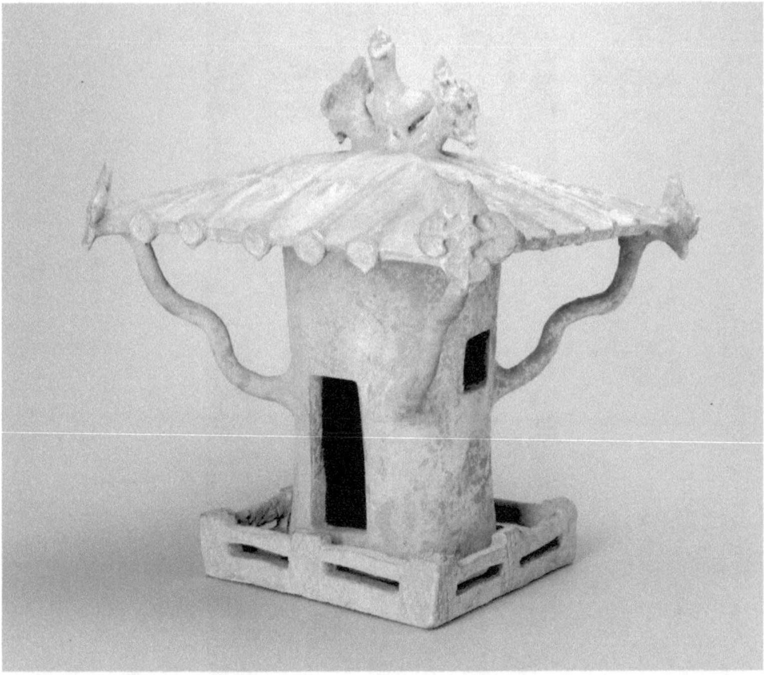

FIGURE 3.5. Eastern Han granary (tomb model). Art Institute of Chicago Lucy Maud Buckingham Collection, The Art Institute of Chicago.

might find useful in the next life. The astonishing army of statues in the tomb of the emperor Qin Shi Huangdi is more technically polished than much of Han funerary art. The faces of the soldiers reflect a variety of ethnic groups and individual personalities; but the army itself represents the emperor's utilitarian, military concerns, as well as his hope to escape his enemies after death. The army of soldiers faces east, toward Qin Shi Huangdi's enemies. However, two bronze chariots, one to carry the Emperor's soul and the other serving as an escort or guard, face west. (See fig. 4.3 for an image of the larger, "spirit" chariot.) Although at the time of Shi Huangdi's death souls fortunate enough to survive death generally went to the Eastern Paradise on the Islands of Penglai, the Western Paradise of the Queen Mother of the West on Mount Kunlun was another destination for souls seeking immortality. By the time of the Han Dynasty tomb murals frequently depicted "soul chariots" carrying the spirit of the deceased to the Queen Mother's Western Paradise. Given the location of Shi Huangdi's enemies, he would probably prefer not to journey east after death.[23]

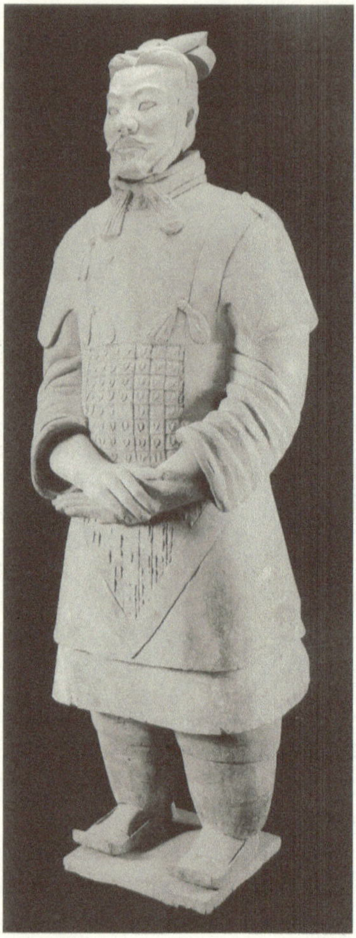

FIGURE 3.6. Terra Cotta Soldier from the Tomb of Qin Shi Huangdi. Image courtesy of the International Museum of the Horse, Lexington, Kentucky.

With few indigenous models to guide them, the earliest Chinese Buddhist statues were clumsy copies of Gandharan, Indian, and Central Asian models. In the middle of the fifth century, however, a distinctively Chinese Buddhist art began to develop. Early examples of the "Dunhuang style of the Northern Wei" appeared in the cave temples and grottoes along the Silk Road during the Western Jin (265–317) and the beginning of the period of the Sixteen Kingdoms (304–439). The gigantic highly stylized Buddhist figures found at the Yungang cave temples near the Northern Wei capital of Pingcheng (the present day city of Datong) represent the relatively unsophisticated Dunhuang style. (See fig. 3.11.) This style is an eclectic mix of Indian and Central Asian forms. The influence of the simple style of Han dynasty stone carving distinguished these figures from the "more delicately and realistically modeled Gandharan and Mathuran sculpture from India."[24] Representatives of this style had gentle affable smiles, recalling the smiling faces of the figures of Han musicians and dancers. They wore smooth robes with pleats suggested by intaglio carvings and modeled after Central Asian examples from Buddhist centers along the Silk Road; but while the Dunhuang style imitated Central Asian models, the faces of the Buddha and bodhisattvas usually reflected the Xianbei (Mongolian) ethnicity of the Wei Dynasty. At the end of the fifth and early sixth centuries the mature Northern Wei style emerged as a truly Chinese sculptural style in both northern and southern China. How had a uniquely Chinese Buddhist art evolved in this particular time and place? The story begins with the arrival of Buddhism in China.

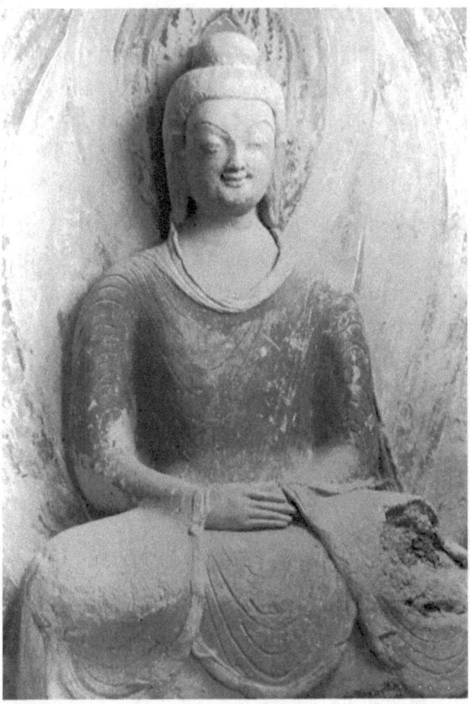

FIGURE 3.7. Seated Buddha in Grotto 16, Dunhuang. Sixteen Kingdoms (366–385).

From India to China

About two hundred years after the death of the Buddha, Buddhism began to move northwest from India into the central Asia kingdom of Gandhara, located in what is now northern Pakistan and eastern Afghanistan. Although Gandhara had been conquered by Alexander the Great in 326 BCE, Greek rule was quickly ended by Indian armies. Nevertheless, the kingdom remained in close contact with Greek and later Roman civilizations for centuries, and the Hellenistic aspects of Gandharan civilization, including classical Greek philosophy and art, had a significant impact on the development of Central Asian Buddhism.[25] Eventually Gandhara was absorbed by the Kushan Empire, a vibrant multiethnic society that blended Buddhist and Hindu religions, languages, and cultures, and included parts of northern India and modern-day Tajikistan, Afghanistan and Pakistan.

Early Buddhism was aniconic, representing the Buddha symbolically by an empty throne, a lotus, a *bodhi* tree, some footprints or a wheel.[26] The first images of the Buddha were produced in the Kushan Empire and were immensely popular. Modeled on Greek originals and their Roman copies, Gandharan statues of the Buddha and bodhisattvas had Western faces and stood in classical poses wearing robes whose pleats and folds made them look like Roman aristocrats dressed in togas.

At the eastern end of the Kushan Empire, Buddhist icons were influenced by the art of the Indian empire of Gupta. Images of the Buddha appeared with Indian features and seated in positions of meditation, their bodies clearly visible through transparent robes. As Buddhism traveled east along the Silk Road local artists began with Gandharan and Indian models, but created images reflecting the ethnic characteristics of the indigenous populations who adopted the new faith.

Buddhism spread rapidly, carried in the caravans, knapsacks, and minds of the merchants, soldiers, missionaries, adventurers, and captives who traveled the Silk Road, taking Buddhist texts and images over the Tian Shan and Kunlun Mountains, through the Karakoram Pass, and across two of the most formidable deserts on the planet. The caves and grottos bordering the Taklamakan and Gobi Deserts, including the enormous complex of cave temples at Dunhuang, became resting places and shrines where travelers gave thanks for journeys past and prayed for safety ahead. The dangers were real—ranging from ferocious sandstorms, extremes of heat and cold, and the frequently hostile inhabitants of the desert.[27] Eventually the hostilities increased to the point that the Chinese empire was

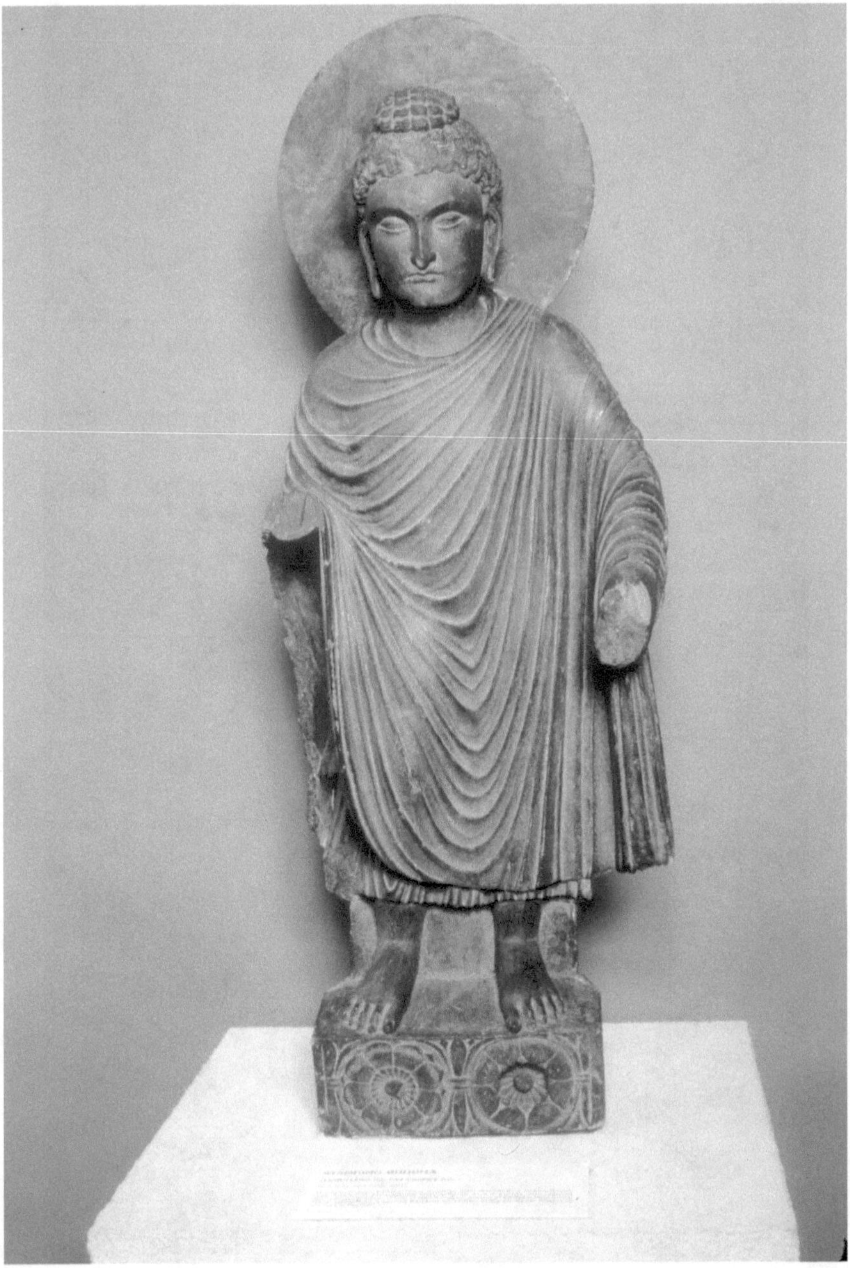

FIGURE 3.8. Standing Buddha, Gandhara, India. Second century CE. Courtesy of Penn Museum, image #60986.

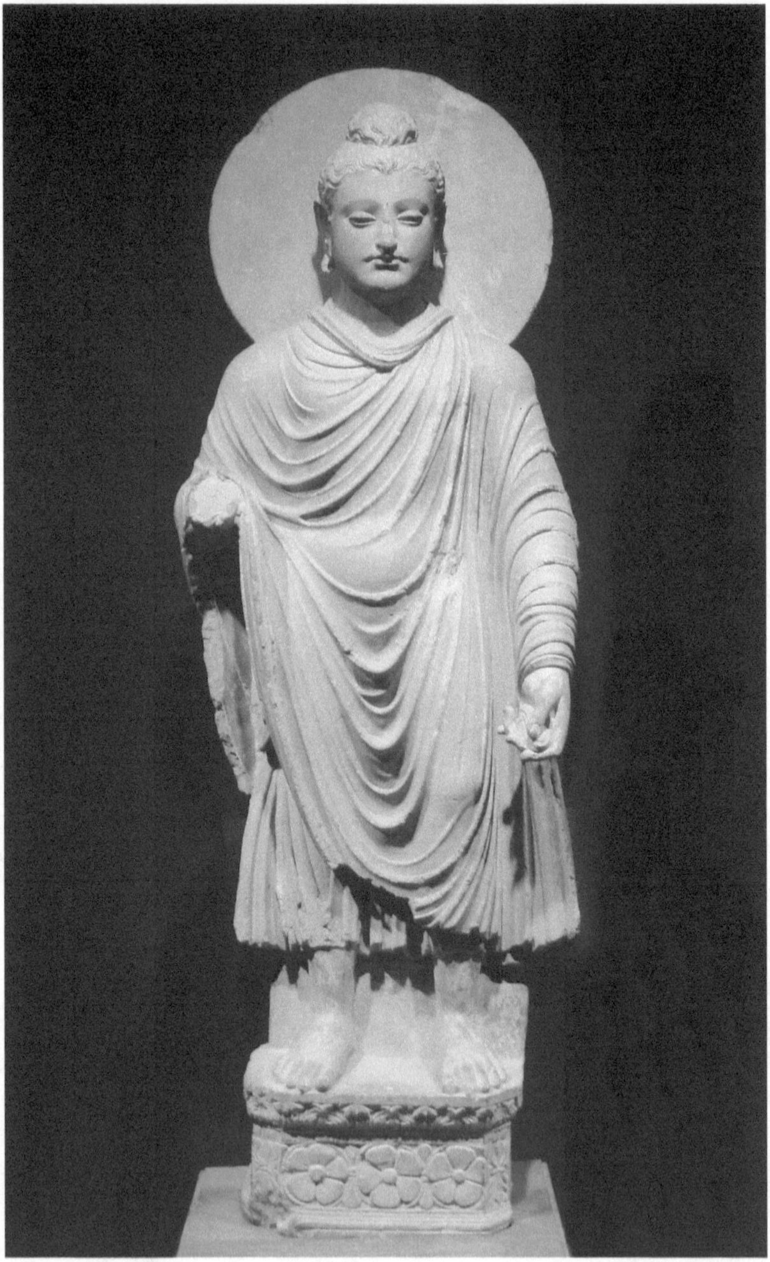

FIGURE 3.9. Gandharan Buddha, first and second centuries CE, Tokyo National Museum. Personal photograph by World Imaging, 2004.

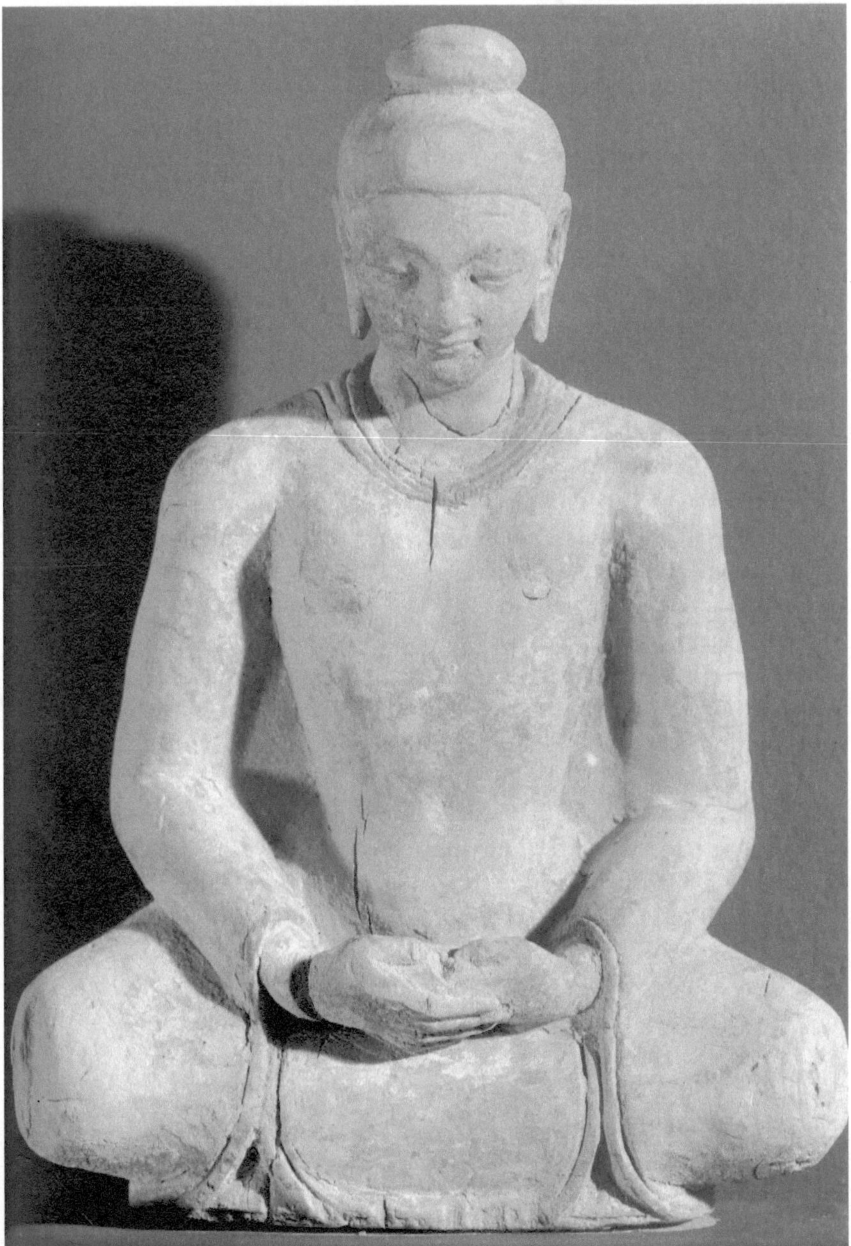

FIGURE 3.10. Indian Buddha, Seated Buddha, fifth century. From Tumshuk (Xingiang province China). Central Asia. Photo credit bpk, Berlin/(Museum fuer Asiatische Kunst)/(Juergen Liepe)/Art Resource, New York.

unable to protect travelers and the importance of the northern Silk Road (through the mountains and deserts of central Asia) declined. The magnificent statues, murals, and manuscripts collected in the cave temples and grotto shrines were abandoned, preserved for centuries by the dry desert air and the extreme isolation of the caves themselves.[28]

The first contact between Buddhism and Chinese civilization is surrounded by myth. In one account it occurred in 65 CE when the Han Emperor Ming dreamed of a "golden man great and tall, the light of the sun and the moon issuing from the nape of his neck."[29] Hearing that the Buddha was a golden person, the emperor sent messengers to India to bring Buddhist scriptures and images to China. When the messengers returned the emperor founded the White Horse Monastery in Loyang to house the treasures they brought back.[30] This story is almost certainly legendary. Not only was the White Horse Monastery founded long after the Emperor Ming's reign, given the political and military situation in the territory between China and India during the Emperor's reign, the story of his dream and the envoys it inspired him to send to India is almost certainly apocryphal.

Another popular account is even less credible. According to *Laozi's Conversion of the Barbarians* (*Laozi Huahu Jing*), a text written during the Western Jin Dynasty, after Laozi left China for the West he was reincarnated in India as the Buddha. Although the story began as an attempt to demonstrate that Buddhism was simply a form of Daoism, it quickly evolved into a vitriolic condemnation of India and its religion and was used to argue that Laozi-Buddha preached the most un-Chinese doctrine of celibacy as a form of genocide against the inferior Indian population.[31]

Buddhism was first mentioned in official Chinese history in an incident involving Prince Ying, the half-brother of the Emperor Ming. Having been sent in disgrace to the dukedom of Chu, the Prince sent the Emperor thirty-nine rolls of silk to atone for an offense he had been accused of committing. The Emperor argued that the Prince should be forgiven and the silk returned because

> [t]he prince of Ch'u [Chu] recites the obscure words of the Yellow [Emperor?] of Lao [-tzu], he does honor to the Buddha's temples of forbearance. Having purified himself and fasted for three months, he makes a vow to his god. Why should we doubt him? Why should we suspect him? He must have

> some regret. Let his ransom be returned, therewith to aid the elaborate feast of the *upāsakas* and *Śramaṇas*.[32]

The passage indicates that as early as the first century CE the Chinese recognized Buddhism as a legitimate religion, and that there was even a group of Buddhists at Loyang. Nevertheless, for a long time Buddhism was practiced primarily in communities of foreigners living in the Gansu-Shaanxi area, in the large Chinese cities that traded goods along the Silk Route, and on the western edge of the Chinese empire. As increasingly sophisticated translations made Buddhism accessible to the Chinese *literati*, however, interest in Buddhism grew at the elite level of Chinese society.

Translators and Missionaries

For many centuries Buddhist texts were unintelligible to Chinese readers.[33] Buddhist scriptures were written in the myriad languages of the Silk Road: Sanskrit, Tibetan, Uygur, Turkic, Xi-Xia, and perhaps even classical Greek. Many of the manuscripts that arrived in China were only fragments of the original text; scriptures were often not written at all but simply recited by travelers who had memorized them.

The first translators of Buddhist texts were foreign missionaries whose Chinese was barely literate. Chinese scholars refused to learn any languages other than their own, considering it the only language worth learning—all others being the mutterings of semi-civilized "outer barbarians."[34]

Although the early missionary translators were from Central Asia, from the beginning translations were done by teams, using a system that remained pretty much the same throughout the early history of Chinese Buddhism.[35] The process began with either a manuscript of an original text or with a foreign monk, missionary, or other visitor reciting a text from memory. If the visitor had enough knowledge of Chinese, he gave an oral translation of it. More often, however, bilingual intermediaries made the preliminary translations. Chinese members of the team transcribed the translations and revised them into a final form. Oral explanation and discussion of the texts provided during the work of translation were often included in the translation itself.[36] This system ensured that while the missionaries provided the original text, the Chinese organized the rest of the process. In this way Buddhist missionaries were very different from the Christian missionaries who came later. The Christians controlled the whole process of disseminating their sacred texts—translation, interpretation and adaptation. The Buddhists only provided the original text—written or recited. After that what happened was controlled by the Chinese. Zürcher speculates that this explains why Buddhism became Chinese and Christianity failed to do so.[37]

There was an enormous gulf between the religious and philosophic concepts of Indian Buddhism and those of the literary Chinese elite, a gulf that reflected the differences in the languages involved. Written Chinese was uninflected, ideographic, and had little or no formal grammar. The languages of Indian Buddhism were highly inflected, alphabetic, and relied on an elaborate formal grammar. Chinese literary style was concise and terse; its metaphors came from nature and ordinary life. Indian literature was discursive and abstract, relying on imaginative and exaggerated metaphors.[38] Moreover Buddhist scriptures were difficult, technical, and repetitive. Translators had to make difficult decisions about whether to render the scriptures in polished and shortened versions suited to the taste of Chinese readers or in versions that were faithful, literal, and unreadable.[39] Translators had to choose whether to provide texts that would further the mission to "save all beings" by appealing to Chinese literary tastes or to present a more authentic version of "authentic Buddhism" that Chinese readers would find incomprehensible. Since it is impossible to completely separate philosophical and religious systems from the languages in which they are written, even the most "faithful" translation had to make some concessions to Chinese language and thought.

Chinese encountering Buddhist texts for the first time were attracted to *dhyana* (*chan* 禪), a system of meditation and breathing exercises, and to the explanation of various numerical categories.[40] Buddhism seemed to provide more efficient versions of Daoist practices and more powerful, magical spells for longevity. Moreover, Buddhist explanations of numerical categories felt quite familiar to Chinese scholars accustomed to borrowing elements of the ancient Yin-Yang school and relating the principles of Yin and Yang, the five elements, the four seasons, the five notes, the twelve lunar months, etc., with each other.[41]

Early in the fourth century a process of explanation known as *geyi* 格義 was developed. *Geyi* is usually translated as "matching concepts" and, while it is sometimes considered a translation method, it was primarily used to help Chinese students understand Buddhist concepts by associating ("matching") them with ones from traditional Confucian and Daoist philosophy. *Geyi* is said to use some rather simplistic equations:

bodhi = *dao* 道
arhat = *zhen-ren* 真人
nirvana = *wu-wei* 無 為[42]

Thus, one of the first Chinese responses to Buddhism was to see it as something Chinese. Centuries later Western missionaries returned the favor by translating "*tian*" as "God" and arguing that the Chinese philosophical and metaphysical system was consistent with the (Christian) Western one. The argument, known as the Rites Controversy, was defeated in Rome, but a version of it seems to be returning in the claim that Confucianism is just as much a "world religion" as Christianity is.[43]

Translation of Buddhist scriptures and development of Buddhist institutions continued to flourish at the imperial capital of Loyang until the Han Empire disintegrated into the Three Kingdoms (220–265 CE). The Western Jin (265–317) briefly reunified China but the dynasty came under increasing pressure from non-Chinese people and was ultimately forced to flee south of the Yangtze River. As northern China fell to various non-Chinese tribes, warfare and destruction forced many of the Buddhist leaders to flee south also, beginning a new phase of Chinese Buddhism.[44]

The defeat of the Chinese empire and the attendant miseries of war and exile seriously undermined *literati* confidence in traditional Confucian values. Disheartened and dismayed, living in an alien region of China, the refugees turned to philosophy and religion for solace and entertainment. Daoist theories of aesthetics and religion formed the basis of an abstruse metaphysics known as *xuan xue* (Dark Learning 玄學). *Xuan xue* is often identified as "Neo-Daoism," "Daoist metaphysics," or "Mysticism." Its name refers to the Sixth chapter of the *Daodejing*

The Valley spirit never dies
It is called the Mysterious (*xuan*) female
The entrance to the Mysterious female
Is called the root of Heaven and Earth

Endless flow
Of inexhaustible energy.[45]

Based on the *Yijing*, the *Daodejing* and the *Zhuangzi*, *xuan xue* explored esoteric, abstract, and mysterious truths including the relationship between "original non-being" (*benwu* 本無) and the phenomenal world. *Xuan xue* scholars taught that verbal, linguistic expressions were always inadequate ways of understanding fundamental reality. Thus the Neo-Daoist Wang Bi (226–249) claimed that it was necessary to "forget the symbols in order to grasp the ideas" and referred to the passage in the *Yijing*, "Writing does not completely express speech, nor does speech completely express ideas."[46]

Although the South was relatively isolated from the influx of Central Asians, Buddhist missionaries and monks continued to travel between northern and southern monasteries—sometimes as envoys, often as refugees from the fighting in the north. As they traveled south Chinese Buddhist scholars and translators encountered *xuan xue* beliefs in original non-being and the inexpressibility of truths about ultimate reality. Although these beliefs resonated with Buddhist beliefs about emptiness and the inexpressibility of Buddha Knowledge, Buddhist scholars were concerned that the meaning of Buddhist texts were being distorted by the association with Daoism, and thus they held the *geyi* translation/explanation method in contempt.[47]

The missionary translator Dao An (312–385) was particularly aware of the inadequacies of previous translations methods. His life almost precisely overlaps the period between the fall of the Western Jin (317) and the founding of the Northern Wei (386).

Dao An was a Chinese Buddhist monk from a family of Confucian scholars. He studied Buddhism in the north at Yeh where he may have been a disciple of Fotudeng. Warfare and devastation frequently made refugees out of communities of monks and Dao An eventually settled at Xianyang, which was then part of the Jin Empire. There he became familiar with *xuan xue* and was credited with being one of the early masters to develop a theory of "Fundamental Emptiness" (*pen-wu* / *ben-wu* 本無), a doctrine which seems to have roots in *xuan xue* learning

After fourteen years at Xianyang Dao An was brought to Changan by Fu Jian, the ruler of one of the most powerful kingdoms of the time who supported a translation project at Changan. Although Dao An's linguistic skills were not good enough for him to do any actually translating, he was thoroughly familiar with the ancient texts and literary traditions and advised the large translation team at Changan, discussing and correcting the versions produced by the foreign masters and writing important interpretive prefaces.

Concerned for the purity of Buddhism, Dao An struggled with the problems of translating the Buddhist scriptures into versions that were both faithful and readable by the Chinese public. Although he initially relied on the *geyi* system to understand and teach Buddhist thought eventually Dao An criticized *geyi* as being not "fit and proper," as "diverging from the original texts" and being "contrary to reason," i.e., opposed to the deeper meaning of Buddhist principles.[48] At Chan'an Dao An rejected *geyi* and developed his own rules for when translations should deviate from the original texts and when they had to follow the Sanskrit faithfully.[49]

Nevertheless, it was almost inevitable that Chinese Buddhist monks who knew only Chinese would continue to rely on *geyi* categories, continuing to see Buddhism as something Chinese.[50] It was not until Kumārajīva was brought to Changan in 401 that Chinese Buddhists began to distinguish between the original Indian Buddhism and the Chinese versions that had assimilated Buddhism to Daoism and *xuan xue* metaphysics.[51] Kumārajīva (350 or 344–413) was born in Kucha (west of Turfan, east of Kashgar) in 350 CE. He studied Buddhism at Kashmir and Kashgar, but in 384 Kucha was conquered by a Tibetan tribe. Kumārajīva was captured and taken to Liangzhou (in Gansu Province). In 401 another Tibetan ruler, Yao Xing, took Kumārajīva to Changan where he produced a great many excellent translations.[52] However, if "authentic Buddhism" is transcendental Indian Buddhism, it was too late for Chinese Buddhism to return to authenticity. The monk Huiyuan, a disciple of Dao An and founder of the Chinese school of Pure Land Buddhism, indicated as much in a famous correspondence with Kumārajīva. While Kumārajīva's influence had moved Huiyuan away from the *xuan xue* metaphysics he had learned from Dao An, Huiyuan continued to insist that the *dharmakaya*—something like the eternal Buddha nature or the spiritual body of the Buddhas—must be made out of some "stuff," something that no matter how subtle it is, you must be able to see and hear. Thus, Chinese "practical reasoning" (intuitivism/empiricism) continued to assert itself against Western (Buddhist/Greek) transcendental idealism.[53]

Missionaries in the North

In both the North and South, centuries of chaos undermined belief in traditional Confucian values and made the Chinese open to the teachings of missionaries from Central Asia. The relative isolation from Central Asian Buddhism and the dream of reunifying China under Han Confucian rule, kept Buddhism in the South primarily an activity of the *literati* elite. In the North it was different. The non-Chinese tribes of the Sixteen Kingdoms were constantly fighting each other and the armies of the South. The countryside was ravaged by war, bringing an era of devastation, famines, ruthless killing, and brutality. Although the non-Han dynasties of the North had very little contact with Confucian thought and no reason to want to rescue Confucian political certainties, they were desperate to find a way to rule the divided and demoralized populations they had conquered. Buddhism offered a solution. Buddhist monks, preaching compassion for all living beings, provided a unifying force between the nomads and the peoples they conquered. Ruler and ruled, Han and nomad, were equal in that they all were born, died, and suffered karmic retribution.

Accounts of the rise of Chinese Buddhism often focus on the great translation projects and the philosophical literature the Chinese Buddhist elite wrote in response to these translations; but the relentless warfare in the north brought many of these projects to an end. Nevertheless, Buddhist monks in the North continued to do missionary work among ordinary Chinese and their non-Han rulers. At the popular level Buddhist missionaries undertook to save all beings by establishing Buddhist institutions in China, monasteries or *sangha* (Buddhist communities) which engaged in charitable works, performed rituals, sponsored feasts and processions, and built temples. Because Buddhist magic was considered more powerful, Buddhist medicine more efficacious, and Buddhist fortune-telling more accurate than the Chinese alternatives, Buddhism became the major religion in northern China.

The enigmatic Buddhist monk Fotudeng [Fo-t'u-teng] played a significant role in establishing the tradition of state supported Buddhism in northern China. Fotudeng was probably born in the Buddhist kingdom of Kucha at the northern edge of Taklamakan desert. He arrived in Loyang in 310 when the city was still controlled by the Western Jin and immediately began practicing magic and divination.[54] It is not clear what kind of scholar Fotudeng was, or could have been, but he was a brilliant propagandist, dedicated missionary, and tireless organizer.[55] The year after Fotudeng's arrival in Loyang a group of Xiongnu invaders, led by Shi Le, a general of the Han Zhao Kingdom, sacked and burned the city, massacring the civilian population and killing thousands of Buddhist monks. Having witnessed the horrors caused by Shi Le's slaughter, Fotudeng decided to bring Buddhist compassion to the unusually brutal general, offering to use his knowledge of magic and prophecy to help Shi Le continue his conquests and rule the populations under his control.

A resourceful and loyal counselor, Fotudeng served the Shi family for thirty-eight years, advising them on agriculture, warfare, medicines, and religion. In return he obtained an edict of toleration for Buddhism permitting the establishment of Buddhist institutions and providing for the training of disciples free of state control. Fotudeng established a relationship between Buddhism and the non-Han rulers in the North that led to the participation of monks in all parts of court life and to state sponsorship of temples, translations, artists, and religious institutions. Despite Fotudeng's influence, however, Shi Le's armies, particularly those under the leadership of Shi Le's nephew Shi Hu, were known for their cruelty. At one time Shi Hu punished an assassination plot by executing one of his own sons, his daughter-in-law, numerous children, and hundreds of followers.

Nevertheless, the monks Fotudeng trained, strengthened and spread Chinese Buddhism. The institutions he established and the close cooperation of church and state were invaluable in the development of Buddhism at both the elite and popular level in the North. At the elite level Buddhist clergy and laity discussed both the *xuan xue* metaphysics that gradually made its way up from the South and the translations being produced by the great translation centers. Although most of the translation centers were located in the North, their work was frequently disrupted by war and northern Buddhists did very little of the creative speculative thinking typical of southern Buddhist thought.[56] Northern court and popular Buddhism focused more on Buddhism as magic, seeing its sutras as sources of spells.

As economic and military conditions deteriorated, Buddhist monasteries replaced the large family estates, both as economic powerhouses, running mills, and olive presses, and as sources of charity and safety from the warfare and demands of corvée labor. Chinese and non-Han peasants saw Buddhist institutions as one of the few sources of solace and refuge in a time of chaos and destruction. Buddhist monks ministered to the needs of the suffering population and popular Buddhism absorbed local and family cults. An inscription at a cave temple at Longmen shows just how thoroughly integrated Buddhism was into popular beliefs:

> We respectfully make and present this holy image in honor of the Buddhas, Bodhisattvas, and pray that all living creatures may attain salvation, and particularly that the souls of our ancestors and relatives [names given] may find repose and release.[57]

Rise of the Northern Wei

In the last years before the Jin dynasty was forced to flee south, it formed an alliance with a small, loosely organized Tuoba tribe of the Xianbei, giving the Tuoba chief the title of the Prince of Dai. When northern China fractured into the Sixteen Kingdoms, the Tuoba state was too weak and disorganized to be considered one of the Sixteen Kingdoms, but in 386, after the defeat of one of the most formidable states of the time, the Tuoba ruler changed the name of his state to Wei, indicating his ambition to succeed the Cao Wei—the powerful northern state of the Three Kingdoms (220–265). The Tuoba Wei conquered its neighbors until it had complete control of northern China, including all the major centers of Buddhism: Loyang, Changan, Xiangguo (the capital of Later Zhao Dynasty), Ye, Xiangyang, and Dunhuang. Although many of these centers had been devastated in the fighting and the surviving monks were refugees in remote mountain areas or monasteries in the south, the rule of the Northern Wei provided northern China with over one hundred years of relative peace and economic prosperity and greatly accelerated the spread of Buddhism to the east.

Because northern China had been severely depopulated by continual warfare, disease, and starvation, invading armies were often little more than slave raiders. Conquered peoples were considered spoils of war; and the Northern Wei deported hundreds of thousands of farmers, laborers, and craftsmen from the territories it conquered—usually to the Wei capital Pingcheng.[58] Torn from everything familiar—family, land, and language—they suffered the fate of slaves everywhere. The semi-nomadic Tuoba Wei despised farmers and farming and put their slaves to work on the land around their cities, developing a system of land management (reform) that created a prosperous agricultural base. The forced moves caused incredible hardship and a great many deaths, but the skills of the survivors greatly enriched the ruling dynasty.

The Tuoba Wei had a strong military tradition, but had no experience governing large territories and were greatly outnumbered by its citizens—Chinese, other groups of Xianbei, Xiongnu, and even Koreans; tensions between various ethnic groups often erupted in violence and slaughter.[59] Like the people they ruled, most of the Tuoba Wei were devout Buddhists. Buddhist institutions and the Buddhist belief, generally accepted at the time that all living beings had a Buddha nature, provided a way to unify a society deeply divided among ethnic and class lines.[60] Buddhist ritual, ceremonies, feasts and processions brought the Wei rulers and their subjects together. Buddhist clergy advised the court, and the Wei state sponsored the building of Buddhist temples and monasteries. At the same time, the Wei court wanted to control clergy, limiting the number of monks and nuns, insisting that they be registered, and setting conditions for ordination. The court also tried to prevent, without much success, the practice of ordaining slaves and removing them from their households.[61] In rural areas, where the monasteries and hermitages were small and there were very few official clergy, unregistered "rebel monks" not living in Buddhist institutions, and popular Buddhist associations unconnected to a monastery, worked to save all beings by preaching, reading scriptures, reciting mantras, and practicing healing magic, and occasionally leading extremely bloody eschatological rebellions. Although many scholars agree with the Wei court that unregistered monks were dangerous subversives, Daniel Overmyer challenges the assumption that popular political religion is somehow less "pure" and therefore inferior to officially sanctioned religion, imperial Confucianism, orthodox Buddhism, or mainstream Christianity.[62] Unregistered monks and institutions operating without official sanction were probably serving a real need in their communities.

Officially sanctioned Buddhist institutions were not unproblematic either. Their growing power led to conflict with the ruling military who wanted to curb the drain on sources of labor needed for building projects and armies, and with the Daoist clergy who saw the Buddhist monks as direct competitors. The conflict erupted in periodic persecutions; the first of which (446–452) began when the Tuoba Emperor Taiwu established a Daoist theocracy and drastically restricted Buddhist organizations and activities.[63] The persecution ended when the Emperor Wencheng succeeded Taiwu and made amends for the persecution by starting construction of the cave temples at Yungang. These temples contain some of the most impressive Wei Dynasty Buddhas. In return for the emperor's support, the Buddhist clergy resolved the problem of conflicting loyalties by announcing that the reigning emperor was a Buddha incarnate. This was not the last persecution, but popular Buddhism was too strong in northern China to be seriously threatened, at least as long as the chaos caused by disunity, war, starvation, and conquest continued.

Like many northern dynasties, as the Tuoba Wei became increasingly powerful and secure it began to sinicize. In 494, in a deeply symbolic move, the emperor moved the Wei capital from Pingcheng to the ancient Chinese capital city of Loyang. The court also encouraged intermarriages between the Tuoba Wei and Chinese, and adopted Chinese court dress. With the move of the capital work on the Yungang cave temples stopped and construction of new cave temples near Loyang began. The most

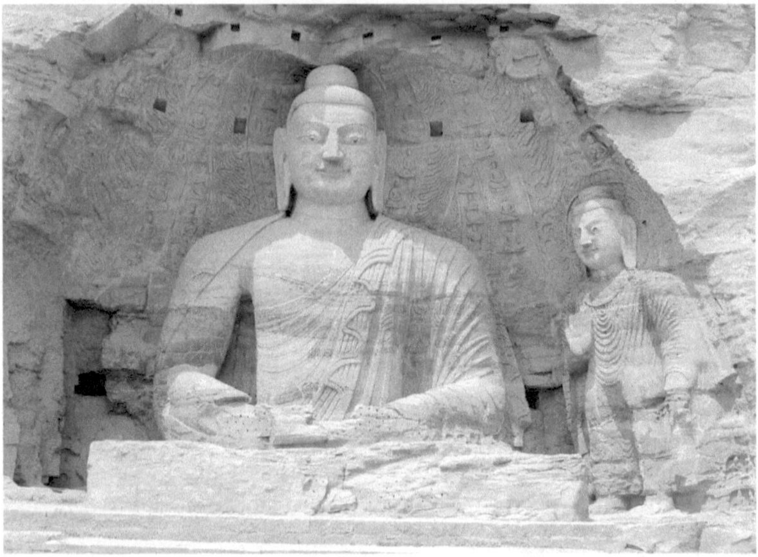

FIGURE 3.11. Buddha and aureole, Cave 20, Yungang, Datong. Second half of the fifth century. Photographer: Marcin Białek.

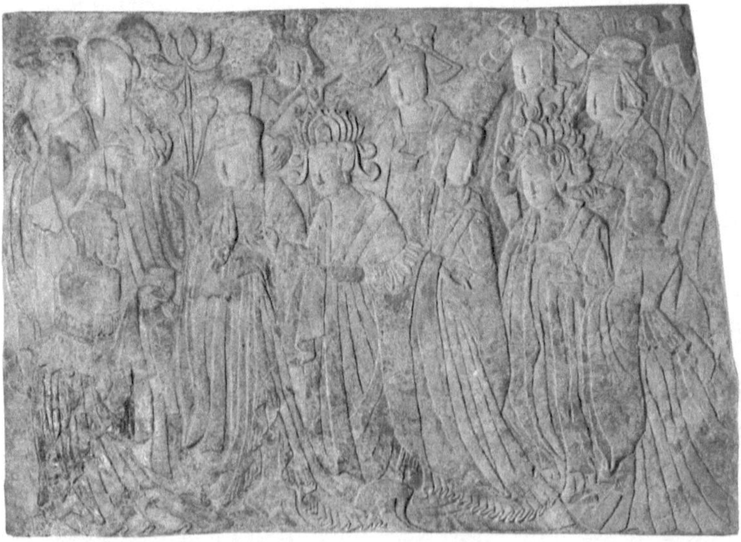

FIGURE 3.12. Offering Procession of the Wei Empress with Her Court, from Longmen, Binyang Central Cave, Henan Province, ca. 522 CE. The Nelson-Atkins Museum of Art Kansas City, Missouri. Purchase: William Rockwell Nelson Trust. Procession: Longmen Caves, Northern Wei Dynasty.

important of the Loyang caves was at Longmen where the Northern Wei Buddhist style in which Buddhas and bodhisattvas, like the Tuoba aristocracy, wore Chinese court robes, predominated.

The iconography of the beautiful east wall relief from the Binyang central cave at Longmen presents a clear vision of Northern Wei Buddhism.[64] There are four layers in the relief. Over the doorway the top of the relief presents the debate between Vimalakīrti and Mañjusrī, in which Vimalakīrti, a wealthy and compassionate layman who lived at home with his family, defeats Mañjusrī, reputed to be the wisest enlightened being.[65] The Vimalakīrti sutra was extremely popular among Chinese *literati* and the sinicized Wei court, at least as much for its presentation of Vimalakīrti as an unordained and respected Buddhist layman, as for the explanation and defense of the doctrine of non-duality.[66] To many *literati* Vimalakīrti seemed to be an ideal to which they would aspire, wise and devout but living at home with his family. In the upper right of the wall Vimalakīrti, accompanied by female attendants, holds a fan and leans comfortably against a pillow. On the left Mañjusrī is surrounded by bodhisattvas. As

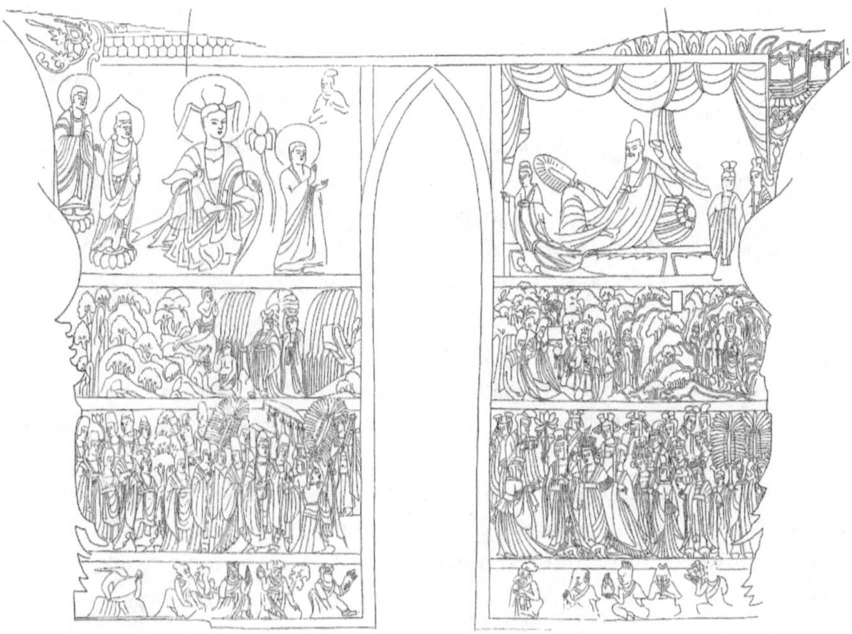

FIGURE 3.13. Reconstruction of the east wall relief of Binyang Central Cave, Longmen. Drawing courtesy of Amy McNair.

befitting their status as holy beings the figures are idealized, with the thin bodies and flowing robes of the Northern Wei style. The second level of the wall illustrates two of the best known Jataka stories. To the left the Prince who sacrifices his life to feed a starving tigress and her cubs is shown jumping gracefully off the cliff toward the hungry animals. The right panel shows the tale of a Prince who gave away a prized white elephant. Below the Jataka stories are two imperial processions—one led by the Emperor and the other by the Empress.[67] The Court figures are more realistic than those of the top panel, with details of court dress, headdresses, flowers, shoes, and fans carefully depicted. Nevertheless, the square heads, long necks, and flowing robes of the Imperial couple and their entourage identify these beautiful panels as examples of the Northern Wei Buddhist style. The lowest level of the wall depicts a series of unidentified "spirit kings," nature deities who probably had connections to the semi-human dwarf sculptures of the Han dynasty, to Sogdian monsters, and perhaps even to Roman gods and figures from the worship of Dionysus and Zoroaster. Highly skilled artists considered how worshipers leaving the temple would perceive these figures and sculpted their facial details to take advantage of the natural light coming through the doorway creating a sense of three dimensions. Now that the figures have been removed from their intended setting in the temple the wall, museum curators are not always able to reproduce the effect.[68]

The layers of the wall depict Northern Wei Buddhism as a sedimented whole combining abstract Buddhist philosophy, popular stories of the Buddha; imperial piety, and public support of Buddhism; and echoes of earlier folk religions from all the areas through which Buddhism had traveled and which had been assimilated into popular Buddhism. The graceful figures in the wall suggest that the disparate elements of the Northern Wei Empire had been unified by Buddhist worship.

Unfortunately, this pleasantly idealized picture was not to last. The move of the capital to Loyang and the sinicization of the Wei court helped the dynasty control its Chinese subjects; but ultimately it led to the fall of the Wei Dynasty. The Wei military that remained in the northern garrisons defending the dynasty against competing tribes resented an imperial court which was more appreciative of Chinese civilization than the older military traditions. At the same time, the Wei court was weakened by scandals and intrigues. When her son disapproved of her affairs, the Empress Dowager Hu poisoned him and tried to replace him with his daughter, pretending she was a son. The northern garrisons rebelled and the generals responsible for protecting the Empress turned against her, slaughtering thousands of courtiers, almost the entire Wei aristocracy, and drowning the Empress and the child emperor.[69] As the Wei Empire collapsed, the wars, devastation, treachery, cruelty, and turmoil of the period before the Northern Wei returned to northern China.

The end of the Wei Dynasty was also the end of the Northern Wei style of Buddhist sculpture. Construction in the Longmen caves ceased with the destruction of the dynasty. When the Sui dynasty reunified China, building at Longmen resumed, but by this time Buddhist sculpture, like Buddhist scriptural interpretation, had become increasingly concerned to return to a "genuine Indian" style. Because the constant warfare in Central Asia and northern China had thoroughly disrupted trade along the Silk Road, trade between China and India increasingly followed the water route around Southeast Asia, resulting in a Chinese Buddhist art that was influenced by the sensual art from Southeast Asia rather than by Central Asian models.

After the fall of the Northern Wei, Buddhist sculpture became more realistic and secular. By the time of the Tang dynasty Buddhas and

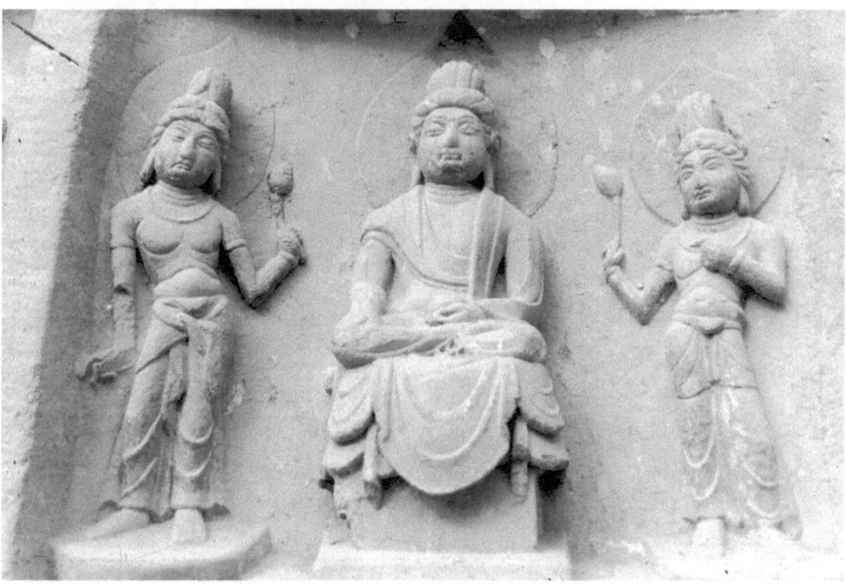

FIGURE 3.14. Buddha and Bodhisattva, Tang Dynasty (618–906), Binglinsi Caves, Grotto 30, Gansu, China.

bodhisattvas had human faces, sensuous bodies, and looked very much like members of the Tang court. The Bodhisattva in figuse 3.15 could easily pass for a Tang Dynasty noblewoman. Sensual as Sui and Tang Dynasty sculpture was, however, it never approaches the sensuality—sexual and scatological—of Southeast Asian religious art.

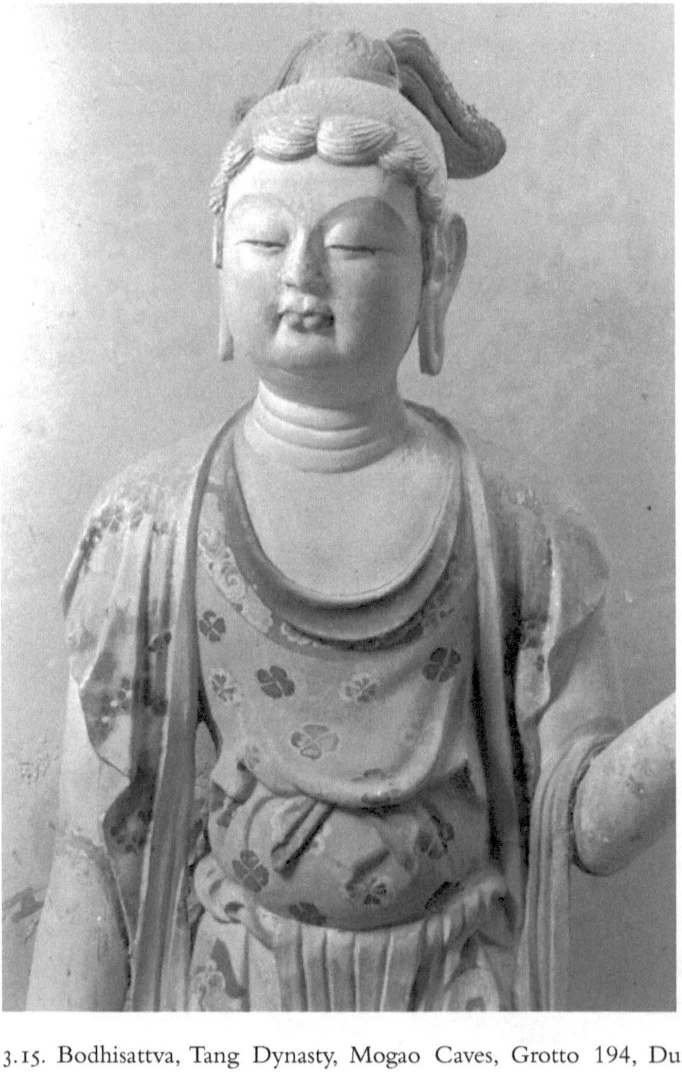

FIGURE 3.15. Bodhisattva, Tang Dynasty, Mogao Caves, Grotto 194, Dunhuang, Gansu, China.

Although a discussion of the philosophical influence of Indian Buddhism on Chinese thought is beyond the scope of this chapter, the attempt to return to "genuine Indian Buddhism" resulted in a Buddhism that was not only artistically, but philosophically and religiously, even more Chinese than ever.

Aesthetic Experience and Religion

On Li Zehou's theory of aesthetic experience (pleasures of the will and spirit *yue zhi yue shen* 悦 志悦神), we must know the historical, cultural, and philosophical context of the Northern Wei Buddhas in order to have a genuine aesthetic experience of them; but intellectual understanding is not sufficient for aesthetic experience.[70] The cognitive element of an aesthetic experience is simply the most easily described part of a complex experience which provides intense pleasure. Although this pleasure is "disinterested" in the sense that aesthetic objects are not immediately useful, our emotional responses to aesthetic objects—pleasure and pain, delight and frustration—cannot be divorced from the sedimentation of thousands of years of human history, of productive, social, and sensuous life in the world. In aesthetic experience all the elements of aesthetic attention (pleasure of the heart-mind and mood): sensation, emotion, imagination and understanding come together in a complex harmony—with different elements predominating in different experiences.[71]

All that we have learned about the Northern Wei Buddhas may seem to fade away as we look at their thin bodies, elegant flowing robes, and mysterious smiling faces. What are they saying about those brief experiences of peace and calm in generally disastrous and chaotic times? The aesthetic experience of the Northern Wei Buddhas implies a relationship between art and religion, aesthetic and religious experience.

Aesthetic and religious experiences are often distinguished by what is being experienced. Aesthetic experiences are of particular sensuous objects. Religious experiences on the other hand, are often described as experiences of a Transcendent Other, the Sacred, a reality beyond the empirical, phenomenal sensuous one. This description of religious experiences appears to entail an ontological commitment to the existence of two "realms" or worlds: the immanent, sensuous, world; and a transcendent reality that is nonsensuous and timeless.[72]

Li argues that what we identify as the transcendent ontological realm is a human creation.[73] It was not created by a particular individual, or society, or culture, but by the species as a whole while we became human. The construction of a realm of "timeless truth" began in rituals in which we attempted to communicate with nonhuman spiritual forces and developed the sense of social unity required for moral communities. The realm of "timeless truth" was created as we learned mathematics, looked for universal scientific laws, and came to understand the moral principles that sustain a humane society. The transcendent realm is a product of the psychological, cognitive, emotional, and sensuous structures that make us human. The structures allow us to imagine things beyond our experiences, freeing us from time to "experience an event in the past as though it were present" and to transcend space when we respond to distant objects as "if they were with us."[74] Li values aesthetic experiences precisely because they do not attempt to transcend the sensuous by negating or repressing it. A Confucian version of religious or aesthetic experience is not one of moving away from the sensuous, phenomenal world of pleasure and pain to an utterly different nonsensuous world, but rather of a harmony between particular human experience, the past and present of the human species and the cosmos.[75]

Great artworks are historical because they belong to a particular time and place, and timeless because they continually renew themselves by revealing new meanings in different eras to different audiences. Because art merges past, present, and future, Li claims "art is eternal, as long as the human species survives."[76] But this, of course, is "not really eternal" since we know our species will become extinct long before the universe itself dies. On the other hand, participating in the sedimented transcendent ontological world—through mathematics, through science, through life affirming religions and aesthetic experience—can give us great pleasure and is as close as sensuous beings can come to immortality.[77]

Conclusion

How then are we to interpret the smiles of the Northern Wei Dynasty Buddhas? Having begun by being haunted by their smiles, aesthetic attention turned us to their historical, social, and theological context. From one perspective these smiles can be seen as expressing an ascetic life denying Buddhism, or as a way to temporality relieve and even justify the oppression, wars, starvation, slaughters, and forced migration of one of the most violent periods in human history. Moreover, we remain twenty-first-century thinkers with particular religious histories and political upheavals sedimented into our individual and cultural consciousness.

On the other hand, aesthetic attention allows us to imagine life during the Northern Wei Dynasty. The era had been preceded by, and would be followed by, periods of horrifying violence; the society was divided by class and ethnicity. Terrible as these times were, they are sadly not unique in human history. There have been, and undoubtedly will be, many such times. Nevertheless, the Northern Wei Dynasty was a time of relative peace. The Northern Wei aristocrats had the wealth and leisure to build great temples, and to wonder if there would be retribution, perhaps after death, for some of the actions that brought them to positions of wealth and power. Like reflective citizens of almost any age of peace and material prosperity, they may have noticed that once material survival at a certain level of comfort has been attained, "more things" do not make us happier, much less immortal. Buddhism preached compassion for all living beings at a time when it was desperately needed. Buddhist rituals and institutions brought members of the divided society together; providing relief from suffering, and a sense of being one community. Looking at these Buddhas we are transported into the Northern Wei, identifying both with the Wei, who massacred and enslaved the populations they had defeated and who would soon be conquered and slaughtered themselves, and with their subjects, who suffered terribly, but who endured to build new lives, material prosperity, and great beauty. Although the particular circumstances, the temples and rituals of Northern Wei Buddhism, have disappeared into the past, some of the religious emotion of the time remains in these smiles. The religious aura of these Buddhas is greatly diminished with their removal from the ceremonies and the culture in which they played such an important role, but it is not completely gone, or at least, it can remind us of something about contemporary religions.

The traditional function of religious institutions includes helping people face death, fight poverty, and relieve suffering.[78] While these institutions may also provide refuge from oppressive states and families, when religious institutions become rigidly orthodox they can become oppressive themselves. At such times, perhaps particularly in a relentlessly secular age such as our own, people look for alternatives. As we saw in chapter 2, faith and participation in religious ritual is only one of many paths to religious or spiritual experiences.

There are, for example, a growing number of Americans who identify themselves as "Spiritual but not Religious." These people generally reject traditional religious institutions but retain an ontological commitment to a "higher power" and a belief in some sort of afterlife. Many of them appear to experience a version of the "nature mysticism" described in chapter 2 when they "see God" on the beach, or in a sunset. The concern is that these experiences, like the often puzzling experiences we have with "foreign religions," or during brief visits to museums to view "great art"—are typically private and transitory. Without any sort of discipline, cut off from any context or community, these experiences threaten to result in isolated individuals, complacently pleased with the "deep thoughts" they share with themselves.[79]

The path to a genuine religious, spiritual, or aesthetic experience involves a process which may begin in many ways: faith and the practice of religious rituals; dedication to scholarship or scientific research; the sense of union with nature typical of nature mysticism expressed by Wordsworth in "Tintern Abbey."[80] It may start with an interest in adjusting one's body and mind to the rhythms of nature by practicing qigong, tai chi, yoga, or meditation.[81] Aesthetic experience begins with an aesthetic attitude, "pleasure of the ear and eye." It requires the intellectual and emotional exploration of aesthetic attention, "pleasure of the heart-mind and mood," and results in an aesthetic experience, "pleasure of the will (*zhi*) and spirit (*shen*)." Calling these pleasures *shen* (spirit) clearly makes them spiritual, not in the sense of negating sensual pleasures but of including more than sensual pleasure. Once we have moved beyond the sense of strangeness, we see that the Northern Wei Buddhas are beautiful. Furthermore, since as I argued in chapter 1, *zhi* is always in some sense moral, these pleasures also have a moral aspect. Aesthetic experience involves recognizing that one is part of the human community, and has a commitment to Li's version of the categorical imperative, to the thriving of our species, which cannot help but include compassion for suffering human beings.

The smiles of the Northern Wei Buddhas reflect this compassion. The world of the Northern Wei was a human world, full of suffering—personal, national, cultural, global. Suffering is inevitable. Christians describe life as a "veil of tears." Buddhists point to the First Noble Truth. These gentle smiles tell us that life is not always suffering, there is also great pleasure. They are a message of sympathy and hope, although not perhaps for a better "life after death." They remind us that we are living in a world where compassion exists and is sedimented not only in these absolutely beautiful statues, but also in the political and intellectual institutions that produced them. Rather than demanding an ontological commitment to a transcendent world, these smiles promise that there is a way out (for some of us, some of the time) in terms of an experience that makes us see ourselves part of a vast human community, a community capable of creating great beauty and sharing it with us over long distances in space and time.

If, however, there is an insurmountable ontological distinction between religious and aesthetic experiences. . . .

If the claim made by Confucian philosophers to be able to reconcile the two worlds and make sense of something like "transcendent-immanence" or the harmony of humanity and cosmos as long as humanity survives, is ultimately incoherent . . .

If we have to distinguish the spiritual goals of religion, and art, and science—and of the various religions, arts, and sciences, and to prioritize their paths to these goals, making one more meaningful than the other, then the argument of this chapter won't work.

If it does work, however, then Deutsch is wrong and at the deepest level the artist and the saint *are* doing each other's job.

4

The Meaning of "Horse"

> To "read" a Chinese painting is to enter into a dialogue with the past; the act of unrolling a scroll or leafing through an album provides a further, physical connection to the work. An intimate experience, it is one that has been shared and repeated over the centuries.
>
> And it is through such readings, enjoyed alone or in the company of friends that meaning is gradually revealed.[1]

During the height of the Tang Dynasty the Emperor Xuanzong (712–756) commissioned a famous painter of horses, Han Gan (ca. 720–780), to paint one of his favorite war horses, Night-Shining White. Night-Shining White appears in his portrait as a powerful and spirited horse fighting against the post to which he is tied. The painting is done in monochrome with ink shading, called *baihua*, "white painting," along the horse's back, neck, chest, and belly to make the horse's powerful legs and impressive rump stand out in three dimensions. Night-Shining White's twisting body and thrashing hooves create a sense of strength and movement. His head is raised; his nostril flared; his mouth is open; his eyes are fierce and his mane stands up.[2] The horse is glaring at us indignantly. Is he asking for sympathy and help? Is he complaining about having to stand for his portrait? Is he protesting that he, the Emperor's favorite horse, should not be treated this way?

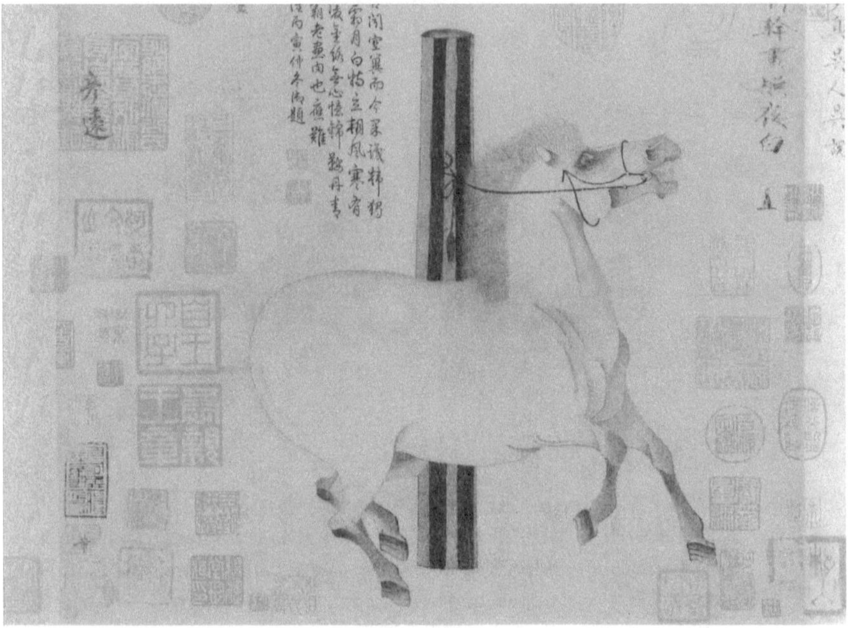

FIGURE 4.1. *Night-Shining White* by Han Gan, ca. 750. Purchase the Dillon Fund Gift, 1977. Image copyright © The Metropolitan Museum of Art. Image source: Art Resource, New York.

The original picture of *Night-Shining White* is only about one foot square and has been retouched in several places, but the painting has become part of a much larger work. More than a thousand years after it was painted, Night-Shining White's portrait is embedded in a hand scroll more than 20-feet long containing inscriptions and seals added over the centuries by people who have owned and enjoyed the picture. By the eleventh century the collectors and admirers of the painting understood that its association with Emperor Xuanzong made *Night Shining White* not only a symbol of Chinese pride and power, but a warning against the sort of mismanagement that occurred at the tragic end of the Xuanzong's reign.

The inscriptions and seals indicate that the painting remained in the imperial family for more than a thousand years. When the Qing Dynasty collapsed, however, many works in the collection were sold or given away and taken out of Beijing. In the nineteenth century the Jiaqing Emperor (r. 1796–1820) gave *Night-Shining White* to one of his younger brothers, Prince Cheng (Yongxing), and the painting was eventually acquired by a Japanese collector. In 1977 it was purchased by the Metropolitan Museum of Art.[3] This delightful painting continues to charm audiences. In 2002 it was one of the featured works in the exhibition "A Millennium of Chinese Painting" at the Metropolitan Museum of Art. Night-Shining White's image has appeared on post cards, tote bags, and refrigerator magnets.

The calligraphy and seals on Chinese paintings attest to the intimate relationship between painting and writing. Chinese characters began as pictures and the relationship between the characters and the original pictures has never been completely lost. Although many of the explanations of the origins of Chinese characters is apocryphal, the fact that these explanations are provided is significant. Painting and calligraphy both require the "four treasures": brush, inkstone, ink, and paper. Painters use calligraphic brush strokes and often write poems and explanations on their paintings, while generations of collectors and connoisseurs add verses and appreciative remarks to paintings that inspire them. Indeed Chinese paintings are frequently described as having been "written" rather than painted, encouraging us to "read" a Chinese painting in the way described in the quotation at the head of this chapter. Thus, theories of the meaning of art and of language may illuminate puzzles in both fields.

This chapter will begin by setting out several theories of meaning in language. These theories will then be used to explore the history of horse painting in Chinese art and the evolution of the meaning of horses in Chinese art.

Theories of Meaning in Language and Aesthetics

In his essay "The Meaning of 'Meaning'" (1975) Hilary Putnam argues that meanings are not abstract entities, mental or psychological states "in the head."[4] Instead Putnam claims that the meanings of words are determined by social, contextual, and historical factors. While this may seem uncontroversial, Putnam is challenging a theory that has a long and respectable philosophical pedigree going back as least as far as Plato. The theory identifies the meaning of a word as its "cognitive content," that is, the concept the word is expressing.[5] Thus, I know the meaning of a word when I am in a relationship with its cognitive content, that is, I understand a word because its meaning is part of my psychological state. Knowing the cognitive content, or sense, of a word like "horse" allows me to identify the objects and situations to which the word refers, including individual horses—Night-Shining White, Bucephalus, and Man-o'-War.

A major advantage of this theory is that it explains how translation and historical understanding are possible. At various times and places people use words in different languages to mean "the same thing," that is, to express the same cognitive content. Thus, one way people who only understand modern English can "enter a dialogue with the past" and—with the help of excellent and hardworking translators—communicate across vast distances of space, time, and culture with people who know only ancient Greek or classical Chinese, is to be in the same relationship with the cognitive content of each other's words. This theory does not claim that doing a translation or examining history is straightforward or easy, only that it is, sometimes, possible.

Put this way, the theory Putnam undercuts is an intuitively plausible way to avoid the following kind of skepticism and relativism:

> *No two people, but particularly people of different cultures and historical eras share the same social context. Since meanings are determined by their social historical context, we can never know what someone else means. Translation and inter-cultural communication are therefore fundamentally impossible. We can only hope to understand people who are very much like us; even historians do not write about the past, as it actually was; they only reflect the prejudices of the present.*

Philosophers who identify meaning with language independent, cognitive content reject relativism of this sort, arguing that while various language users may have different interpretations—beliefs about what something means—in many cases there is such a thing as "getting it right," with which anyone with a healthy concern for important matters like truth must be concerned.[6] Differences in interpretations are explained by noting that in addition to their cognitive content, words may have an emotive content reflecting the emotional state of the language user—including her particular social and historical beliefs and prejudices—and creating an emotional response in the audience.[7] Emotive content can be very powerful, but not only is it irrelevant to the any kind of objective meaning, it tends to distract us from that meaning. This theory has significant importance for politics and morality. Without some hope of agreement on what the phrase "human rights" means, a document like the United Nations Declaration of Human Rights makes very little sense. Without shared meanings it seems impossible to distinguish between "justice" and "the way we usually do things."

Putnam challenges this view by noting that the concepts (cognitive content) of ordinary speakers are often too vague and inaccurate to allow us to identify the objects to which our concepts refer. Although Putnam's argument relies on a science fiction example, he buttresses his case, almost as an aside, with the example of the Chinese word for jade which refers to two different minerals, jadeite and nephrite.[8] Without significant scientific knowledge of the chemical composition of jadeite and nephrite ordinary speakers of Chinese and English could incorrectly identify two different minerals as "the same thing," i.e., "jade." Putnam argues that any scientifically interesting sense of meaning is determined by a division of linguistic labor in which ordinary speakers are supported by a community of experts who have the relevant scientific knowledge to properly identify objects and correct or clarify common usage.[9]

One difficulty with Putnam's view is that the "scientific method" used by the community of experts is in fact several methods, all of which are constantly evolving. Thus there may be a number of "communities of experts" whose views differ. This moves the question of linguistic relativism to another level:

> *That is nephrite not jadeite; Pluto is one of many dwarf planets, not a major planet, a whale is a mammal not a fish, at least according to the standards we now accept—although perhaps not according to some past or future standards.*

Putnam rejects this line of reasoning because its relativistic implications threaten the concept of truth, of "getting it right," really, truly, once and for all.[10]

The notion that there is a "community of experts" who can decide what words really mean, and whether sentences containing them are true or not, is quite plausible in science where the community of scientific experts is a genuinely global institution whose members communicate, at least about their research, with little if any linguistic misunderstanding. In other areas, however, the case is more complicated. For example, there seems to be little evidence that there is a global community of experts on matters of international justice. The "court of world opinion" comes to different decisions depending on where it meets. The case of aesthetic meaning is at least as complex as that of the meaning of "justice" and "rights."

Theories of the meaning of language have parallels in aesthetics. The view that meanings are the cognitive content of language is analogous to the claim that a work of art has an "aesthetic content." Many artworks have a "representational content" analogous to the reference of a word, the objects, or the situation it represents. The representational content of pictures of horses is, naturally enough, horses. But not all pictures of horses are works of art. One theory is that something is a work of art if and only if it has an "aesthetic content."[11] Just as two people who do not understand the same language can understand the meaning (cognitive content) of each other's words, people from different cultural contexts appreciate the same work of art because they recognize its aesthetic content. This view is found in what Danto has called "familiar image of the historically ignorant viewer transfixed by the timeless power of artworks"[12] and could be used to explain the popularity of Han Gan's portrait in twenty-first-century New York. This timeless power is an effect of the "aesthetic content" of art, that special quality/property that only works of art possess which makes them meaningful in a way that other objects are not and allows people from different times and places to appreciate each other's art. Sounds, or marks that express cognitive content are meaningful pieces of language; those that do not are only noise or scratches. Deutsch claims that objects that have aesthetic content are art; those that do not may be more or less skillfully executed propaganda, or pornography, but not genuine art.[13]

Recognizing the tremendous emotional power of art, many philosophers identify the emotive content of a work of art as the feelings expressed by its creator or roused in its audience, and go on to claim that the aesthetic content of a work of art simply is its emotive content. In a similar move some philosophers claim that statements about moral values have only an emotive content. On these views aesthetic and ethical judgments only seem to be meaningful; on closer examination these judgments are simply expressions of, or occasions for, emotional reactions.

Identifying the aesthetic content of a work with its emotive content suggests that there is no such thing as "getting it right" in aesthetics. Emotional responses vary so greatly between people and cultures that it is hard to see how such responses, the archetypical case of "subjectivity," could be "right" or "wrong." One reason for not taking art seriously is the suspicion that artistic judgments, unlike those of science and mathematics, are only a matter of taste, personal preference, or transitory and often wildly changing fashions.

Rather than dismiss the emotive content of art as temporary and unimportant, totalitarian thinkers, religious puritans, and advertising executives recognize the power of art and take it very seriously. Political thinkers from Plato to Goebbels and the socialist realists of the former Soviet Union and Mao's China have used this power to stimulate "noble" patriotic emotions and to censor art that rouses "decadent" feelings which threaten the health of the state. The religious right is similarly concerned to proscribe art which appeals to the "lower" sensual emotions encouraging heresy and immorality. A great deal of contemporary advertising relies on the fact that "sex sells."

The relationship between art, politics, and morality is viewed quite differently in other traditions. Medieval European art was supposed to serve, or at least not conflict with, the goals of theology and morality, and as such much of it might be considered propaganda for the Church.[14] Confucius insisted that there is an intimate relationship between art and morality, advising us to "Set your sights on the way, sustain yourself with excellence, lean upon authoritative conduct, and sojourn in the arts" (*Analects*, 7.6). In the modern West, however, art and morality are thought of as independent, and one's artistic values are to be kept quite distinct from one's morality. Defending her negative remarks about Nochlin's *Women, Art, Power and Other Essays*, critic and artist Maureen Mullarkey claims that "[a]n artistic conscience and a social conscience are not the same, and there is too much at stake to confuse them."[15]

In a related vein, Eliot Deutsch writes that the aesthetic content of genuine art "immunizes its subject matter (insofar as it has one in the first place)" by transforming it into something outside the range of "interest-motivated politics and sectarian-political concerns."[16] Deutsch argues that because "genuine art" has an aesthetic content it should be protected from political and religious censorship. On the other hand, nothing he says is incompatible with the commercial, political, or religious control and use of pseudo-art, works without aesthetic content, as propaganda, or more or less disguised pornography. But how do we decide if a work has an aesthetic content?

Since locating the meaning of language in the mental states of individual language users and the cognitive content of their beliefs ignores the significant role of social factors in determining meaning, Putnam argued that the meaning of a word is determined by two groups: ordinary speakers and the community of scientific experts. The Institutional View of Art makes a similar move with respect to the aesthetic content of a work of art. On the Institutional View the status of something as a work of art is conferred by the relevant community of experts who are members of "the art world," people who know a great deal of art history and theory.[17] Although the primary members of the art world are artists, museum curators, collectors, and art critics, in one version of this view, anyone who considers herself to be a member of the institution is one. Thus, the meaning of a work of art, its aesthetic content, is determined by a complex interaction between artists, their audiences, and the set of historical, cultural, and social circumstances in which art is produced and enjoyed.

One difficulty with the view that social institutions and historical context determine whether a work has an aesthetic content is that it would make the issue of censorship a great deal more complex since we could not appeal to a context-independent content to protect artworks from censorship. If anyone who considers herself a member of the art world is one, political or religious authorities could declare themselves members of the art world and decide that works they found offensive or dangerous had no aesthetic content and were simply propaganda or pornography.

On the other hand, narrowing the membership of the art world to a relatively small "community of experts"—collectors, museum directors and academics—isolates art from the experiences that make it meaningful, turning art into the relatively trivial concern of a small group of people and separating art from daily life, greatly diminishing the power of works of art and making them appear remote and academic.[18] Finally, the art world has become increasingly dominated by the art market, so much so that Mullarkey can justify the separation of her artistic and social conscience by noting that "[p]olitical art, fashionable for its radical cachet, is as convertible to cash as any other kind. This should signal art's irrelevance as a political act."[19] One need not be a Marxist to deplore the general trend of modern life to reduce all value to economics and increasingly identifying aesthetic content with "cash value."

The community of scientific experts is more or less able to protect science from censorship by political interests and from the attempt to judge the value of scientific research with how much money it makes.[20] Ordinary language users are generally competent to determine the cognitive content (meaning) of their beliefs and only need to consult the experts when normal standards fail to make important distinctions—Is this jadeite or nephrite? Sometimes the judgment of the community of art experts is accepted—Is this a Song dynasty painting or a modern forgery? Other times, however, their authority is less recognized. Is this object offensive because it is so new that I do not understand it, or is it the kind of material that should neither be displayed in public nor given any kind of public support?

One reason for this lack of confidence in the art community, compared to the almost religious authority of the scientific community, is that, as a social institution, the art world is far less historically stable than the community of scientists. While it is at least plausible that scientific standards, including scientific methods, improve over time, it is more difficult to make a similar claim about aesthetic standards. It is fairly unproblematic to argue that our ability to prevent smallpox has vastly improved in the last two centuries. It makes very little sense to argue that Mahler is "better than" Handel. Moreover, works of art may have different meanings at different times, in different places. The same work might be "art" in one context but not in another. On the other hand, there does seem to be something like "getting is right" in the study of history and culture, and the lack of a universal and timeless "aesthetic content" may not lead to the sort of skepticism—"it is all only a matter of opinion"—implied by emotive theories of art and morality. Indeed another reason for the lack of confidence in art experts may be that unlike the chemical formula for water, or the classification of minerals, art, like morality, is too important to be left to the experts.

Our original delight in Han Gan's painting, our "aesthetic attitude" in Li Zehou's analysis of aesthetic experience (described in chapter 2), leads to a number of philosophical, historical, and political questions, questions that demand what Li Zehou calls "aesthetic attention." This chapter will describe how the meaning of Chinese horse paintings, their aesthetic content, has been created by an evolving community of artists, collectors, poets, and critics working in a particular historical and cultural situations.[21]

Han Gan's portrait of Night-Shining White belongs to a tradition of painting, poetry, and sculpture which have contributed to the meaning of "horse" in Chinese art. Demonstrating how the meaning of these paintings has evolved will contribute to a deeper understanding of the relationship between art, history, politics, and morality.

Horses in Early China

Chinese critics before the Tang Dynasty (618–906), did not believe that painting could express the heart's intent (*shi yan zhi*) of the painter, and painting was not considered a fine art. Since painting was not thought to express the aesthetic feelings, subtle emotions, and philosophical reflections conveyed by poetry and music, painters were considered craftsmen whose works were primarily decorative or didactic. Like poetry and music, the earliest paintings were part of religious ceremonies in tombs and chapels. The magnificent painted silk funerary banner found in Lady Dai's tomb at Mawangdui contains one of the earliest examples of a painted portrait.[22] Paintings were also used to decorate palaces and illustrate stories and poetry. Gu Kaizhi's famous fourth-century paintings (*The Admonitions of the Instructress to the Court Ladies, Nymph of the Luo River*, and *Wise and Benevolent Women*) illustrated popular stories and romantic poems. Portraits of noble rulers were believed to inspire reverence; those of evil men moved viewers to sadness and disgust.[23] Xie He's fifth-century Six Laws of Painting described techniques for capturing the spirit (*qi, shensi*) of the subject of a portrait—of people or horses. Thus, while the Six Laws have been sedimented with centuries of theoretical attention, they were originally intended as little more than instructions to craftsmen, and did not make any philosophical points about expressing the character and feelings of the painter.[24]

Horses, on the other hand, had tremendous symbolic power in China many centuries before the Tang Dynasty. Although most of China is more suitable for intensive agriculture than for raising horses, the steppes of Central Asia north of China are ideal for raising livestock. Since the nomads of the steppes needed agricultural products and the Chinese needed horses, trade was an obvious solution; but the Chinese refused to recognize commercial relationships with "barbarians." Therefore, trade was conducted under the guise of "tribute" from and "gifts" to the steppe nomads. When one side or the other became dissatisfied with the terms of exchange and wanted to renegotiate them, there were raids, military expeditions, and conquests. The "renegotiations" were often quite horrendous, and the steppe tribes terrorized the Chinese peasants who came to associate horses with some very unpleasant experiences.

Despite the feelings of Chinese peasants, horses had a number of more positive associations. The *Shuo Gua*, one of the earliest commentaries on the *Yijing* identified the first trigram, *Qian*, the Creative, with horses. "The Creative is symbolized by the horse, swift and tireless as it runs."[25] "The Creative is heaven. It is round; it is the prince, the father, jade, metal, cold, ice; it is deep red, a good horse, an old horse, a lean horse, wild horse, tree fruit."[26] Various horses are associated with human qualities: the good horse with power, the old with endurance, the lean with firmness, and the wild horse with strength.

The *Analects* continues the tradition of referring to horses to as metaphors for human situations. In *Analects* 2.2:

> The Master said: "Although the *Songs* are three hundred in number, they can be covered in one expression: 'Go vigorously without swerving.'"

The phrase "Go vigorously without swerving" is from the "Hymns of Lu," section of the *Book of Songs*, celebrating a herd of fine horses particularly well-suited to pull chariots.[27]

Although the text of the *Yijing* [*I Ching*] itself associates the Creative with dragons rather than horses, in Central Asian tradition water-dragons could change themselves into horses and emerge from rivers with their wings folded at their sides.[28] From this tradition grew the legend of Heavenly Horses (*tianxia ma* 天 下 馬), magical and powerful creatures who were either the offspring of dragons or actual dragons disguised as horses. These wonderful creatures could be recognized, and perhaps captured, as they rose out of the water to take up life on land.

People who could recognize superior horses were as legendary as the horses themselves. In the seventh century BCE a famous judge of horses, Bole, was able to look at horses and tell their quality. With one glance he could identify a Heavenly Horse or "*qianli ma*, 'thousand-*li* horse'" who could run a thousand *li* (about three hundred miles) in a single day. Not only could Bole recognize superior horses in humble surroundings, the horses responded to him. When Bole noticed a particularly good horse pulling a salt cart, the horse cried out to him and Bole began to weep over the animal's fate.[29]

Bole's talent for judging horses became a metaphor for identifying talented men, leading the Tang Dynasty writer Han Yu to yearn for the appearance of a new Bole to correct the failure of the government to recognize talented scholars. In a famous allegory Han Yu wrote:

> Only when the world has someone like Bole [Po-le] are there thousand-*li* horses. Thousand-*li* horses are common, but Boles, on the other hand, are rare. Thus even though there may be famous horses, they are only abused under the hand of the man to whom they are enslaved, and they die in the stables—never having been recognized as thousand-*li* horses. . . . With whip in hand the man approaches them and says, "There are not any good horses in the whole world!" Alas! Is it that there are really no good horses or is it that perhaps there is no one who really understands horses?[30]

A number of popular texts identified the principles used to determine if a horse was a superior thousand-*li* horse. One such text described an ideal horse:

> In judging a horse one begins with the head. The head should be high and erect; it should look as if it were shaved. . . . The eyes should be full and bright; the eye sockets should be small. Above they should be curved like a bow, and below they should be straight . . . The ears should be small and sharp, like a trimmed bamboo tube. The distance between them should be narrow . . . the jaw should be round; the upper lip should be square; the lower lip should be round; the spine should be level; the forelegs should be straight; the kneecaps should be round.[31]

Although Han Gan's painting of Night-Shining White presents a particular, individual horse, the shape of his head, his eyes, his ears "like a trimmed bamboo tube," and his round knees clearly indicate that he is a thousand-*li* Heavenly Horse.

In addition to their other qualities Heavenly Horses were valued for their magical-religious associations, a team of them having carried the Yellow Emperor off to immortality with the Queen Mother of the West in the Kunlun Mountains. Thus, the tomb of China's first emperor, Qin

Shi Huangdi, contained not only thousands of terra cotta warriors and horses, but also a pair of bronze chariots probably intended to take the Emperor's spirit to the Queen Mother's Western paradise.[32]

Lecturing in front of Shi Huangdi's chariot, the American art historian Steve Goldberg complained that it was "too utilitarian to be beautiful." Since Goldberg had been talking about the horrible brutality of Shi Huangdi's reign, it was not clear whether he was making an aesthetic judgment or a political one. Despite Mullarkey's insistence that an artistic conscience is different from a social one, if the meaning of a work of art depends at least in part on its context, it may not always be possible to distinguish aesthetic judgments from political ones.[33]

Several centuries after Shi Huangdi's reign, the Han Emperor Wudi (r. 141–87 BCE) shared his predecessor's interest in immortality and Heavenly Horses. Wudi was eager to obtain these special animals to use in magical-religious ceremonies and to give him an advantage against the

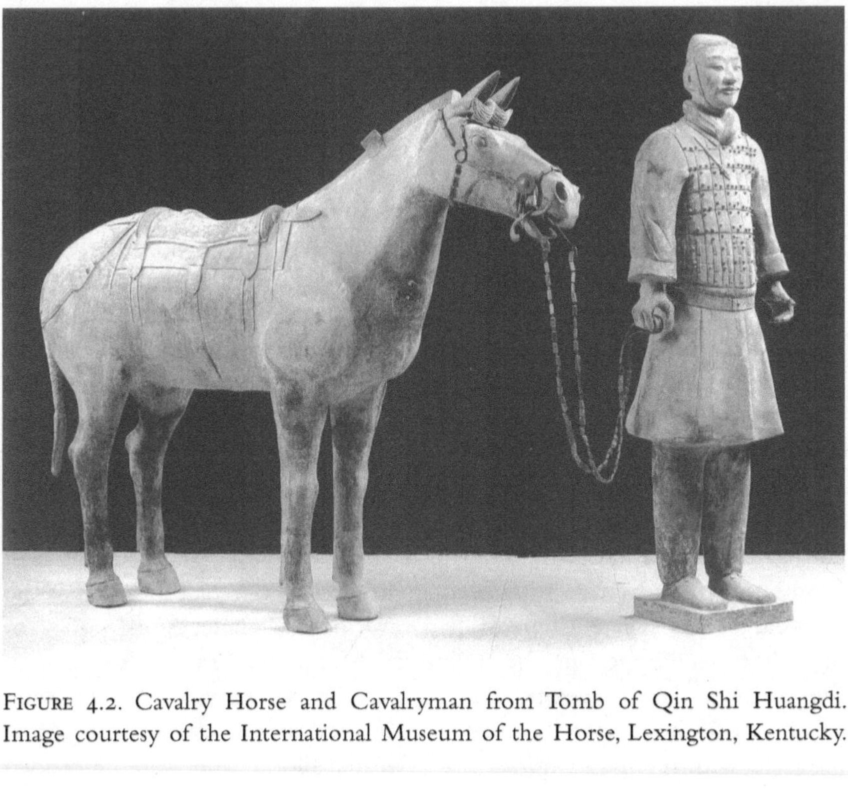

FIGURE 4.2. Cavalry Horse and Cavalryman from Tomb of Qin Shi Huangdi. Image courtesy of the International Museum of the Horse, Lexington, Kentucky.

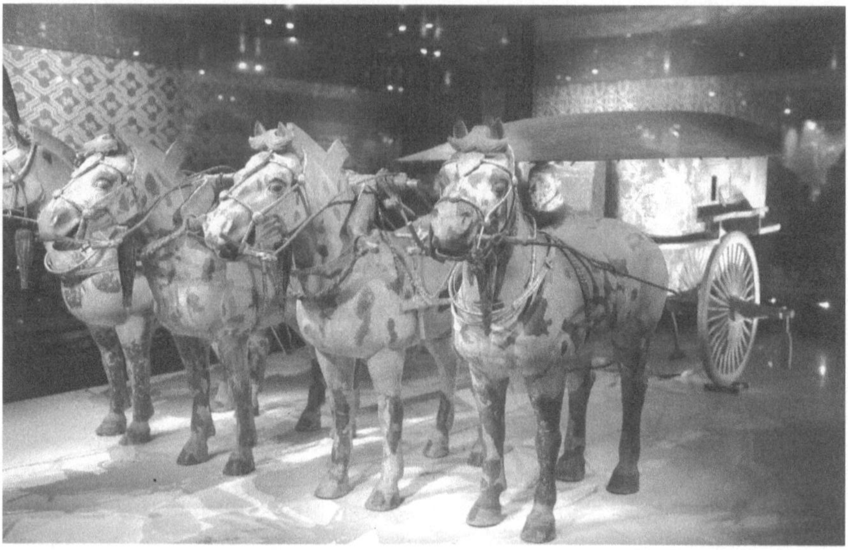

FIGURE 4.3. Qin Bronze horses and Chariot from the Tomb of Qin Shi Huangdi. Photographer: Jean-Marie Hullot.

steppe ponies of the Xiongnu, nomadic steppe people who raided the agricultural Chinese for centuries.

Relations between China and the Xiongnu were relatively peaceful when Han Wudi inherited the empire. Peace had brought prosperity. The granaries were full and the imperial treasury had so much cash and gold there was some problem of where to put it. Life was so good that the historian Sima Qian wrote: "[H]orses were to be seen even in the streets and lanes of the common people or plodding in great numbers along the path between the fields and anyone so poor as to have to ride a mare was disdained by his neighbors."[34]

Han Wudi began a series of military campaigns to expand his empire, bringing southern China, northern and central Vietnam, and northern and central Korea under the control of the Chinese empire. One of Han Wudi's military adventures involved an attempt to purchase or capture the Heavenly Horses. The Emperor had reversed his predecessors' policy of negotiating and appeasing the steppe tribes and attacked the Xiongnu to the north of China. Seeking allies against the Xiongnu, Wudi sent Zang Qian west to the kingdom of Ferghana, in modern Uzbekistan. Zang Qian returned with reports of horses that "sweated blood" and were descended from water-dragons. Until he heard of the Ferghana horses Han Wudi believed that the Heavenly horses, *tian ma*, were raised by the Wusun, a steppe tribe living in the grasslands in Western Gansu and the Tarim Basin. These "dragon horses," "celestial horses," or *tian ma* depicted in Qin and Western Han painting and pottery—including the horses in Qin Shi Huangdi's tomb—had large heads, thick necks, and short legs. Since the horses raised by the Wusun were only 140 cm to the shoulder, they were probably Mongolian steppe ponies that were given particularly good care.

The Ferghana horses were larger, 150 to 160 cm to the shoulder and had small heads, long and curving necks, and long legs. Legend has it that the Ferghana horses were related to the large Persian horses Alexander the Great brought to Central Asia, and are the ancestors of the contemporary breed of Akhal-Teke horse.[35]

Wudi dispatched an envoy with sacks of gold to buy the prized horses, but the King of Ferghana refused to part with his horses, attacking the emperor's envoy and appropriating the gold. Wudi then sent a military expedition for the horses, but the general in charge seriously underestimated the difficulties of the task and the mission was a disastrous failure. When a second, better equipped, Chinese army arrived in Ferghana, the local lords beheaded their recalcitrant king and convinced the Chinese to leave with thirty Heavenly Horses and three thousand ordinary horses.[36]

Although the story of the Ferghana Horses is one of the great romances of Chinese history, Wudi's military expeditions were extremely expensive and brought the once prosperous empire to the brink of ruin. Later Han emperors resumed the more Confucian policy of obtaining the horses they needed by the system of tribute and gifts, returning the empire to its former prosperity. Eventually, however, the Han Dynasty fell; the empire was divided for over three hundred years, and large parts of China were conquered and depopulated by raiding nomadic tribes. (Chapter 3 describes one of the most successful of these tribes, the Northern Wei.)

Horse Painting in the Tang Dynasty

Tang Royalty and Their Horses

Despite the havoc wreaked by the steppe tribes in northern China, both cultures, steppe and Chinese, changed each other profoundly. In the process of becoming sinicized the nomads had a significant influence on China.

Indeed while the Tang Dynasty is praised for restoring Chinese culture and values to the empire after centuries of barbarian rule, the Dynasty itself was founded by a military family from the northwestern frontier. Tang royalty were an ethnic mixture of Chinese, Xianbei, Xiongnu, and Turk, and remained loyal to their steppe heritage. They were so closely tied to the nomads that the first two Tang emperors were accepted by both Chinese and steppe people.[37] Tang royalty rode, hunted, and played polo enthusiastically, celebrating their beloved horses in poetry, painting, sculpture, and the famous tri-colored pottery statues. The seventh Tang Emperor Xuanzong (reign 712–756) summoned the most eminent painters in the empire to make portraits of his magnificent animals and had a troop of horses specially trained to dance on important ceremonial occasions. Xuanzong's dancing horses were praised in poetry and legend, but they met a tragic end in the aftermath of the An Lushan rebellion.[38]

Aside from delight in their prized horses the Tang valued their horses for many very practical reasons. Their empire controlled over a million square miles and depended on horses for communication, transportation, and support of its increasingly large military.[39]

Under the Emperor Xuanzong, China reached unprecedented levels of wealth, prosperity, and artistic creativity, but the Dynasty never completely recovered from the economic and military disaster of the An Lushan Rebellion (755–763) at the end of Xuanzong's reign. Although the rebellion was ultimately defeated, the Dynasty gradually declined. When the Empire was doing well the emperor, and his people, had fine healthy horses and "anyone so poor as to have to ride a mare was disdained by his neighbors." When things went badly the horses were often blamed. In 806 a government official, Liu Ke [Liu K'o] composed a "Farmer's Prayer" decrying the increasingly desperate situation:

> Alas, if only the horses would not gorge themselves on millet and concubines would not be surfeited with silken garments, our taxes would indeed be small. How else can their reduction be achieved? We hope that the gods will not be neglectful and we pray: 'Do not make thin the farmers in order to fatten the stabled horses. Do not make cold the cocoon-tending women in order to reward singing girls and concubines. Do not melt down ploughs to multiply weapons of war. If the farmers are not hungry, the world will be fat. If the cocoon-tending women are not cold, the world will be at peace. If the ploughs are not

melted down, the whole world will prosper. If concubines are kept warm, they are proud. If weapons multiply, they bring destruction. If horses are fat, they are haughty. If the unrighteous do not gallop, it will bring sufficiency of food and clothing.'[40]

But all this is in the future for Xuanzong's favorite horses. Night-Shining White may be complaining about being tied to a post, but other animals Han Gan painted are more content. For example, in Han Gan's painting of *Pasturing Horses* neither horse is trying to escape, and the groom is holding the black horse with only a lead rope. The horses are interacting with each other, paying little attention to their human caretaker, and ignoring the viewers of the painting. In Chinese painting and pottery the people in charge of horses are often foreign; this groom's beard, nose, and deepset eyes suggest that he is probably not Han. Like Night-Shining White, however, these hoses are clearly well-cared for, and very well fed.

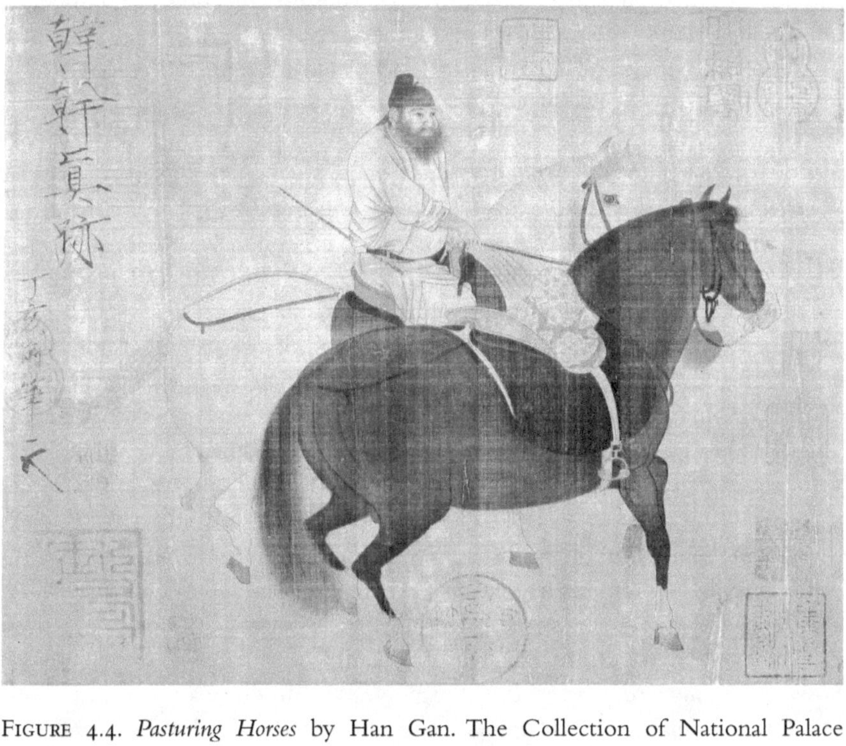

FIGURE 4.4. *Pasturing Horses* by Han Gan. The Collection of National Palace Museum, Taipei, Taiwan.

Although Han Gan was well known for his ability to depict horses, not all of his contemporaries were impressed with his skills. The poet Du Fu (712–770) wrote,

> Han Gan was . . . good [also] at painting horses, catching their strangest forms; but Han Gan paints only the flesh; he does not paint the bone, and will let the fire of the boldest steed melt away and be lost.[41]

Since this remark appears in a poem praising a rival painter of horses, we might discount the complaint. Night-Shining White's fire and spirit is anything but lost. But there may be something to the remark about "painting the flesh." These horses are *fat.* As pampered warhorses in a peaceful court, the emperor's horses lived well. Perhaps too well. Like Liu Ke, Du Fu used horses to criticize the decadent life of a wealthy and powerful court which, along with its warhorses, had become lazy and lost its martial spirit.[42] Nevertheless, despite his political concerns, Du Fu described Xuanzong's horses themselves as the companions and messengers of dragons.[43] The painter poet Zhao Mengfu (1254–1322) also wrote about the happy lives of imperial horses

> How elegant are these [five] horses,
> Standing freely and relaxedly facing the autumn breeze!
> Since the monarch was not interested in military arts,
> They were well fed with hay and corn in the year of harvest.
> In the morning they entered the Heavenly Gate;
> In the evening they fed at the twelve imperial stables.
> Their splendid air was as bright as the morning sun;
> Running, they disappeared into the flying mists.
> Looking backward, they displayed their high spirits,
> Playing with the dragons in the heavenly fields. . . .[44]

Han Gan's horses are doing well. Night-Shining White is playing with dragons, eating corn, getting his portrait painted. The painter has caught the spirit and personality of this very individual horse, captured it well enough to create a symbol of Tang confidence and power. We, however, living long after the Tang dynasty, might want to return to Du Fu's complaint that Han Gan is not quite the "realistic, naturalistic" painter he is reputed to be. Is Han Gan's portrait of Night-Shining White a "realistic" horse? Night-Shining White's portrait is not an anatomically faithful horse as it "really is." For that sort of "ideal" horse we have to look at the work of another artist who, like Han Gan, loved horses and worked at the artistic and cultural peak of his civilization.

Ideal Horses in Chinese and Western Painting

Leonardo da Vinci painted during the Italian Renaissance, when Florentine, Italian, pride and independence were at their height. Leonardo's horses are ideal horses in a number of ways. Not only did Leonardo have a thorough knowledge of horse anatomy, he was concerned with the mathematics of horses, both in terms of the complex calculations required by linear perspective and the techniques of foreshortening, but also in the ideal, mathematical ratios between the physical parts of horse and human bodies.

The demand that paintings of horses be anatomically correct suggests that a painting should be judged on how well it duplicates the

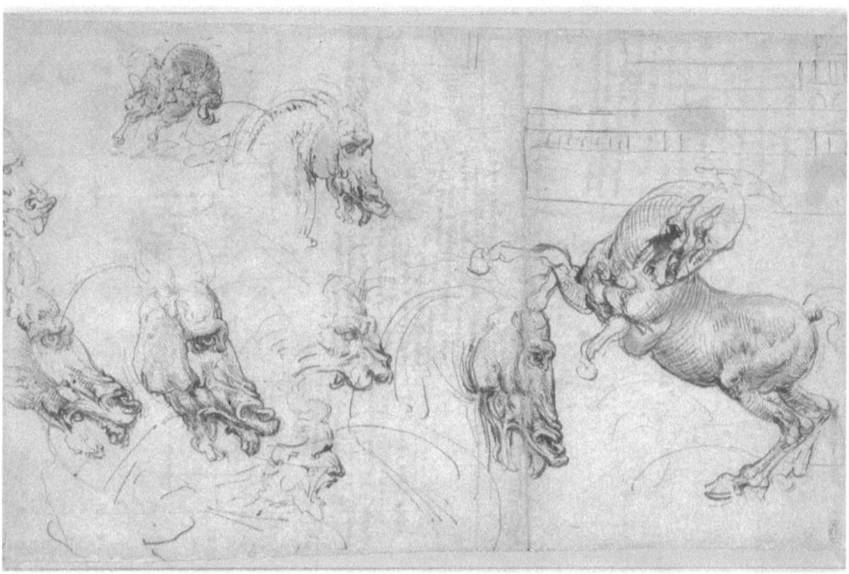

FIGURE 4.5. *Horse Sketches* by Leonardo da Vinci. Royal Collection Trust. © Her Majesty Queen Elizabeth II, 2015.

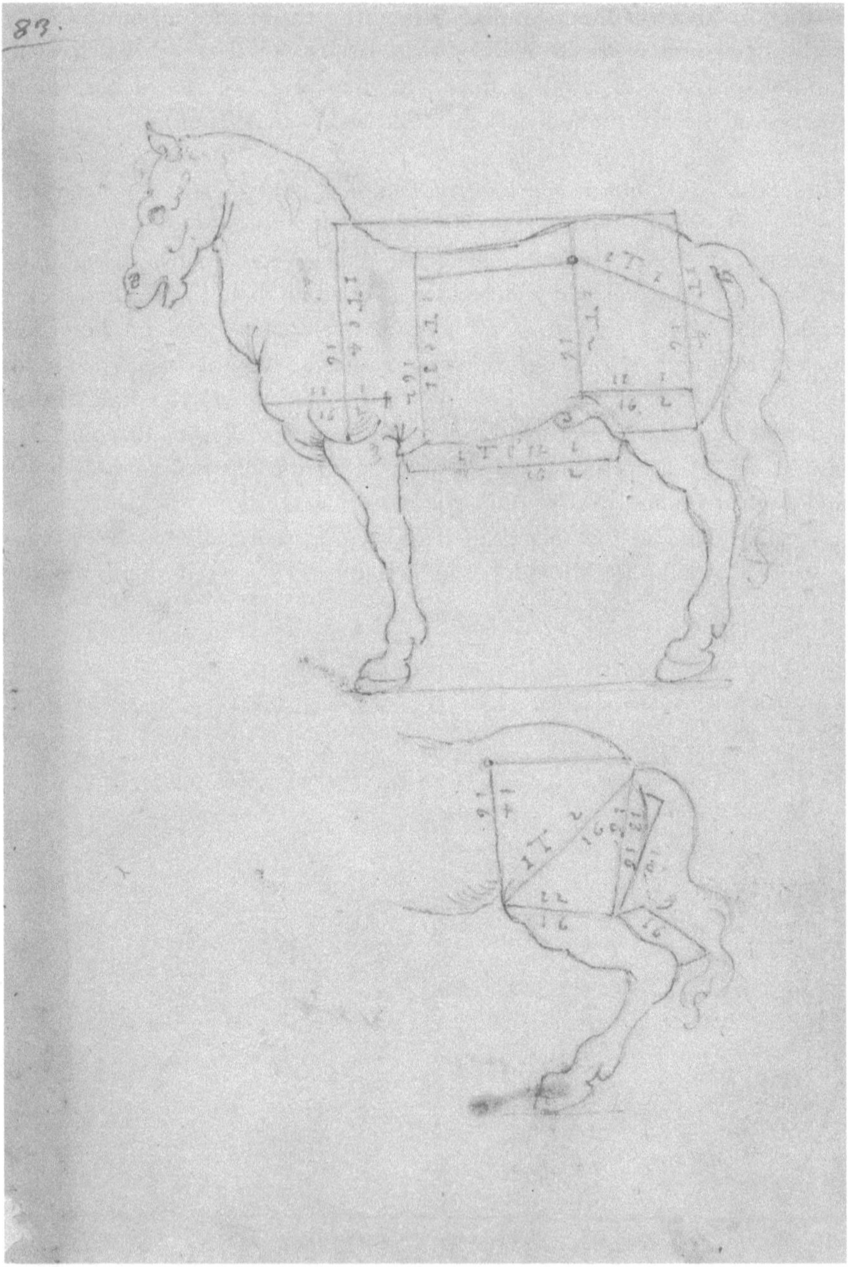

FIGURE 4.6. Carlo Urbino. *Horses in Profile, Standing; Hind-Quarter of the Same Horse.* The Pierpont Morgan Library, New York. 2006.14:83. Purchased in 1938.

experience of perceiving the object it represents. As far back as Plato the thesis that art was an imitation of reality has been a common theme in Western painting theory. Western painters developed increasingly sophisticated techniques of representing nature as painting became increasingly naturalistic and scientific. During the Renaissance, painters and the men of the nascent scientific revolution believed that mathematics and careful observation would reveal the laws of nature and the Neo-Platonic Ideal forms that lay behind the transient, imperfect, and often corrupt world of appearances. We can distinguish between two senses of "idea" or "realistic." Neo-Platonists believed that the ideal Platonic forms were the ultimate reality, which was ideally beautiful. Scientists believed that "reality" corresponded to scientific (and mathematical) accuracy. Given the ancient Platonic belief that Truth and Beauty were the same, these two ideals often merged. Thus, Renaissance scientists sought the eternal laws of nature; Renaissance artists created lush works of art reflecting a timeless idea of beauty.[45]

Although *Night-Shining White* is not an "ideal horse" in an anatomically accurate Neo-Platonic sense, Han Gan and Leonardo were both painting ideal horses. Night-Shining White's square head, small eyes, round knees, and "ears like a trimmed bamboo tube" identify him as a superior horse, but in addition to painting an ideal, superior horse Han Gan has captured the personality of a particular animal, showing us just how annoyed this pampered pet is at being tied to a post. One might accuse Han Gan of anthropomorphism, but this would be assuming that only people have emotions, personalities, spirits, or souls.[46] Chinese painting makes no such assumption and aims to capture the spirit (*shensi* 神似) of people and animals, and, as the tradition evolved, of plants, trees, and landscapes. While Han Gan focused on the feelings and spirit of the horses he painted, the humanism of Renaissance Italy was concerned with the human personality, individual human feelings, and character, not with depiction of emotions and personalities in the nonhuman world.

At first glance this sketch of the *Battle of Anghiari* by da Vinci seems to refute this claim. Leonardo's *Battle of Anghiari* was destroyed, but even in this copy there is clearly a great deal of horse emotion. These horses are obviously in a fury. Note, however that while Han Gan's horses are responding to each other, or to their situations, Leonardo's horses reflect the feelings of the human warriors in battle.

The individualism of our own era has its origins in the humanism of the Renaissance in which individual human personalities were valued

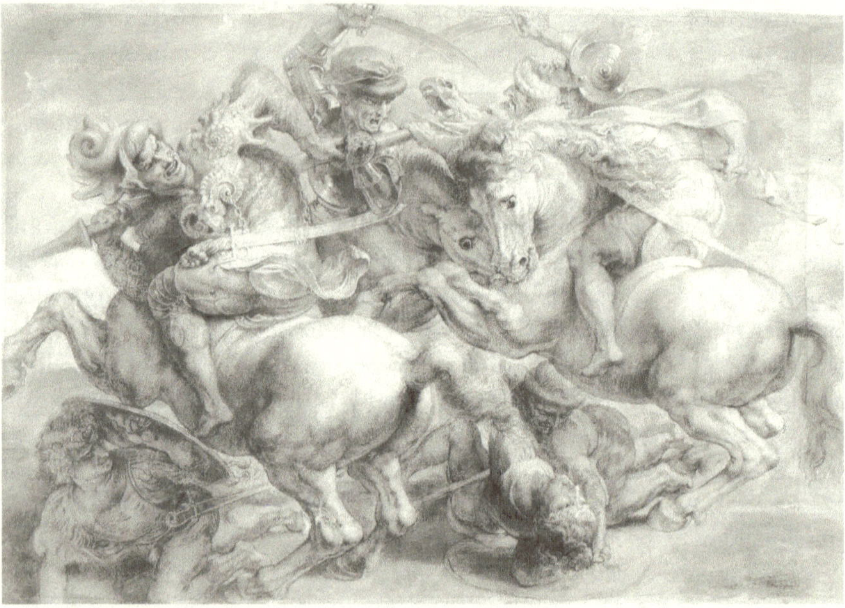

FIGURE 4.7. Peter Paul Rubens's copy of the lost *Battle of Anghiari*.

almost to the exclusion of the nonhuman world. At the same time the scientific revolution began the "conquest of nature" which has had such spectacular results in the ensuing centuries. While Renaissance art reflected this humanism, it was also increasingly naturalistic.

Chinese and Western Painting Theory

Arthur Danto argues that until the beginning of the twentieth century (Western) painters learned increasingly sophisticated techniques of representation, making paintings visually accurate, perceptual equivalents of the natural world. The advent of cinematography, however, caused a crisis in this way of looking at painting since film was so very much better at being visually accurate than painting.[47]

Danto interprets modernism in twentieth-century painting as an attempt to represent "invisible" things. This led to an explosion of styles of painting depending on what these non-perceptual things were: the structure and form of painting, colors, and shapes; the artist's responses to the things she was representing, perhaps her emotional responses to them, but more and more often some theoretical or philosophical idea. The list Danto presents of the most familiar twentieth-century movements in art is dizzying: "Fauvism, the Cubisms, Futurism, Vorticism, Synchronism, Abstractionism, Surrealism, Dada, Expressionism, Abstract Expressionism, Pop, Op, Minimalism, Post-Minimalism, Conceptualism, Photorealism, Abstract Realism, Neo-Expressionism."[48] He concludes that art—at least contemporary American art—has become increasingly pluralistic, relativistic, and postmodern. Anything is possible—under the aegis of the eccentric tastes and vast resources of the art market.[49]

Wen Fong writes of a parallel crisis in Chinese art history. He describes the tension between the traditional view of Chinese art history as a matter of careful analysis, dating, and evaluation of works which is primarily concerned with identifying the painter of a particular work, or at least of the period in which it was painted. Traditional Chinese art history involves a great deal of detailed scholarship, and even then experts often cannot come to any definitive conclusions and frequently disagree. Younger scholars, impatient with the painstaking and often indecisive work of traditional scholars, are less interested in the history of Chinese art than they are using Western techniques and vocabularies—becoming deconstructionists and relativists.[50] They may even go so far as to dismiss the question of whether a painting was actually done by a particular artist or was produced "under the influence" or "in the style of" that artist by someone else. Such an approach is an anathema to traditional historians.[51]

This tension reflects a distinction Fong makes between Chinese and Western art history. The Western approach, grounded in Plato and Aristotle's theory of art as imitation, takes the point of view of the audience or viewer of the work of art. Did the audience recognize what was being presented? Was it seen as an accurate representation? The primary relationship is between the audience and the work; artist is absent.[52] Thus, Danto can claim that Andy Warhol's *Brillo Box* is in some sense "about the viewer of it."[53]

Chinese art, on the other hand, always contained traces, intimations of the artist himself. Color and light are not as important as line. Chinese painting was considered an extension of calligraphy in which the artist's personality could be read from his brush strokes.[54]As we saw in chapter 1, Chinese art expressed (the artist's) intent: *shi yan zhi*.

A standard comparison between Western and Chinese painting reflects this distinction by contrasting "form likeness" (*xingsi* 形似) with "spiritual likeness" (*shensi* 神似).[55] Western painters were said to be good at the "realistic portrayal of natural objects" (*xingsi*) while Chinese painters captured "emotional response" (*shensi*). This way of framing the discussion, however, distorts the Chinese case by viewing it through a lens of an opposition between "objective" nature and "subjective" emotions.

In Chinese thought harmony (*he* 和) is more important than the need for clear distinctions between categories. As the comparison of correlative and causal thinking in chapter 2 indicates, Chinese philosophers often do not understand the relationship between various contrasting pairs the same way Western thinkers do. Polar opposites are seen as complementary rather than logically contradictory, engaging in a continual process of merging into each other. The ideal of harmony requires that many different things exist in a balanced relationship.

Given the aesthetic ideal of an evolving harmony between many elements rather than the representation of something (a natural object, timeless beauty, an emotion or a philosophical concept), Chinese theory never asked painters to choose between accurate representation (form likeness) and personal expression (spirit likeness). From the beginning of the Chinese painting tradition, painting was considered an important way to preserve the visual appearance of things and Chinese painters were concerned with accurate representation or form likeness.[56] Even in the earliest writings about painting, however, serious painters worked to capture the spirit or personality of their subjects. The third-century Chinese painter, Gu Kaizhi (ca. 345–ca. 406), described the goal of his art as "transmitting the spirit by means of form" (*yixing-xieshen* 以 形 寫神).[57] Gu Kaizhi made his portraits a believable likeness because that was the best way to depict his subject's inner life and personality.[58] Indeed Han Gan's paintings were said to be so lifelike that one of his painted horses flew off the page and became an invincible warhorse until the horrors of war distressed him so much that he returned to the painting.[59]

"Concern for "form likeness," is analogous to the attention to representational accuracy in Western painting. On the other hand, insisting on *shensi*, or spiritual likeness, shifts the focus away from the viewer who is to be convinced that a painting presents "things as they really are."

Representing spiritual likeness requires looking at things from the point of view of the subject of the work.

Since the Renaissance horses in the *Battle of Anghiari* are as fully involved in the fighting as their human counterparts, their point of view is the same as that of the humans. Night-Shinning White's obvious irritation at being tied to a post, however, reflects his own view of the situation while the horse in Han Gan's folk tale has a quite different perspective from that of the human warriors, and indeed is morally critical of the warriors.

Because of its concern for emotions, *shensi* (spiritual likeness) includes a subject's emotional responses, Chinese painting theory is suggestive, ambiguous, and vague rather than a definite statement of how things really are, or should be, "once and for all."[60] Moreover, the understanding of whose spiritual nature was to be expressed and how it was to be done changed over time.

When Han Gan was painting, Chinese critics were just beginning to recognize that painting could be as emotionally expressive as poetry. Thus Han Gan's painting of *Night-Shining White* went beyond the representation of an ideal thousand-*li* horse to capture the feelings and personality of a particular horse. According the Northern Song poet Su Ziyou,

> The artist Han Gan, did he really know the Dao?
> When he painted these horses he painted more than their skins.
> He painted what is in the minds of these three horses.[61]

Tang Dynasty painters generally painted the spirit of their subjects; their portraits revealed the Dao by expressing moral quality of sages, the wisdom of good rulers, and the pride and confidence of the emperor's horses.

Nevertheless, as long as painting was not considered a fine art, painters were more limited in the feelings their works expressed than other artists were. While the writings of a poet like Du Fu expressed the poet's moral judgments and personal character, Han Gan's beliefs and feelings were not as significant as those of the horses he painted. Having been commissioned by the emperor himself, Han Gan almost certainly intended his portrait of Night-Shining White to capture precisely how the horse was feeling, rather than express a judgment about Xuanzong's court. Nevertheless the feelings and personality of horses, and painters, include their emotional and moral responses to the societies in which they lived. Night-Shining White is indignant *because* he is the well-fed and pampered pet of a very powerful emperor. If painters could express the feelings, spirit, and situation of their subjects, it was not difficult for them to begin to express their own emotional responses to their world.

Moreover, what it meant for poetry to fulfill its mission of "expressing the heart's intent" (*shi yan zhi* 詩言志) and painting to fulfill the traditional injunction to "convey spiritual nature is by instilling vitality" (*qi yun sheng dong* 氣韻生動) began to change.[62] In ancient China the arts were assumed to encourage morality, that is, Confucian political values—making their audience revere and follow the good and noble rulers and condemn the evil deeds of decadent and corrupt officials. In early texts the heart's intent (*zhi* 志) generally meant a fairly specific moral commitment, and was frequently associated with emotions (*qing* 情), so much so that sometimes *zhi* and *qing* were said to be the same.[63] During the Six Dynasties (220–589) the aesthetic tradition became less didactic and more romantic, and the meaning of *qing* was broadened. Emotions, *qing*, were detached from their association with *zhi* and came to include emotions in general without any explicit political or moral implications.[64] At the same time the status of painting rose from that of a craft to that of a fine art.

Literati Painting of the Song and Yuan

By the Song Dynasty (960–1279) painting had come to have as much prestige as poetry and calligraphy. Scholars believed that all three arts of the brush—painting, poetry, calligraphy—could express subtle emotions and the cosmic patterns of the Dao. Indeed Su Shi, a leading Song Dynasty scholar official, identified poetry and painting:

> When one savors Wang Wei's poems, there are paintings in them;
> When one looks at Wang Wei's pictures, there are poems . . .
> Du Fu's writings are pictures without forms,
> Han Gan's paintings, unspoken poems. . . .[65]

During the Song Dynasty scholar officials with the classical Confucian educations required for government service practiced calligraphy, painting, and poetry in their leisure hours. These scholar-officials or *literati* distinguished themselves from the court artists who painted to please the people who hired them. Unlike professional court painters, the *literati* or *wenrenhua* painters were self-consciously amateurs. They valued spontaneity and creativity over meticulous attention to detail, describing the best painters as ones who attained an almost mystical union with their subjects. Su Shi wrote "[w]hen the retired scholar was in the mountains, he was not preoccupied with any single thing, and thus his spirit communed with all things, and his knowledge encompassed all the arts."[66] One of Su Shi's most often quoted remarks on painting insists on the importance of spirit over representation:

> If any one discusses painting in terms of formal likeness,
> His understanding is close to that of a child.[67]

Nevertheless, Song *literati* theory did not ignore the importance of study and skill in all areas of life, politics as well as painting. Later in the same text Su noted,

> . . . when it comes to people who look at things but fail to see them correctly, even as painters they will be incompetent. How much worse it would be with things of major importance! Therefore, a gentleman must emphasize study and be fond of asking questions. . . .[68]

Moreover, despite their emphasis on spontaneous creation, the *literati* did not encourage unrestrained expression of emotion. Although artists felt things deeply, they tried to avoid the danger of emotional extremes and over attachment. Like poetry and calligraphy *literati* painting conveyed intuitive truths, truths that could not be expressed directly in words—either because they were ineffable, or so strong that expressing them would threaten the ideal of mental harmony described in the *Zhongyong* (*The Doctrine of the Mean/Focusing the Familiar*):

> The moment at which joy and anger, grief and pleasure, have yet to arise is called a nascent equilibrium (*zhong* 中); once the emotions have arisen, that they are all brought into proper focus (*zhong*) is the great root of the world; harmony then is the advancing of the proper way (*dadao* 達道) in the world. When equilibrium and focus are sustained and harmony is fully realized, the heavens and earth maintain their proper places and all things flourish in the world.[69]

Qing (情) were emotional responses to things in the world; things which often became the representative content of a painting. In the Northern Song (960–1126), *literati* painting theory began to focus less on the painter's emotional response (*qing*) to the representational content of a painting, and began to consider the painter's character. A *literati* painting revealed the lofty mind and refined emotional responses of the artist.

Literati painters simply "borrowed" natural objects as means to convey their feelings. Thus Wen Tong [Wen Tun'g], a famous painter of bamboo, was said to remark, "What I love is the Dao which I release in bamboo [painting].'"[70] His friend Su Shi noted that Wen Tong's paintings expressed his noble character,

> Bamboos chilled but preeminent,
> Trees lean but enduring,
> Rocks homely but distinctive,
> These are "the three beneficial friends."
> Their brilliance makes us befriend them;
> Their independence forbids their being constrained.
> I think of this man—
> Alas, can I ever meet him again?[71]

Thus Wen Tong's painting of bamboo expressed the spiritual nature (*shenyun* 神韻) of the painter at least as much as that of the bamboo.

Although *literati* painting was originally a leisure time activity of Confucian scholar officials, the fall of the Song Dynasty changed everything. As the Song Dynasty lost control of northern China to the non-Chinese Jurchen Jin Dynasty early in the twelfth century, the Song retreated to the south. The Southern Song battled the Jin for more than a century until the Mongol forces joined the Song armies and ended the Jin Dynasty in 1234. The Mongols then turned their attention to the Song and in 1279 Kublai Khan destroyed the last remnants of the Southern Song Dynasty, establishing the Yuan Dynasty (1206–1368) and becoming the first non-Chinese emperor in Chinese history. Since the Mongols, like the Tang emperors, honored their nomadic heritage and loved their horses, court painters produced many portraits of Yuan nobility on horseback and pictures of large herds of imperial horses to celebrate the Mongol's power and success.

The *literati*, however, had been driven into poverty and exile by the Mongol conquest and painted horses for other reasons. For the defeated loyalists of the late Southern Song and Yuan Dynasties *Night-Shining White* was more than a portrait of a spirited horse. He represented the vanished glories of Chinese culture at its height, a poignant reminder of a time when China was a vast empire, independent, proud, spirited, and confident. Unable, or unwilling, to serve the foreign government, *literati* painters turned to symbols and allusions to convey feelings of bitterness and regret, emotions it would have been contrary to the Confucian ideal of loyalty to the sovereign, not to mention politically dangerous, to express explicitly. Since the audience for *literati* paintings was other *literati*, these symbol allusions were easily recognized.

Gong Kai (1222–1307) was a well-known Song Dynasty *literati* until the Mongol conquest forced him into a life of hardship and obscurity. Although Gong Kai used Tang Dynasty models for his paintings of horses, his *Emaciated Horse* is anything but a fat and spirited symbol of imperial power. Du Fu could not criticize Gong Kai for showing only the horse's flesh and not his bones. This horse is pathetic; its head is bowed; its mane is wispy. Its ribs and backbones showing, the horse is practically a skeleton. Nevertheless, like Night-Shining White, this horse's ears are "small and sharp, like a trimmed bamboo tube" and its kneecaps are round. This is a thousand-*li* horse that has fallen into poverty and misery. Like Bole, we are moved to tears at the sight of the sufferings of this superior horse. The inscription at the top of the painting reads in part:

> Ever since the clouds and mist fell upon the Heavenly Pass, empty have been the twelve imperial stables of the former dynasty. Today who will have pity for the shrunken form of his splendid body? In the light of the setting sun, on the sandy bank, he casts his towering shadow—like a mountain![72]

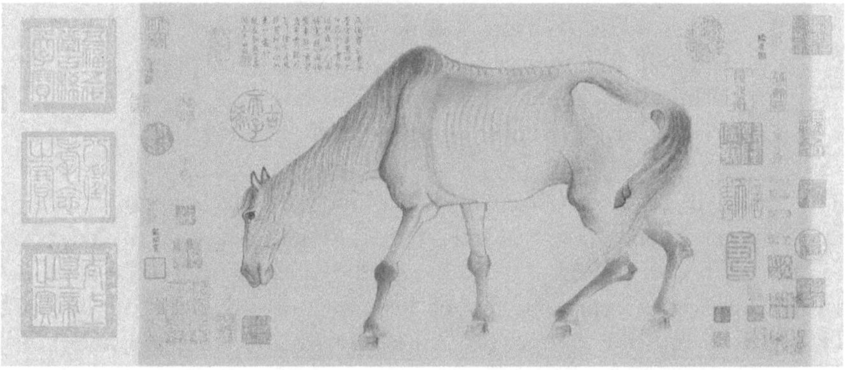

FIGURE 4.8. *Emaciated Horse* by Gong Kai. Osaka City Museum of Fine Arts.

But while Han Gan's portrait of Night-Shining White celebrated the spirit of a particular horse, the *Emaciated Horse* is not exactly about a horse. Its representative content is a horse, but its aesthetic meaning or content is more complicated. Not only does the inscription clearly encourage us to be nostalgic for the lost glories of the Tang Dynasty; one of the colophons on the painting claims that the horse represents the painter himself, a talented artist who was reduced to misery, anger, and despair by the loss of his country.[73] An ancient text on Chinese painting theory claims that a painting is animated "*qi yun*" (氣韻) or "sympathetic responsiveness of the vital spirit."[74] The *qi* or "spiritual nature" of the painter and the horse he is painting are in harmony with each other because they are fundamentally the same. The aesthetic content of Gong Kai's painting, unlike its representative content, is produced by an interaction between the painter, his subject, and his audience. The painting, the inscription, the colophons, and our knowledge of Chinese history let us share the painter's sense of sorrow for the defeated Chinese empire. The experience of the horse and the painter is extended and broadened until it resonates with us. Even without any particular attachment to the Tang Dynasty, the painting leads us to feel Gong Kai's nostalgia, as we think, personally or politically, of the contrast between times of health, pride, and happiness and those of humiliation, poverty, and obscurity.

Zhao Mengfu was another *literati* painter of horses and a contemporary of Gong Kai. Zhao was a prince of the Song royalty whose poem describing the happy life of the emperor's horses was quoted earlier. The poem concludes:

> These noble coursers will never die,
> But will live forever in this painting and calligraphy,
> While the vaunted stones of Chao-ling
> Have had to crumble as the years have gone by.[75]

The "vaunted stones of Chao-ling [Zhaoling]" are the Imperial Tombs of the Emperor Xuanzong's great grandfather, Emperor Taizong. By referring to the six horses carved on the tomb, the poet associates Tang power with Tang horses, expressing regret for the vanished glory of the Tang Dynasty, and thus for the loss of Chinese power and independence under Mongol rule.[76]

Like Gong Kai, Zhao Mengfu was a *literati* painter, but, unlike Gong Kai, Zhao compromised his loyalty to the Song Dynasty and served the

Mongol empire. During his years of service to the court in Beijing, Zhao became familiar with the masterpieces of Tang painting and was thoroughly aware of what had been lost. The painters of the Tang Dynasty celebrated the pride and power of the imperial stables with portraits of particular imperial war horses—inscribing the names of the horses, their lineages, measurements, and origins on the paintings. Zhao Mengfu, on the other hand, painted anonymous horses for his friends, claiming to paint simply for his own pleasure and insisting that *literati* painting reflect the spirit of the past, writing: "the spirit of antiquity is what is of value in painting. If there is no spirit of antiquity, then though there may be skill, it is to no avail . . . the result will not be worth looking at."[77]

Zhao's painting *Groom and Horse* is far more subtle than Gong Kai's Emaciated Horse. The painting is the first section of a series of three paintings of horses and grooms. Although the other two paintings were added later and follow the tradition of depicting grooms as foreigners, the groom in Zhao's painting appears to be Han Chinese and may even be a self-portrait of the artist himself.[78] The round, fat shape and white color of the horse remind us of Night-Shining White, but the horse and groom stare at us placidly, showing neither Night-Shining White's spirited struggle, nor Gong Kai's bitterness. The brushwork in the painting and calligraphy are simple and unassertive. Like Han Gan's portrait of Night-Shining White, Zhao's painting is basically a line drawing, but while Han Gan used monochrome painting with ink shading (*baihua*, white painting)

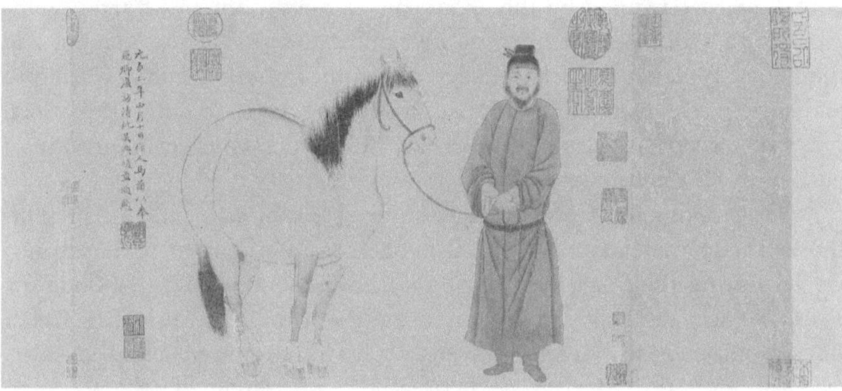

FIGURE 4.9. *Groom and Horse* by Zhao Mengfu, dated 1296 and 1359. Gift of John M. Crawford, Jr. Image copyright © The Metropolitan Museum of Art. Image source: Art Resource, New York.

to suggest depth and motion, Zhao's used a simple line drawing minimal shading (*baimiao*, white drawing), suggesting a contrast between Han Gan's status as a professional painter and Zhao's as an amateur.

Zhao's inscription says simply:

> On the tenth day of the first month of the second year of Yuanzhen (1296) I painted this picture of a man and a horse for the pure enjoyment of Surveillance Commissioner Feiqing. Zhao Mengfu of Wuxing[79]

The horse and the groom are presented for Feiqing's inspection, implying that Feiqing, like Bole, is a judge of horses and men. Thus the painting seems to be a fairly conventional, albeit exaggerated, expression of respect for a superior.[80] The simple line drawing and vague, washed-out colors, however, make the painting disturbingly bland. Calm and still as the figures appear, there is more going on.

Jonathan Hay argues that the picture is structured as a series of interlocking circles. There are large circular arcs in the horse's body, the rein, and the groom's belt. The horse's jaw and the groom's collar contain parts of smaller circles. The arcs provide a dynamic rhythm suggesting some of the movement in Night-Shining White's portrait, even while the groom and horse quietly gaze at us. The straight lines represented by the erect posture of the horse and groom recall the post against which the Emperor's horse struggled while the composition is grounded in the horizontal line determined by the alignment of the groom and horse's feet.[81]

Circles and straight lines are metaphors for moral measurement and the neo-Confucian respect for rules, decorum, and self-control. The horse and groom are completely aligned with the overall cosmic and moral order of Confucian ideology, reflecting the proper Confucian attitude of harmony with nature and respect toward rulers.[82]

The dominant mood of the painting—plain, calm, still—represents the aesthetic value of blandness that became important in Chinese aesthetics during the Song Dynasty under the influence of Chan Buddhism. *Dan* (淡) is translated variously as blandness, simplicity, insipidity. Other translations include "flavorless, weak." It is important to avoid associating *dan* with the Western aesthetic value of "restrained." "Restrained" suggests that there is something being held back; something that might break free—for better or worse. *Dan*, blandness, is neutral, able to take on and absorb anything, in an appropriate manner, responding to the circumstances without being committed to anything particular. From a certain point of view, therefore, the negative connotations of "insipid" and "weak" are not entirely incorrect. *Dan* had long been part of Confucian and Daoist thought. For example in the *Zhongyong*:

> The *Book of Songs* says:
> Over her brocade skirts
> She wears a plain robe.
> This means she hates to make a display of her refinement.
>
> Thus the ways of exemplary persons (*junzi* 君子) while hidden, day by day become more conspicuous; the ways of petty persons while obvious, day by day disappear.
>
> The ways of exemplary persons are plain (*dan* 淡) and not wearisome,
> Simple and refined,
> Amicable and coherent.[83]

And in the *Daodejing*

> Music and sweets
> Make passing guests pause,
> But the DAO emerges
> Flavorless and bland (*dan* 淡).
>
> Look—you won't see it.
> Listen—you won't hear it.
> Use it—you will never use it up.[84]

Li Zehou argues that Chan Buddhism took this early praise for the value of blandness and made preference for blandness a major and continuing part of Chinese aesthetics.[85] Li describes blandness, *dan*, as "something that is without taste, but at the same time full of flavor; in other words, 'the flavorless flavor is the perfect flavor.'"[86]

For the Confucians blandness had political value. The third-century work "Annals of Public Figures" (*Renwu zhi*) remarked, "Of all the human qualities, the most valuable is moderation and harmony. A moderate and harmonious character will be bland and unflavored, so that it can then be 'seasoned' into the five talents, or adapted to the needs of the situation."[87] Chan took this political attitude and raised it to a spiritual state of mind, one of "lingering flavor" (*yunwei*), of unfathomable meaning beyond words.[88]

The aesthetic value of blandness contrasts sharply with both the Western value of heroic intensity and the tragic bitterness of Gong Kai's *Emaciated Horse.* The Chan goal of emptiness and "non-attachment" is not any sort of "golden mean" or "happy medium," nor is it allied with Zhuangzi's quest for personal freedom. Li Zehou writes that the aesthetics of blandness "attempts to describe the most ordinary natural scenes, so as to portray the empty illusoriness of life and the spiritual realm in a way that arouses thought and deep feeling."[89] Looking at the figures in Zhao's *Groom and Horse* who look at us, placid, calm, bland, we sense a state of spiritual enlightenment from which all spirit and emotion have been emptied.

Jonathan Hay argues that the painting also represents "the dark side of Zhao Mengfu's political identity, the price of success."[90] Zhao was continually torn between a desire to retire from the court and live a life of unfettered freedom, and pressure from the Mongol Court to fulfill his Confucian commitment to duty and use his talents for public service. Zhao painted the *Groom and Horse* just before he left retirement to take up yet another court-appointed position. The era of Chinese independence, power, and pride, the world of Night-Shining White, were gone, and Zhao responded neutrally, blandly to the situation. In the spirit of Chan enlightenment he rejects both self-serving careerism and fanatical loyalty to the old, Chinese dynasty. Hay concludes that the painting is Zhao's justification for his decision to serve the court, despite the personal sacrifice involved.[91]

The Confucian injunction is to serve when the Way prevails in the world, to hide when it does not. But even by the time of Mencius there was a problem of how to know when it is time to hide and when there is still important public work to be done; a problem Mencius's followers recognized if he did not. Thus, Chan enlightenment is tempered with the ironic understanding that no matter how much the Daoist/Chan aesthetic draws us away to a metaphysical realm, Confucianism is always there to remind us of the practical concerns of the world in which we live.

Like Zhao Mengfu, Ren Renfa (1255–1328) was a *literati* painter who worked for the Mongol administration; but Ren was even more closely tied to the Yuan Dynasty, having married his daughter to a central

Asian official. Ren Renfa took Tang and Northern Song models (Han Gan and Li Gonglin) and relied on the tradition dating back to the *Yijing* of associating horses with human characteristics. His painting *Lean Horse* and *Fat Horse* is clearly a political protest. The painting depicts two horses: a well-fed piebald, prancing alertly, followed by a thin horse with its head down. Both horses have the round knees and bamboo ears of superior Heavenly Horses, and while the second horse is lean with some of its ribs showing, he is not the skeletal wreck painted by Gong Kai (figure 4.8).[92] Renfa's inscription on the painting tells us that the *Lean Horse* represents the loyal and honorable official who wears himself out in unappreciated service to the people, while the fat one represents the corrupt official who uses his position to enrich himself.[93]

Although both the *Emaciated Horse* and the *Lean Horse* express the sufferings of *literati* under the Yuan Dynasty, there are significant differences between the two. The *Emaciated Horse* is painted in a deliberately unsophisticated style, demonstrating Gong Kai's sincerity and his status as an amateur.[94] Ren Renfa's style, on the other hand, is highly polished and almost professional. Where Gong Kai's painting is a bitter lament over his fate and that of China, Ren Renfa's pictures justify his own decisions. The *Lean Horse* does not represent a tragic defiance of the Yuan rulers but a principled accommodation to distasteful reality. The obvious self-serving nature of these paintings may be part of the reason one critic complains that they are clumsy and overdone and another that they are "mediocre."[95]

Ren Renfa's paintings are so decidedly political that a Western viewer might be reminded of a political cartoon rather than of *Night-Shining White* and wonder if the aesthetic content of these paintings sufficiently immunizes them from politics to justify protecting them from the ire, or at least censorship, of the Yuan authorities. This worry assumes, however, that aesthetic values can be distinguished from political and moral ones. As we have seen, Deutsch and Mullarkey believe we can make such a distinction, but it would not have occurred to Song and Yuan Dynasty *literati* painters to do so. These painters had moved beyond the early Confucian view that paintings had to be morally inspiring to a more complex view of the relationship between painting and morality. Unlike Han Gan who captured the spirit of Night-Shining White for his imperial patron, and the professional court painters who painted horses to please their employers, *literati* painters of the Song and Yuan Dynasties painted to express their personal beliefs and feelings, presenting themselves as highly refined and morally sensitive people who were deeply concerned about their lives, their society, and their government. The *shenyun* (神韻) "spirit resonance" their paintings expressed included their political and moral values.

China Modernizes: Ming and Qing Dynasties

Modern China began in the Ming Dynasty (1366–1644). According to Li Zehou, at that time the old feudal society was disappearing in favor of a more complicated social order that encouraged a spirit of individualism.[96] The examination system and the growing wealth of the merchant class increased social mobility and the newly rich began to value scholarship, manners and connoisseurship in art. As education became more widespread, however, there were more educated people than there were government jobs, and scholars who succeeded at the examinations were forced to create new places for themselves in society.

Since the Ming Dynasty had reestablished Chinese rule, *literati* painters were no longer defined by their position as exiled members of the defeated Song Dynasty. *Literati* painting evolved from an expression of the beliefs and moral characters of painters who considered themselves alienated from the ruling elite into a particular painting style, one that was self-consciously amateur, using simple ink washes with little or no color and relying heavily on the brush techniques of calligraphy to express the artist's personal feelings through allusions. *Literati* painters began to make a living from their art; but because *literati* were traditionally amateurs who painted for pleasure rather than economic ends, they risked losing their status as artists. Thus *literati* painters were seldom paid directly for their work, instead they were given "gifts" and "traded" their work for goods and services.

The Ming Dynasty (1358–1644) provided more than a hundred years of relative stability in Chinese history, but by the seventeenth century the dynasty had begun to decline. The civil service was increasingly embroiled in ideological disputes, and the army was stretched to the breaking point fighting bandits, peasant guerrillas, and the Manchu cavalry.[97] Terrified that the Manchus would imitate the Mongols and become conquerors, the Ming refused to follow the usual strategy of negotiation and compromise with the Manchu nomads. This mistake led to precisely the outcome it was intended to avoid. In 1644 the Manchu Qing Dynasty replaced the

Ming. The Qing were conservative to the point of being reactionary in politics, economics, and culture, and the modernizing trends of the Ming came to an abrupt end.[98]

Although fighting between Ming loyalists and Manchu conquerors destroyed the city of Yangzhou, on the north bank of the Yangzi River northeast of Nanjing, the city was rebuilt in the eighteenth century. Ambitious businessmen took advantage of the salt monopoly and Yangzhou's position as the gateway to South China to make Yangzhou one of the richest cities in China.

The painters known as the Eight Eccentrics of Yangzhou were among the artists attracted to the city to serve the newly rich. The Eight Eccentrics had little in common except that they ignored the models of the past, emphasized creativity, and cultivated their individual styles.[99] Jin Nong 金農 (1687–1763) was one of the Eight Eccentrics who started his career as a calligrapher and did not begin painting until he was fifty. After some early success, most of Jin Nong's life was difficult and unhappy. In his old age he became cynical and withdrawn and painted only portraits, Buddhist images, and horses.[100]

Although Jin Nong probably knew very little about Ferghana when he painted the *Ferghana Horse*, he was familiar with the stories of Bole and the tradition of expressing human feelings by painting horses. The brushwork in the painting is energetic and complex, reflecting the painter's vigorous and creative calligraphy. The bamboo ears and rounded knees identify the *Ferghana Horse* as a superior Heavenly Horse. The painting of horse's hooves and the muscles in his neck suggest strength and power, while the horse's wild and fierce appearance represents the painter's bitterness over his lack of recognition.[101]

Ren Xiong (1823–1857) lived at the end of the Qing Dynasty and his short life coincided with an incredibly turbulent period in Chinese history. Ren was very successful, but his life was far from peaceful. He had a tragic affair with a courtesan and fought on the side of the Manchus during the Taiping Rebellion. As a young apprentice Ren Xiong worked in a studio, painting ancestor portraits for clients who had lost their ancestral images in the Rebellion. In a practice known as "buying an ancestor," painters used ancient pictures as models for portraits to replace the lost images. Bored with the process, Ren changed the models, removing dignified official robes and hats, replacing formal postures with casual ones, and emphasizing physical defects to produce some very unflattering

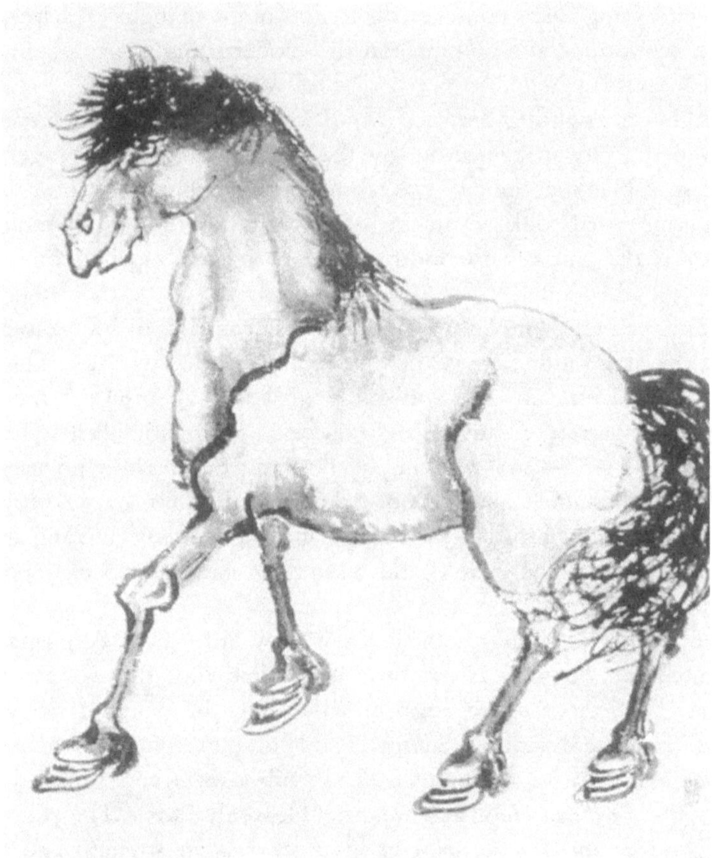

FIGURE 4.10. *Ferghana Horse* (ink on paper) by Jin Nong (1687–1763). Private Collection. Photo © Christie's Images/Bridgeman Images.

portraits. Although his enraged teacher chased the young man out of his studio, Ren Xiong's paintings eventually sold well and he was generally optimistic and cheerful.[102]

Ren's *Ferghana Horse after Jin Nong* makes the same sort of changes to the original that his early "ancestor" portraits made to the original models. The structure of *Ferghana Horse after Jin Nong* is the same as Jin Nong's painting with parts of the tails of both horses out of the picture; moreover Ren's horse has the round knees and bamboo ears of a thousand-*li* Ferghana horse, but the pictures reflect the radically different personalities of

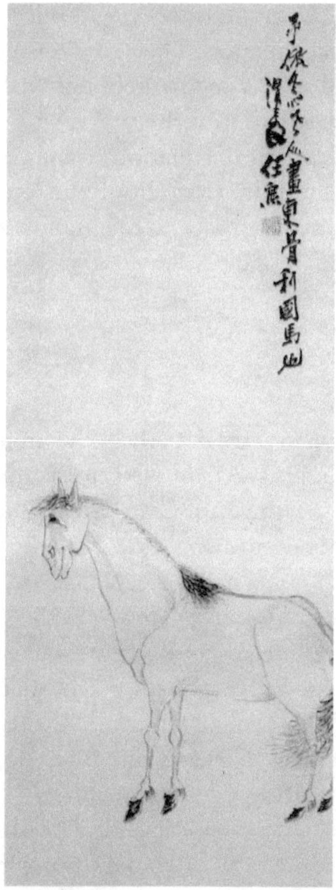

FIGURE 4.11. *Ferghana Horse after Jin Nong* by Ren Xiong. University of Michigan Museum of Art. Museum purchase made possible by the Margaret Watson Parker Art Collection Fund, 1985/2.32.

the painters. Ren's brushwork is simpler and less dramatically calligraphic than Jin Nong's and Ren Xiong's horse, like Ren Xiong himself, seems cheerful and friendly. Marshall Wu notes that the horse's dainty hooves seem almost to be dancing, while his "whimsical and humorous expression" and his "raised head, upstanding ears, and playful smile make Ren Xiong's interpretation of the animal more lively and amiable."[103]

Despite the radically different feelings expressed in these paintings, both paintings are consistent with the growing sense of individual freedom in early modern China. The paintings express the artist's personality and respond to his particular circumstances without making any judgments about the wider political situation. The Confucian aesthetic tradition that serious art expressed the artist's deeply held political values seemed to have come to an end.[104] *Literati* painting began as an expression of the artist's social class. When the political situation changed, the *literati* expressed nostalgia for the past and concerns about the present. Finally, as China modernized, the tradition turned to a celebration of individualism rather than communal political morality.

China and the West

Although the Qing Dynasty tried to halt the modernization that began in the Ming, the attempt was doomed to failure and China became increasingly influenced by the European West. One of the earliest painters to bring Western techniques to China was the Italian Jesuit Giuseppe Castiglione (1688–1768) who took the Chinese name Lang Shining and served as a court painter in Beijing from 1715–1766. Unlike the *literati* painters who defined themselves as amateurs and in some sense outsiders, court painters were obliged to express the values of their imperial patrons. Since the Manchus of the Qing Dynasty, like the Tang and Yuan before them, retained their nomad heritage and their love of horses, many of Castiglione's paintings portrayed imperial horses.

While Ren Renfa's *Lean Horse* and *Fat Horse* makes us uneasy because of its overtly political content, Castiglione's horse paintings are disturbing in a different way. The themes and composition of these paintings are clearly Chinese, but Castiglione uses Western techniques of foreshortening, atmospheric perspective, and modeling. The meticulous treatment of the landscape in the painting *A Hundred Horses* presents an illusion of three dimensions and introduces a new kind of realism in Chinese painting.[105] Nevertheless, the painting is a strange hybrid of Chinese and Western styles and sensibilities that doesn't seem "right" from either point of view. Castiglione's *Afghan* (*Ferghana*) *Horses* are visually accurate representations and probably pleased the Chinese Emperor, but they look more like the work of the British painter, George Stubbs (1724–1806), who painted the horses and dogs owned by English aristocrats, than the idealized superior horses with round knees and bamboo ears. Castiglione's horses exhibit neither the spirit of Night-Shining White, the political commentary of Zhao Mengfu, nor the personal feelings of Jin Nong and Ren Xiong.[106]

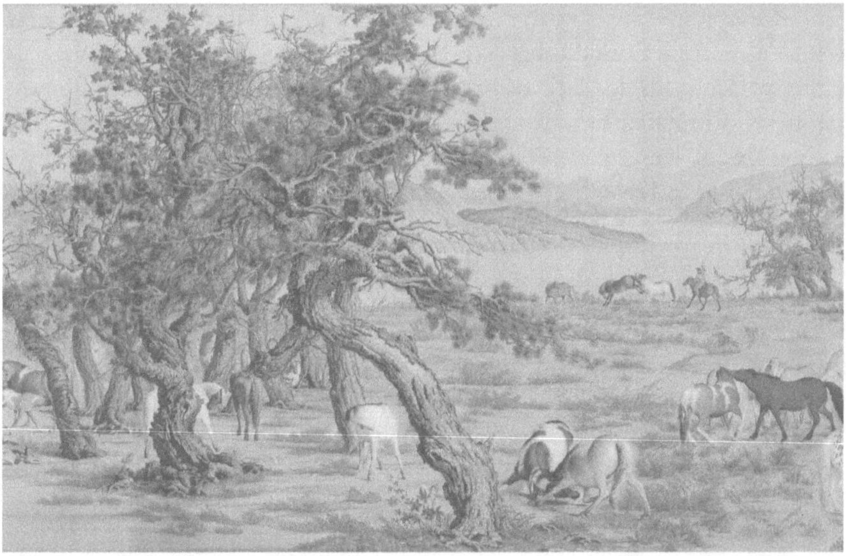

FIGURE 4.12. *A Hundred Horses* (detail) by Giuseppe Castiglione [Lang Shining]. The Collection of the National Palace Museum, Taipei, Tiawan.

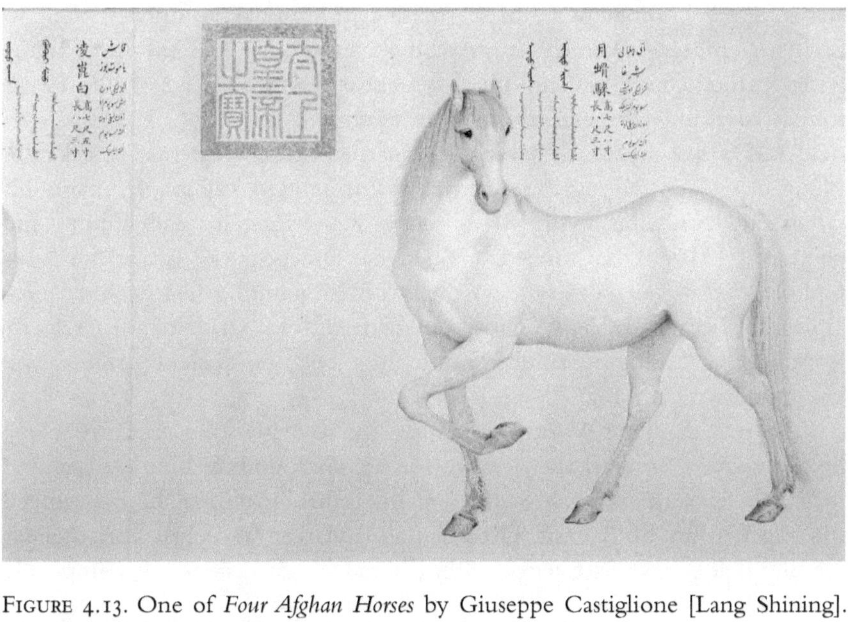

FIGURE 4.13. One of *Four Afghan Horses* by Giuseppe Castiglione [Lang Shining]. The Collection of the National Palace Museum.

Castiglione was greatly admired during his lifetime, but Chinese critics ultimately decided that although his work was acceptable for decorating palace walls, his lack of brushwork prevented him, and the Chinese artists who imitated him, from being serious artists.[107] In criticizing court painters who had to please their patrons, Castiglione's critics may have been defending the Chinese *literati* tradition and raising elitist objections to popular taste. A court artist in the Qing court summed up his view of western painters: "The student should learn something of their achievements so as to improve his own method. But their technique of strokes is negligible. Even if they attain perfection it is merely craftsmanship. Thus foreign painting cannot be called art."[108]

Nevertheless, Western techniques could not be "unlearned," and Chinese painting eventually assimilated them. One scholar echoed a remark often credited to Mao Zedong by noting that while Castiglione "made Chinese things serve the west," Chinese painters after Castiglione "made foreign things serve China."[109]

For many Chinese the slogan "make foreign things serve China" voiced deeply held Chinese xenophobia, but as China was forced to deal with ideas, and armies, from the West, it became increasingly urgent to appropriate foreign things to avoid Western domination. Some Chinese artists, like a number of Chinese social critics and philosophers, went so far as to embrace Westernization wholeheartedly. One of the most influential painters in China in the last century, Xu Beihong (1895–1953), fought to bring Chinese art into the twentieth century, although, as we shall see, it was not clear which *part* of the century he meant. Like Jin Nong and Ren Xiong, Xu learned painting and calligraphy from his father and made his living for a while as an itinerant calligrapher and painter.[110] In 1914 Xu moved to Shanghai and became part of the New Culture Movement. Announcing that Chinese painting had declined precipitously because of its commitment to tradition, Xu demanded reform, insisting that Chinese painters should stop copying ancient painters and use modern technology.[111]

When the First World War ended Xu went to study in Paris where he completely ignored the avant-garde art surrounding him and painted in the style of the French Salon. On his return to China he denounced the modernism of Renoir, Cézanne, and Matisse as vulgar and shallow, arguing that Western art, particularly in France, was degenerate, completely controlled by capitalism and the art dealers.[112]

In 1933 Xu Beihong returned to Europe with a collection of Chinese paintings which were shown in Paris, Berlin, Rome, Moscow, Leningrad, and Kiev. In Russia Xu met a number of Soviet artists with whom he continued to correspond and whose friendship helped him encourage Chinese academic painting to adopt Socialist Realism.[113]

On a visit to India in 1940 Xu painted a picture that was to have a dramatic effect on his career. *The Foolish Old Man Moving the Mountain* illustrates the story of a man who believed that by working away year after year he could remove a mountain blocking the view from his house. The story was Chinese, but because many of the figures were Indian, Xu probably considered the painting a celebration of pan-Asian resistance to Japanese aggression. Mao Zedong interpreted the painting differently and praised it as a "parable of the power of communal effort to accomplish any goal."[114] A Western art critic called this painting "uncomfortable and tasteless." One cannot help but wonder if this judgment, like Goldberg's criticism of Shi Huangdi's chariot, is aesthetic or political.[115]

Mao's support ensured Xu's power and influence. As president of the Central Academy of Fine Arts and chairman of the Artists' Association, Xu used his position to require that Chinese painting students spend two years learning Western drawing.[116]

Xu's most famous paintings are of horses and, like Leonardo da Vinci, his work was based on a scientific study of horse anatomy.[117] Although most of his horse paintings are in traditional ink washes with expressive brushwork, Xu's brushwork owes more to his skill in drawing than to traditional calligraphy. Like Castiglione's paintings, Xu's work is a hybrid of Chinese themes and Western techniques. Yet while Castiglione's paintings appear to be a pastiche of two distinct traditions, Xu's horses are painted in a distinct individual style. One of his most famous paintings, *Galloping Horse*, was painted in Singapore in 1941. Xu's inscription reads

> The second battle was fought in Changsha on August 10 of the year Xinsi; my heart was burning with anxiety. Probably the outcome of the battle would be the same as the previous one. I am hopeful.[118]

Like so many Chinese paintings of horses, Xu's *Galloping Horse* is not exactly about a horse. The representative content is a horse; the aesthetic meaning (or content) goes deeper. As a celebration of the victory of

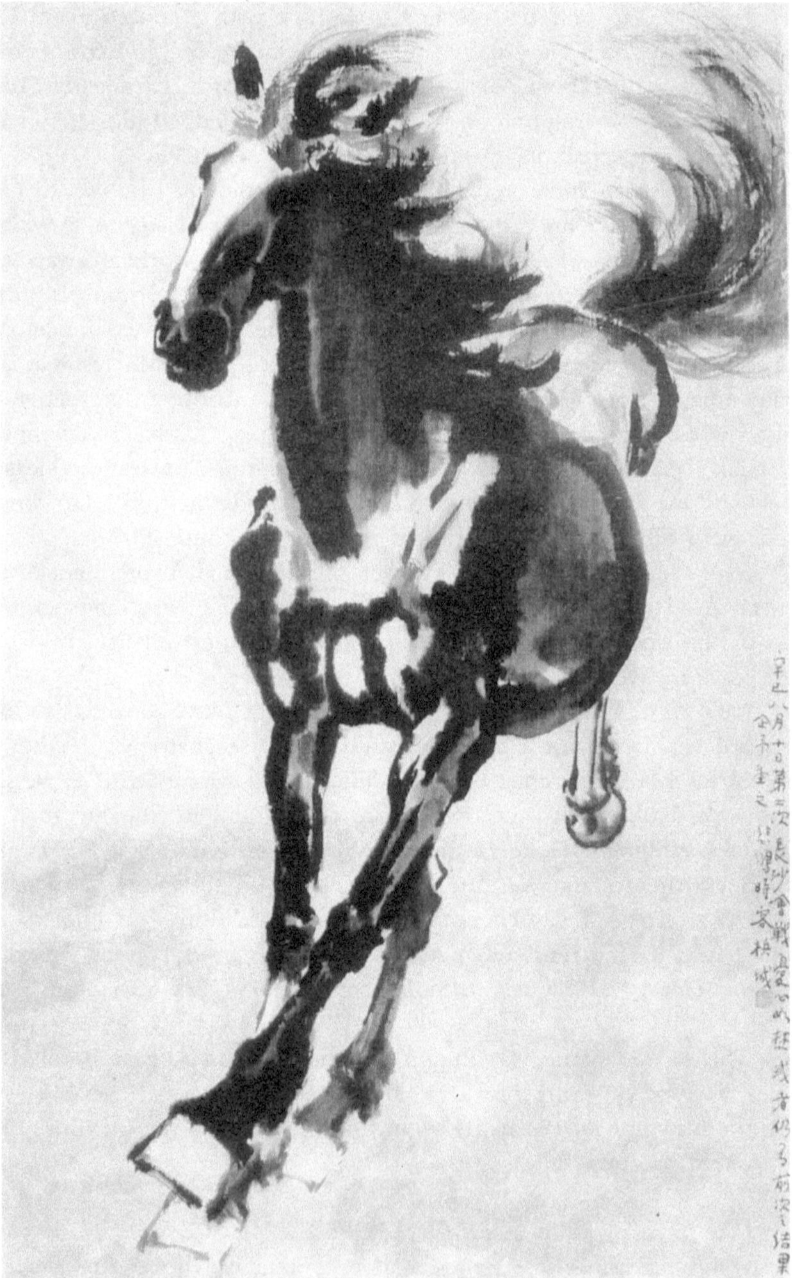

FIGURE 4.14. *Galloping Horse*, Xu Beihong, 1941.

Chinese soldiers in a great battle, the painting became a symbol of the fighting spirit of the Chinese and the hopes for China's future. Like *Night-Shining White*, the *Galloping Horse* represents a proud and independent China. On the other hand, *Night-Shining White* belonged to a powerful emperor in a time of peace. Xu's painting honors a military victory at a time when China was fighting a desperate battle against Japan and beginning to disintegrate into chaos and civil war. How important is location of the battle it celebrates? Does the identity of the enemy matter? Would the aesthetic meaning change if it celebrated a battle that had been between the Communists and the Guomindang, or against the Americans in Korea? Chinese, Japanese, and American responses might be very different under different circumstances and would probably change over time. The aesthetic meaning of the *Galloping Horse* mirrors the confusing history of China in the twentieth century and its complicated relationship with the West. Thus, despite Xu's attack on traditional Chinese painting, his work, like that of the other paintings in this chapter, reflects the political times in which they were painted.

Xu's career displays a number of such ironies. Although he was dedicated to modernizing the Chinese painting tradition and his supporters praise his insistence on Western drawing techniques, his detractors argue that his conservative hostility to modern art set Chinese art back by at least forty years.[119] Moreover, because many of his paintings were so similar, he was accused of painting in an assembly-line manner, a charge that severely damaged his reputation among serious artists. He soundly condemned the domination of Western art by the capitalistic art market, yet his own paintings have been thoroughly exploited by that market. Images of his horses are far more widespread than those of *Night-Shining White*, having poured into popular culture on inexpensive posters, postage stamps, refrigerator magnets, and charms. Ultimately Xu's project to modernize Chinese painting was wildly successful in at least one respect. Xu's condemnation of international capitalism, notwithstanding, contemporary Chinese artists are full participants in the global art market.

Chinese Revolutions and the Global Art Market

Xu's sponsor, Mao Zedong, would also have found late twentieth-century Chinese painting disconcerting, to say the least. In his 1942 "Talks at the Yenan Forum on Literature and Art" Mao announced that "a thing is good only when it brings real benefit to the masses of the people."[120] He denied, however, that there are any "absolute and unchanging" standards in politics and art, insisting that in every society artistic criteria have always been subordinated to political ones. Mao opposed two kinds of art in particular. He decried the "poster and slogan style" of politically progressive art that had no artistic merit because it was "lacking in artistic power." On the other hand, works with high artistic merit but an incorrect reactionary political content were particularly "poisonous" and had to be vigorously rejected.[121] Thus from the founding of the People's Republic of China (1949) until the end of the Cultural Revolution (1976) literature and visual culture in China were severely restricted. Nevertheless, even under Mao the arts were not monolithic. Western modernism was forbidden, but works in many styles and traditions were permitted.[122]

Eventually Mao's intolerance of art that did not serve the ends of the Revolution and the Communist Party was replaced by the more moderate views of Deng Xiaoping and Hu Yaobang: art that was not politically harmful was permissible.[123] Nevertheless, the political repression of the late 1980s convinced a number of Chinese artists to emigrate. At the same time the rapid expansion of China's economy in the 1990s created new demands. Like the businessmen of eighteenth-century Yangzhou, the newly rich wanted to purchase art for collections or as investments; moreover, the Chinese government was looking for exportable commodities. Encouraged by these events the international art market expanded into China and Chinese painting became more available and much more expensive.[124]

The paintings of Wang Huaiqing (1944–) reflect these changes. During the Cultural Revolution Wang Huaiqing made woodblock propaganda posters, but by the 1980s he was a member of a group of modern oil painters called the Contemporaries, *Tongdairen*.[125] He painted *The Picture of Bole* (*Bole, a Wise Old Man Who Knows How to Choose Horses*) in 1980.[126] The picture shows Bole, stoking a superior thousand-*li* horse which has been starved and abused. Both Bole and the horse are painted in naturalistic detail. Bole is wearing only a loincloth. His gaunt face is lined, and his wispy hair and beard are white. His thin body and agonized expression are in decided contrast to the plump and smiling faces presented in propaganda posters by Socialist Realist painters of a previous generation. The horse is also very thin; his ribs and the bones in his spine are clearly showing and we are immediately reminded of the *Emaciated*

Horse. Nevertheless, he paws the ground to indicate that despite his miserable condition, he is as energetic and spirited as Night-Shining White. Bole's head is tilted back and his eyes are raised upward. While the two figures are painted realistically, the background is flat and abstract with a faint inscription that seems to be in ancient Shang Dynasty seal script at the top of the painting. The political meaning is clear: although the Cultural Revolution was a waste of the Chinese people, there is hope for the Chinese future. A Western collector writes "Bole's aesthetic lines convey his experiential wisdom: the raised chin and searching eyes of the frontal image suggest his continuing quest for truth."[127]

The phrase, the "quest for truth," suggests certain Western philosophical and narrative traditions; Bole is more likely to be pleading for a revival of *tian ren he yi*, the ancient Confucian ideal of the union of heavenly morality and human life, rather than looking for an abstract concept like "truth."[128] The painting combines Chinese and Western traditions. It is an oil painting in the formalist tradition, and the horse is very western—it does not have the square head, round knees, short legs, and wispy tail of a thousand-*li* Ferghana horse. On the other hand, the story of Bole is a traditional Chinese folk tale; the characters on the top of the painting are placed where the inscription appears in Gong Kai's *Emaciated Horse*. However, while Gong Kia's inscription explains the painting, the characters in Wang Huaiqing's painting appear to be scattered randomly without any semantic meaning, although the choice of seal script from ancient bronze and bone writings recalls both ancient Chinese religious tradition as well as the Epigraphic Movement *jinshixue* (bronze and stone studies) of the Qing Dynasty.[129] There is something slightly discordant in the combination of traditions. While the ink paintings of Han Gan and Xu Beihong provide a sense of drama and movement, the oil painting of Wang Huaiqing is relatively static, without any of the deliberate "blandness" of Zhao Mengfu's *Groom and Horse*. The background is flat, but unlike the blank space of traditional Chinese painting, it is not empty, it is painted. The seal script characters seem out of place on a flat painted background; but they refer back to the tradition of writing on Chinese painting, and point to the contemporary, avant-garde use of Chinese characters as a source of abstract forms. In the 1980s many Chinese painters began experimenting with Chinese characters as abstract forms—mixing styles, distorting traditional forms, inventing meaningless characters.[130] These artists had grown up in the chaos of the Cultural Revolution surrounded by the huge red and white "big character" posters. Many of them began their artistic careers producing these posters. Their work was both humorous, albeit often black humor, and biting social criticism of the political distortions of language and social forms. Thus many of these artists immigrated to the United States in the aftermath of the political turmoil of 1989. Wang Huaiqing, however, insisted that because his work was not political there was no reason for him to leave China. He claimed that having once had his work subject to political control he refused to have it subjected to the control of the international art market.

Wang Huaiqing has since become an internationally known artist whose later works include abstract paintings of parts of Ming Dynasty furniture and the roofs of Chinese villages whose subdued almost monochromatic colors echo the tradition of Chinese ink painting. In these paintings Wang sometimes seems to have achieved a harmonious merger of Chinese elements with the Western tradition of abstract, formal art; other times he seems simply to be painting in a familiar international style. Wang has also played a highly symbolic role in the global art market. In the spring of 2008 his painting, *Homeless Furniture*, sold for a record of over 4 million dollars.[131] A few months later the failure of one of his pieces to sell at an international auction was reported as a sign of the effect of the worldwide economic crisis on the Chinese Art market.[132]

The Chinese aesthetic tradition, like China itself, has undergone vast changes in the last century. From Mao's Yenan lectures in 1942 until the end of the Cultural Revolution Chinese art was highly politicized. Now that it is a valuable commodity in the global market the future of Chinese art is vigorously debated. Does the entrance of Chinese artists into the global art world mean the end of a distinctively Chinese aesthetic tradition as *guohua* (traditional Chinese painting) is replaced by *xihua* (Western painting)? Will the importance of calligraphic brushwork decline and disappear or will there be a "convergence" of Western and Chinese painting traditions? Perhaps more significantly for this chapter, will Chinese artists adopt the modern liberal view expressed that artistic values and political morality are, and ought to be, quite independent? Although the spirit of individualism appearing in Ming Dynasty paintings of Jin Nong and Ren Xiong is consistent with the separation of aesthetic content from political content, Chinese painters like Xu Beihong and Wang Huaiqing continue to make more or less subtle political references.[133]

Conclusion: Art or Propaganda?

What can this reading of Chinese horse paintings teach us about their aesthetic meaning? In particular, what do Chinese horse paintings say about the relationship between art and politics? Do works of art have an aesthetic content which distinguishes them from propaganda and protects art from censorship? In liberal theory, censorship is almost always condemned as a violation of the right to free speech. As Henry Rosemont has persuasively argued, however, I can respect your right to free speech simply by ignoring you. Deutsch claims that treating the social impact of art as an example of "free speech" usually results in treating art as a matter of "public indifference . . . something essentially superfluous, a harmless luxury."[134]

Although Deutsch recognizes that works of art are neither ahistorical nor independent of their cultural contexts, the aesthetic content of a work of art somehow transcends time and place since

> [o]ur experience of artworks enables us to enter cultures, times, and places other than our own and eventually to appropriate them precisely as our own and thereby to extend the self into an ever-widening community of humankind.[135]

How is this possible?

Of course we cannot experience the painting *Night-Shining White* precisely the same way the Emperor Xuanzong did. Like Xuanzong we see the Emperor's powerful, well-cared-for warhorse struggling against a post. Our initial feelings of delight and amusement (the first level of aesthetic experience Li Zehou identified as an "aesthetic attitude") might be roughly similar to those of Xuanzong, but the aesthetic meaning of the painting has changed. Not only has almost 20 feet of inscriptions and seals been added that the Emperor never saw, but the aesthetic content of this painting has grown over the centuries as the tradition of horse painting has been sedimented into Chinese art history. The meaning (aesthetic content) of the painting continues to expand by the contribution of thousands of years of interpretations and viewers' responses.

For Chinese viewers, *Night-Shining White* represents one of the highest points of Chinese culture. The horse, the Emperor, and the Tang Dynasty were proud and confident. They faced the world secure in their own superiority but with open-minded curiosity about foreign peoples and foreign ideas. After the decline of the Tang Dynasty, a feeling of nostalgia for an era of naïve optimism became part of the aesthetic meaning of the painting. Western viewers may also come to feel a sort of nostalgia for the Tang, just as nonbelievers can appreciate religious art. Uighurs, on the other hand, who had a more or less adversarial relationship with the Tang Dynasty, and a decidedly unfriendly one with the present Chinese government, may feel anything but nostalgic about symbols of Chinese power. But the Tang were not the only culture that rose to great heights to learn, only too late, the warning hidden in the fact that "if horses are fat they are haughty." Enlightenment Europe believed that science and liberal thought would bring an end to war, hunger, ignorance, and disease. We know better; but we can appreciate the feeling of hope.[136]

The aesthetic content of Zhao Mengfu's *Groom and Horse* includes a reference to the sedimented meaning of *Night-Shining White*. There is nostalgia for the independence, power and pride of the Tang. The calm, bland expressions of the horse and groom contrast with the fire and spirit of the earlier age and earlier painting. What does a *literati* scholar-gentleman do when times are bad? The *Analects* advises: "Be known when the way prevails in the world, but remain hidden away when it does not" (*Analects* 8.13). The Chan value of resignation and acceptance is added to the Confucian admonitions, both of which are sedimented in the aesthetic meaning of this painting. Again, Western viewers can empathize with Han culture under the Yuan, particularly if we recall times when things have not gone well, when knowing what has been lost, we wonder how to survive.

The two Ferghana horses from the Ming Dynasty refer to the ancient past—Han Wudi's expeditions and the history of China and its horses since then. But a modern feeling of individualism pervades the painting. Personal life is not always a direct reflection of the politics of the times. Individuals live—bitterly or optimistically—in any time, and modernity celebrates that fact.

The aesthetic meaning of Xu Beihong's *Galloping Horse* and Wang Huaiqing's *The Picture of Bole* includes the glorious victories and devastating losses of war and revolution. Buried under sedimented layers of Western painting techniques—oil painting and the study of anatomy—are references to *Night Shining White*, the work of Zhao Mengfu, ancient oracle bones, and the calligraphic tradition. The political content of Wang Huaiqing's painting may encourage Western viewers to compare the devastation of the Cultural Revolution with the Holocaust.[137] Moreover, Xu

Beihong's *Galloping Horse* is about victory in the war with the Japanese, an experience Americans share with China, although since the next series of Chinese military victories was against the Americans in Korea, the meaning of Xu's painting resonates with the complex relationships—military, economic, political, and artistic—between our two cultures.

Wang Huaiqing's economic success indicates that the art world has indeed become global, raising troublesome questions about the elitist implications of the increasing domination of the art market by wealthy capitalist collectors. Of course, the relationship between artists and their wealthy patrons has always been complex. Han Gan was employed by the emperor. The Song Dynasty *literati* began as members of the privileged elite. The relationship between the painters of Yangzhou and their newly wealthy patrons was fraught with complications. On the other hand, the appearance of *Night-Shining White* and Xu's horses on refrigerator magnets and tote bags demonstrates the continuing interaction of elite and popular culture.

Finally, we might briefly consider some examples of horse painting in Western cultures. The eighteenth-century British painter, George Stubbs (1724–1806) painted the horses of the landed gentry to celebrate their status and power—for much the same reasons Han Gan painted Emperor Xuanzong's war horses.[138] American horse painters often celebrate the cowboy tradition—a life of independence, adventure, and freedom. And here our two cultures converge in a moment of historical irony. In 2001 descendants of the Ferghana horses took part in what George W. Bush, a United States President from Texas, another part of the world famous for its love of horses, described as "the first cavalry charge of the twenty-first century." American CIA agents and Northern Alliance soldiers rode Central Asian horses in their fight against the Taliban in Afghanistan. Sadly these horses were not fat, and vast numbers of them died carrying heavy loads of modern weapons and supplies over the mountains.[139] Since the military prowess of a modern empire depends on its air power, the twenty-first-century analogue for Xuanzong's warhorses are jets and helicopters rather than the descendants of the superior horses, the Heavenly Horses. But if the meaning of *Night-Shining White* reaches out to us, as Deutsch claims it must, we may be reminded of what a powerful empire forgets at its peril. If the horses are fat, they are haughty.

In conclusion, the aesthetic meaning of a work of art is not static. Whether a painting has an aesthetic meaning, what precisely that meaning is, and whether it protects the work from political censorship is determined

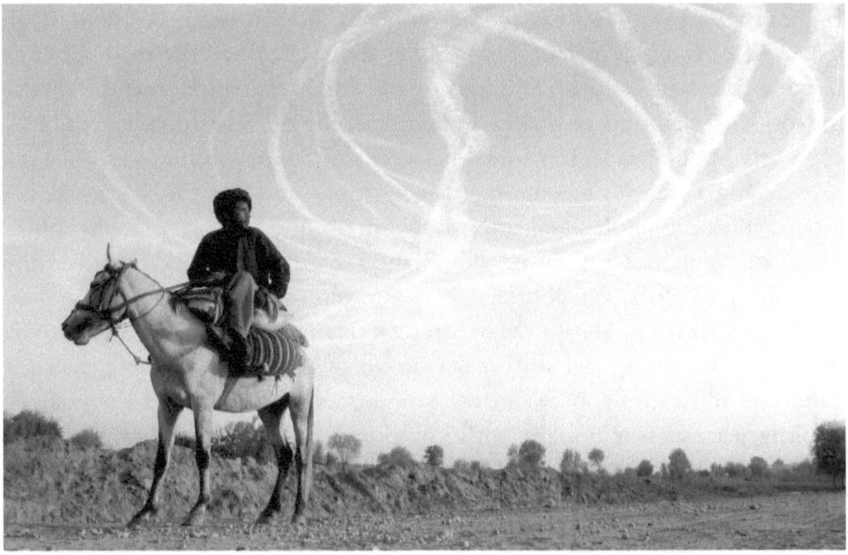

FIGURE 4.15. Northern Alliance Soldier watching the jet trails of American planes, Afghanistan, 2001. Photograph courtesy of James Hill.

by a community which includes connoisseurs, patrons, collectors, directors of art museums, gallery owners, academics, political authorities—and indeed anyone who takes an aesthetic attitude toward the work—responding to it in almost any way at all.

On Putnam's theory the meaning of a word is determined by a linguistic division of labor between the scientific experts and ordinary language users. Analogously we might argue that the meaning of a work of art, its aesthetic content, is determined by interaction between the experts of the art world and the nonexperts who respond to works of art. The relationship is obviously more complex than Putnam's theory suggests. There are many more than two groups involved and their judgments may conflict and change over time. At the level Li Zehou identifies as "aesthetic attention" we may look at many different sources to expand our understanding of the aesthetic content of a work of art. This chapter considers a relatively limited number of such sources. In the end the distinction between genuine art and pseudo art, propaganda, or pornography, often depends less on an "aesthetic content" than on whether one approves of the political and moral values it expresses; and there are times when viewers—the *literati*, the Yuan Emperor, museum directors, gallery owners, and big city mayors disagree. On Li Zehou's theory of aesthetic experience the second level of the experience is "aesthetic attention" where careful consideration of the formal properties and historical context of a work of art may resolve some disagreements, but almost certainly not all of them.

Moreover while the formal properties of a painting—questions of composition, geometry, brushwork, shading, color, perspective—contribute to the aesthetic meaning of the work, as we have seen judgments about these properties may change.[140] Nevertheless, the evolving aesthetic content of a work like *Night-Shining White* can reach out to viewers over vast stretches of time and place because all human beings live in societies in which we play a number of personal and political roles. We are more or less self-conscious that our societies and our place in them are the creations of history. Empires rise and fall. Personal and political times of prosperity and confidence are often followed by decline and moods of cynicism, bitterness, and despair. We cannot separate the aesthetic content of a work of art from its political and moral messages. They are sedimented in its aesthetic meaning. Han Gan's painting skills and sophisticated techniques have made the spirit, *shenyun*, of a particular horse resonate with audiences thousands of years and half the globe away. But the aesthetic meaning of *Night Shining White* reminds us to celebrate times of peace and the ideal of good government, to smile at the self-importance of a horse, or a leader, and to be wary of the dangers of political corruption and the devastation of conquest and war.

5

The Red Cliff Odes

Poetry and Philosophy

Philosophy and poetry have had an uneasy, sometimes openly hostile, relationship in the West. Although one of the early texts of Western philosophy, Parmenides's "On Nature," was written as a poem and Plato himself frequently quoted poets, Plato's quotations were generally illustrations of his point rather than part of his argument; moreover, the *Republic* contains his infamous claim that poets tell dangerously seductive lies. While the condemnation of poetry in the *Republic* is tempered in the *Symposium* and *Phaedrus*, Plato remained deeply suspicious about the role of art, emotion, poetry, and music in the education of citizens of a just and moral society. With the growing importance of science in modern Western philosophy the role of the arts was increasingly marginalized, until in the mid-twentieth-century analytic philosophers often dismissed their continental colleagues as "just writing poetry."

On the other hand, traditional Chinese culture assumed that there was an intimate connection between poetry, philosophy, and the practical concerns of political life. Confucius was believed to have edited the *Shijing* (*Classic of Poetry* or *Book of Songs*) and recommended its study on several occasions.

> Reciting the Songs can arouse your sensibilities, strengthen your powers of observation, enhance your ability to get along with others, and sharpen your critical skills. Close at hand it enables you to serve your father, and away at court it enables

> you to serve your lord. It instills in you a broad vocabulary for making distinctions in the world around you. (*Analects* 17.9)
>
> The Master said to his son, Boyu, "Have you mastered the 'Zhounan' and 'Shaonan' sections of the Book of Songs? Striving to become a person without doing so is like trying to take your stand with your face to the wall." (*Analects* 17.10)

For more than a thousand years aspiring government officials studied for the Imperial examinations by memorizing vast amounts of classical text, including the *Shijng*.[1] Given the importance of poetry in the examination system it began to seem natural for statesman and philosophers to write poetry themselves, a tradition followed well into the twentieth century by many Chinese leaders including Mao Zedong. Li Zehou, writing for both Chinese and Western audiences, defines philosophy as "science plus poetry."[2]

Nevertheless, one of the leading figures of Neo-Confucianism, Zhu Xi (1130–1200), echoed Plato in his criticism of the Song Dynasty poet-philosopher Su Shi (1037–1101). Zhu claimed Su's writings were dangerous because they were so beautiful and so well-written, that readers accepted his views without realizing that they were "wrong from the start."[3]

Su Shi, who took the literary name Su Dongpo, was a poet, politician, art critic, painter, calligrapher, and herbalist whose intensely thoughtful and reflective poetry was often decidedly "philosophical." Thus, Su's work provides an excellent context for examining the relationship between poetry, philosophy, morality, and politics. This chapter will examine Su's poetry, focusing in particular on three poems he wrote about the Red Cliff, poems that raise a number of questions about the relationship between poetry and philosophy in China and the West.

The first part of this chapter describes the development of Su's writing and his political career. When his politics resulted in imprisonment and exile, he became a farmer and claimed that he wanted to model his life on that of Tao Qian (365–427). At the same time, however, he studied Daoist meditation techniques and Buddhist sutras. The second part of the chapter examines the Red Cliff poems; and the third part discusses Su's relationship with the philosophers, who were developed the Neo-Confucian synthesis. Many of these men withdrew from active politics to work out the complex and abstract Neo-Confucian metaphysics. Su, on the other hand, remained actively engaged with the world and his work was firmly rooted in his political experience and the historical and social conditions of his time. Su and his followers are not considered part of the Neo-Confucian tradition, at least in part because of the hostility of Zhu Xi who thought Su's work suffered from the influence of both Daoist and Buddhist thought. I argue that Su's philosophical poetry identified the problems the synthesis was intended to resolve and the strains of thought it brought together. I conclude that the hostility of the founders of that synthesis toward Su Shi reflected a failure of the synthesis itself, and indeed the failure of a certain kind of philosophy in general.

Su Shi's Life and Exile in Huangzhou

Su Shi was born in Meishan, a city in present-day Szechwan province. His father was a relatively wealthy landowner and his mother a devout follower of Pure Land Buddhism, a sect more concerned with Buddhist practice than any particular intellectual doctrines. Although Su and his brother received Confucian educations, their father introduced them to a number of Buddhist monks and sent them to a school run by a Taoist priest.[4] After Su and his younger brother Su Zhe [Su Ch'ei] passed the *jinshi* degree, they were appointed to a series of government positions in what appeared to be the beginning of brilliant public careers; but their lives ran afoul of court politics.

In the last decades of the Northern Song Dynasty, pressure from the Jurchen tribes to the north was putting a severe strain on the Dynasty. Financial and administrative reform was desperately needed, and in 1060 the controversial statesman, Wang Anshi, arrived in the capital city of Kaifeng and rapidly rose to power. Wang instituted the New Laws: a series of radical reforms of the military, the government, and the economic and educational systems.[5] Wang complained that the traditional examination system rewarded people with prodigious memories who could write literary essays quoting long passages of classical texts, abilities which had little to do with the practical skills required for the posts assigned to the men who passed the imperial examinations.[6] To remedy this defect Wang added practical subjects like mathematics, geography, and administration to the imperial examinations, reduced the emphasis on the classics, and replaced the traditional commentaries with his own interpretation of the Confucian texts.[7] Arguing that the *Chunqiu* (*Spring and Autumn Annals*) had been corrupted by too many layers of unreliable commentary, he banned its study completely from the curriculum of the imperial examinations.[8]

Infuriated by the New Laws, the conservative cultural elite vigorously defended China's ancient culture. There were three groups opposed to Wang's reforms. The first, the *shi* (士 gentry scholars) were the most conservative. They held governmental positions and were concerned that not only would the changes in the examination system weaken Chinese culture as a whole, but the financial reforms would end their own freedom from taxation.[9] The second group was centered in Loyang and headed by the neo-Confucian scholar Cheng Yi (1033–1107). These men were more interested in studying and teaching metaphysics and self-cultivation, than they were in active political involvement.[10] Although Cheng Yi passed his *jinshi* degree, he refused to enter government service, remaining in Loyang to become a well-known scholar and an important Neo-Confucian in the generation before Zhu Xi. The third group, the Shu School, centered around Su Shi, his brother, and father. The Sus were generally moderates—agreeing with Wang Anshi that reforms were necessary, but condemning the New Laws for being too drastic and the other two groups for being dogmatic extremists. Although the politics of the Shu group was pragmatic and utilitarian, they were often quite critical without offering many practical alternatives.[11]

Early in Su's career he joined Cheng Yi in opposing Wang Anshi's educational reforms. Su and Cheng defended the historical accounts in the *Chunqiu* for teaching important moral lessons that were critical in the education of government officials.[12] Moreover, the emotional and philosophical orientation Su expressed in his poetry was deeply involved in an understanding of history.

While Su's opposition to Wang's reforms was generally practical—the reforms often had devastating unintended consequences on the people they effected—Cheng Yi was more concerned with abstract principles and theoretical knowledge. The *Da Xue* (*Great Learning*) argued that good government required education and self-cultivation through "the investigation of things."

> In ancient times, one who intended to carry forward all the inherent virtues in the world and to rid them of material desires had first to rule his state well. To rule his state well, he had first to educate his family. To educate his family, he had first to cultivate himself. To cultivate himself, he had first to set his heart right. To set his heart right, he had first to be sincere and honest. To be sincere and honest, he had first to

> perfect his knowledge and the perfection of his knowledge depended on his investigation of things.
>
> It is only when one is able to investigate things that knowledge can be perfected. It is only when one's knowledge is perfect that one can be sincere and honest. It is only when one is honest and sincere that he can set his heart right. It is only when the heart is set right that a man can educate his family. It is only when his family is educated that he can rule the state. It is only when the state is ruled that the world can be governed well.[13]

For Cheng Yi the best way to investigate things was to study the ancient texts, discovering the moral principles in them and evaluating the actions of important historical and contemporary figures to learn where they were right and where they were wrong.[14]

Although Su had studied the classics and wrote at least one commentary on them,[15] his own writing reflected the circumstances of his life rather than any abstract scholarship. Before he entered public service his poems were quite personal, using relatively idiosyncratic language and metaphors to describe landscapes and commemorate events in his life and that of his family. When he took office his poetry turned outward and he began to write in a more public language. At first Su supported most of the reforms of the New Laws, but soon his poems began to express growing concern about the hardship these laws created for the people for whom he was responsible. In a particularly satiric poem he contrasts an old peasant of seventy who cannot afford to buy salt with Confucius: "When the Master was in the state of Qi he heard the shao music, and for several months he did not know the taste of meat" (*Analects* 7.14).

> *Mountain Village, third of five*
> An old man of seventy hangs a sickle at his waist.
> Praised be, that in the spring mountains the bamboo shoots
> and brackens are sweet.
> How could it be that, having heard the Shao music, he
> became oblivious to taste?
> These past three months he has eaten without salt.[16]

After several years in the capital city of Kaifeng Su began to lose favor with the ruling elite and left the capital for a series of posts in the provinces, ending up as a fairly important official in Hangzhou. As his responsibilities and experience increased, Su became involved in the unpleasant realities of politics; his criticism of the government became muted, and he wrote about the practical problems of drought, famine, locusts, and bandits which took up much of his increasingly busy life.[17]

Nevertheless, Su could not escape the political intrigues of the court. In 1079 Wang Anshi's followers imprisoned him on the charge of writing satirical poems slandering the emperor. Although Wang Anshi had retired and Su's trial was not particularly significant, Su was badly frightened. During the 130 days he was in prison he wrote two poems to his brother Su Zhe. In the first of these poems he clearly believes his life is in danger.

> Under the Heaven of Our Holy Ruler
>
> Because of what has happened, I have been confined to the imperial censorate prison. The prison officials treat me with increasing harshness, and I doubt that I can stand it much longer. If I die in prison, I will have no chance to say goodbye to Tzu-yu [Ziyou], and therefore I wrote these two poems and gave them to the warden, Liang Hsü, to deliver to him.
>
> Under the heaven of our holy ruler, all things turn to spring,
> but I in dark ignorance have destroyed myself.
> Before my hundred years are past, I'm called to settle up;
> my leaderless family, ten mouths, must be your worry now.
> Bury me anywhere on the green hills
> and another year in night rain grieve for me alone.
> Let us be brothers in lives and lives to come,
> mending then the bonds that this world breaks.[18]

In 1079 Su was released and exiled to Huangzhou. His initial response was exuberant.

> A Hundred Days, Free to Go
>
> Twelfth month, twenty-eighth day. I receive the favor of being appointed special supernumerary of the Water Bureau and second officer in the home guard at Huang-chou [both merely nominal posts]: two poems.

A hundred days, free to go, and it's almost spring;
for the years left, pleasure will be my chief concern.
Out the gate, I do a dance, wind blows my face;
our galloping horses race along as magpies cheer.
I face the wine cup and it's all a dream,
pick up a poem brush, already inspired.
Why try to fix the blame for trouble past?
Years now I've stolen posts I never should have had.[19]

But there was little to celebrate. His freedom severely curtailed, his career in ruins, and his income drastically reduced, Su began to reflect on his life and his experience. He spent the first three months in Huangzhou at a Buddhist monastery where he lived simply, ate vegetarian meals, avoided social calls, and wandered in the mountains picking herbs and fishing. In midsummer his family joined him and Su moved out of the monastery into Lingao [Lin'gao] Pavilion although he continued to visit Buddhist temples to meditate and study sutras. At the end of 1080 he went on a 49-day "purifying" retreat at Tianqing Temple where he fasted and studied Daoist breathing exercises.[20]

Su Shi and Tao Qian

Su identified his new life in Huangzhou with that of the reclusive poet Tao Qian [T'ao Ch'ien] (365–427) who was also known by his literary name, Tao Yuanming, and had abandoned public life to make his living as a farmer. Although Tao is now one of the most well-known Chinese poets, he owes his popularity largely to Su Shi's determined advocacy of his talent, and most of Tao's reputation for simplicity and unambiguous dedication to rural life was due to Su's interpretation of him.[21] To celebrate his escape from public service Tao Qian wrote a series of four poems titled "Home Again among Gardens and Fields." The first poem describes the simplicity and beauty of his new life:

Nothing like the others, even as a child,
rooted in a love for hills and mountains,

I fell into their net of dust, that one
departure a blunder lasting thirteen years.

But a tethered bird longs for its forest,
a pond fish its deep waters. So now, my

land out on the south edge cleared, I
nurture simplicity among gardens and fields,

home again. I've got nearly two acres here,
and four or five rooms in my thatch hut.

Elms and willows shade the eves out back,
and in the front, peach and plum spread wide.

Distant-village people lost in distant
haze, kitchen smoke hangs above wide-open

country. Here, dogs bark deep in back roads,
and roosters crow from mulberry treetops.

No confusion within the gate, no dust,
my empty home harbors idleness to spare.

Back again: after so long in that trap,
I've returned to all that comes of itself.[22]

The second of the series of Tao Qian's poems rejoices in the isolation of the farm and the limits of what conversations he does have:

So little out here ever involves people.
Visitors to our meager lane rare, my

bramble gate closed all day, this empty
home cuts dust-filled thoughts short.

And day after day, coming and going
on overgrown paths, I meet neighbors

without confusion: we only talk about
how the crops are doing, nothing more."[23]

The third of the series is about planting and weeding beans and how their cultivation "reminds me never to resist,"[24] a line echoing Tao Qian's deeply Daoist feelings. The series ends in a reflective mood. Out walking with his children Tao encounters "gravemounds and houses deserted long ago" which remind him:

> "Life" is its own mirage of change. It ends
> vanished, returned into nothing. "What else?"[25]

Despite the hardship and poverty of his life as a farmer, Tao Qian is delighted to be an exile from court and to have escaped "that trap." Even when writing about being hungry and cold, Tao had few regrets about his choice of a life of escape from government service. Farming is hard work, but it is infinitely preferable to life in office.

In Su's early poems at Huangzhou, "Moving to Lin'gao Pavilion" and the series of poems on Eastern Slope, Su echoes Tao Qian's relief at having escaped the confusion and chaos of official life.

> I am lucky to have been put out to pasture,
> Like a weary horse that has had its load removed.[26]

Su's language, however, is more intellectual than Tao's and while Tao Qian actively left political life, Su had been forced out.

Soon after his move to Lingao Pavilion, Su was given permission to work a small plot of land known as the East Slope. He took the literary name Dongpo Jushi (東坡居士), the Gentleman of the Eastern Slopes, after this land[27] and wrote some of his best work, including "Eight Poems on East Slope" which were modeled after Tao Qian's "Home Again among Gardens and Fields."

The land at East Slope was an abandoned wasteland out of which Su created a small farm where he raised rice, wheat, millet, and oranges to feed his family and timber to make some extra cash. The poems record Su's transformation of the land into a productive farm and himself into a successful farmer. The preface describes the back-breaking work involved:

> The land had been left untouched for a long time, and was no more than a waste of brambles, stones, and broken tiles. In addition it was a year of severe drought. I came near to

> exhausting every ounce of muscle and energy I had opening it up for cultivation, and letting go the plow with a sigh, I wrote these poems to console myself in my labors.[28]

The first three poems present concrete details about clearing the land of brush and weeds, of finding the right place to plant his crops, and the delightful surprise of discovering a little stream crossing his land. The planting and the stream send him dreaming of the meals he will be able to make from the produce of his farm and the fish he might raise. Working to prepare the land, first alone and then with a young helper, he recognized his dependence on nature for rain and fertile soil. In the fourth poem Su became part of the rhythms of the seasons as he described planting rice in the spring, watching it grow in the summer, and putting the newly harvested grains in his steamer, joyfully anticipating the taste of the first rice he grew for himself. In the fourth and fifth poems Su was less socially isolated. Not only did he have a young helper, he took advice from an old experienced farmer about growing wheat, and "by green-blade paddies I chat with friends."[29] Like Tao Qian, Su talked to his neighbors about their crops, but Su was also talking to more educated friends who continued to serve the government and whose conversation may not have been limited to wheat, mulberries, rice, and the weather.

In the sixth and seventh poems the poet's vision widened beyond the daily concerns of farming, clearing land, planting crops, and enjoying his harvest. He made long range plans for planting trees—pines that cannot be cut for at least ten years, Chinese dates (jujubes) and orange seedlings that would grow and eventually bear fruit. Relinquishing his ambition to be a successful official, Su began to hope he might eventually be known for his foresight as a farmer.[30] These two poems refer to the wider political and intellectual world in several ways. Su alluded to ancient texts: the *Shijing*, the *San Quo Zhi* (*The Record of Three States* 三國志), the *Lunyu* (*Analects*), and to Du Fu, a poet who, like Tao Qian, celebrated the simplicity of rural life.[31] Su also mentioned his friends, local farmers and merchants, as well as more educated men who continued to serve the government. In the final poem Su appeared to be resigned to the loss of his official career and content with his life as a farmer, finding meaning in being part of the natural rhythms of the seasons, dependent on the rain and sun, and accepting the simplicity, and poverty, of rural life.[32]

But while Tao Qian was generally delighted to have escaped from official life, Su was clearly ambivalent. Daoist philosophers argue that the Confucian concern with ancient texts and intellectual understanding interferes with living in tune with nature, and Tao Qian eschewed classical references. The last poems of Eastern Slope series, however, reach out to a wider world, talking about more than "how the crops are doing," making historical analogies and references to the Confucian heroes and virtues.[33] This suggests that Su Shi was not completely willing to reject the life of Confucian duty and government service. Tao Qian's exile was voluntary, and he seemed to accept the cold, the hunger, the poverty, and the fact that his sons would grow up uneducated,[34] but Su continued to be concerned for his sons' education.[35] Although he seemed content to find meaning in life as a farmer, he still hoped to makes a name for himself, albeit by the trees he had planted, rather than a successful government career.

On the other hand, Su is obviously closer to Tao Qian than he is to Qu Yuan, another famous exiled poet. Qu Yuan (ca. 340–278 BCE) was a legendary statesman of the state of Chu. Having been slandered by political enemies he was dismissed from the court of King Huai of Chu. A faithful and loyal servant of the king, Qu Yuan composed *Li Sao,* "On Encountering Sorrow," a long romantic poem describing a magical journey expressing his loyalty to the king and deep sense of having been wronged. Unable to convince the court to return him to his former position of trust and power, Qu Yuan held a stone to his chest, threw himself into the river Miluo [Mi-lo] and drowned.[36] Su, on the other hand, refused to write sorrowful complaints about being rejected and tried to reconcile himself to life in exile. Describing his move to Lingao Pavilion he wrote

> This remote region was opened for me by Heaven.
> Hunger and poverty may increase or decrease,
> [But] they are not manifestly to be mourned or congratulated.
> Mind, without sorrow or joy,
> No harsh words become a [soul summoning] *suo*.[37]

The translator notes that while the last line refers to Qu Yuan, Su's refusal to dramatize his exile may also have been motivated by the desire to avoid getting in trouble, again, for writing poems critical of the government.

Despite his best efforts, however, the intellectual climate of the Song Dynasty made it impossible for Su Shi to embrace either Tao Qian's Daoist withdrawal or Qu Yuan's Confucian sacrifice. Qu Yuan lived in the classical age of Chinese thought, when the "Hundred Schools" vigorously debated the nature of the good life and the relationship between happiness and duty. The repression of the Qin dynasty ended these conversations. After the Han defeated the Qin, the Confucianism that had sustained Qu Yuan became the official state philosophy and degenerated into a sterile and rigid orthodoxy. When the invasion of non-Han tribes caused the Confucian certainties to crumble, Tao Qian was not the only writer to reject Confucian values in favor of a Daoist—"love for hills and mountains." In the centuries between Tao Qian and Su Shi, Wei-Jin *xuan xue* synthesized Confucian social values and Daoist mysticism.[38] When Buddhism arrived in China *xuan xue* scholars accepted it, naïvely believing that Buddhist metaphysics was not all that different from their own. As a result Chinese intellectual life was dominated for almost 600 years by Buddhism. The period changed Chinese thought profoundly.

Su Shi and Buddhism

Traditional Chinese philosophy had no satisfying answer to the question of "What happens after you die?" Confucius refused to consider the supernatural and insisted that his followers focus on practical life:

> Zilu asked how to serve the spirits and gods. The Master replied, "Not yet being able to serve other people, how would you be able to serve the spirits?" Zilu said, "May I ask about death?" The Master replied, "Not yet understanding life, how could you understand death?" (*Analects* 11.12)

The Daoist Zhuangzi provided the bleak prospect that after dying we simply decompose and disappear back into organic matter. When Master Lai lay dying his friend Master Li

> . . . leaned against the door way and talked to Master Lai. "How marvelous the Creator is! What is he going to make out of you next? Where is he going to send you? Will he make you into a rat's liver? Will he make you into a bug's arm?"[39]

The transcendent immortals of Daoism were ordinary human beings who recognized and accepted this view of life and death, withdrawing emotionally from any attachments to making "the body like a withered tree and the mind like dead ashes,"[40] taking the "True Man of ancient times" as his model. Such a man

> . . . knew nothing of loving life, knew nothing of hating death. He emerged without delight; he went back without a fuss. . . . He received something and took pleasure in it; he forgot about it and handed it back again.[41]

Since neither of these views provides any comfort to people afraid of dying, Buddhism appealed to Chinese thinkers because it appeared to responded to questions about life after death in terms of an absolute unchanging reality that transcended the care and suffering of ordinary life.[42]

Having been badly frightened when he was forced to face his own mortality in prison, Su Shi began a serious study of Buddhist texts early in his Huangzhou exile. He had read the *Śūramgama* and *Vimalakīrti Sūtras*, both of which expounded the Buddhist belief that worldly phenomena were delusions foisted on us by our senses.[43] The *Śūramgama Sūtra* presents a relatively dualistic metaphysics that contrasts the illusionary physical world of life and death with the timeless world of transcendent reality that remains after death, "a permanent, unchanging Buddha nature that is not subject to birth and death."[44]

The more logically rigorous *Vimalakīrti Sūtra* describes the material world as a drifting cloud "characterized by turbulence and dissolution."[45] The *Sūtra* insists on a strict monism in which the "the Buddhas are neither past, nor present, nor future; their enlightenment transcends the three times."[46] A central theme of the *Vimalakīrti Sūtra* is nonduality, and the sutra reports a dialogue between Vimalakīrti, a bodhisattva, who had been reborn a wealthy layman in order to save sentient beings, and Mañjusrī, the wisest of all bodhisattvas. After gathering a great crowd of bodhisattvas, kings, gods, and goddesses Vimalakīrti asks, "Good sirs, please explain how the bodhisattvas enter the Dharma-door of nonduality!"[47] The bodhisattvas responded by making a long series of sophisticated metaphysical distinctions demonstrating how to dissolve pairs of opposites into a single reality. When the bodhisattvas had finished they asked Mañjusrī to answer the question. He replied:

> Good sirs, you have all spoken well. Nevertheless, all your explanations are themselves dualistic. To know no one teaching, to

> express nothing, to say nothing, to explain nothing, to announce nothing, to indicate nothing, and to designate nothing—that is the entrance into nonduality.[48]

At last they turned to Vimalakīrti for his explanation of the teaching of nonduality.

> Thereupon . . . Vimalakīrti remained silent. This is known as the "great silence," a powerful demonstration of Vimalakīrti's profound understanding, which Mañjusrī explained had no use for either language or concepts.[49]

Early in his poetic career Su associated Zhuangzi's views of death with Vimalakīrti's wordless teaching. His poem "The Statue of Vimalakīrti, a Clay Figure by Yuang Hui-chi of the T'ang in the Temple of the Pillar of Heaven (1061)" begins by quoting Zhuangzi "What will the Creator make out of me next?" and continues by describing a figure of Vimalakīrti, ending

> Old farmers, village wives never deign to give a glance,
> though field mice sometimes nibble at his whiskers.
> Each time I look at him I'm lost in wonder—
> Who can be like Vimalakīrti, a wordless teacher?[50]

Nevertheless, despite his admiration for Vimalakīrti, given Su's love of words, his almost irresistible urge to write about something to preserve its memory, he could hardly be seriously drawn to the austere monism of the *Vimalakīrti Sūtra* and its celebration of the "great silence." After a visit to the mountain retreat of two Buddhists priests, Su wrote:

> Such trips—simple but with a joy that lasts;
> back home, I'm lost in a dreamer's daze.
> Write a poem quick before it gets away!
> Once gone, a lovely sight is hard to catch again.[51]

Attractive as Buddhism was to Su, his delight in the sensuous pleasures of the world, his deep emotional and intellectual attachment to the historical past, and his love of poetry kept him from accepting the Buddhist path to enlightenment. As he wrote in a letter from Huangzhou,

> Compared to the so-called transcendent and enlightened among the gentlemen of the world, I know nothing. In the past Ch'en Shu-ku [1017–1080] enjoyed talking about Ch'an and considered his [understanding] to be enlightened while disdaining mine for being superficial and limited. I would say to Shu-ku, "What you speak of is, to use the analogy of eating and drinking, like dining on dragon's flesh, while what I have learned is like [eating] pork. Of course, there is a difference between dragon's flesh and pork, but even if you talk the entire day about dragon's flesh, it cannot compare to being able to dine on pork [that is] truly delicious and filling.[52]

In his last exile on Hainan Island Su wrote:

> Do not follow the words of Laozi,
> Do not adopt Buddha's teachings either
> Immortals' mountains and Buddhists' realms
> There are probably no such places.
> I fervently wish to follow Old Tao [Qian]
> And take up residence amid a supply of wine.
> Drunkenness and sobrieties come to an end,
> But it hard to escape one's fate.[53]

It was as difficult for Su to accept Buddhism as it was for him wholly embrace the life of a poor farmer with no ambition or hope for the future. Wherever he was Su was intensely involved in life—whether it was government work, farming, studying sutras, or practicing Daoist breathing exercises.

The Red Cliff Poems

The success of the farm on East Slope improved the Su household's economic situation, and the poet left his fields to make a series of visits to the site of the Battle of Red Cliffs, writing poems to celebrate each occasion.[54]

The Battle of Red Cliff took place in the winter of 208 CE when the Han Dynasty was disintegrating into various territories controlled by local warlords. The most powerful warlord, Cao Cao [Ts'ao Ts'ao] who ruled most of the land north of the Yangtze, attacked the warlords south of the river in an effort to seize control of the entire empire. The southern forces were commanded by a 23-year-old general, Zhou Yu [Chou Yu]. Confident that his superior forces would win the day, Cao Cao made a series of strategic mistakes which culminated in a surprise attack on his navy by a fleet of unmanned "fire ships" filled with kindling, reeds, and oil. Vast numbers of Cao Cao's men and horses were drowned or burned to death. In the confusion, the southern forces attacked, and Cao Cao was forced to make a disastrous retreat, ensuring the division of China into the Three Kingdoms: the northern Kingdom of Wei and the two southern Kingdoms of Shu and Wu. [55]

Su Shi wrote his first Red Cliff poem in the *manci* or "long song lyric" form.[56]

Nien nu chiao—Battle of Red Cliff

The Yangtze flows east
Washing away
A thousand ages of great men
West of the ramparts—
People say—
Are the fabled Red Cliffs of young Chou of the Three
  Kingdoms
Rebellious rocks pierce the sky
Frightening waves rip the bank
The backwash churns vast snowy swells—
River and mountains like a painting
how many heroes passed them, once . . .

Think back to those years, Chou Yu—
Just married to the younger Chiao—
Brave, brilliant
With plumed fan, silk kerchief
Laughed and talked
While masts and oars vanished to flying ash and smoke!
I roam through ancient realms
Absurdly moved
Turn gray too soon—
A man's life passes like a dream—
Pour out a cup then, to the river, and the moon.[57]

The first stanza of the poem contrasts the immediate sights and sounds of the river with what is remembered, or "people say" of the heroes of history.[58] The poet's remark "River and mountains like a painting" reminds us of Su's theory of the intimate connection between poetry and painting:

> When one savors Wang Wei's poems, there are paintings in them;
> When one looks at Wang Wei's pictures, there are poems . . .
>
> Tu Fu's writings are pictures without forms,
> Han Kan's paintings, unspoken poems. . . .[59]

The second stanza of the "Battle of Red Cliff" turns to the victorious general, Zhou Yu [Chou Yu], a scholar ("plumed fan, silk kerchief") who had just married a legendary beauty, the younger Qiao [Chiao]. Despite his youth, charm, and fame, Zhou, like every ancient hero, has vanished into the past. Su is overcome with emotion, "absurdly moved," by the contrast between himself and the valiant Zhou Yu. The life of a graying poet and exiled politician is certainly less significant than that of the brilliant warrior, his beautiful wife, and historic victory, and will vanish even more completely. The poet's sorrowful reflection on the devastating effects of time ends with an offering a cup to the river and the moon. Cai Zong-qi notes that the phrase "cup to the moon on the river" can also be read as "the moon's reflection in the river," a traditional Chinese symbol of "the illusoriness and intangibility of human existence."[60] Although Su's concluding line attempts to reconcile himself to the effects of time and his own ruined hopes with a cup of wine, the mood of the poem is unsettled and melancholy.

Sometime later, in August 1082, Su and some friends took a boat to Red Cliff. The *First Red Cliff Ode* describes this trip.

First Red Cliff Ode

> In the autumn of the year jen-hsu, the seventh month, when the moon had just passed its prime, some friends and I went out in a small boat to amuse ourselves at the foot of the Red Cliff. A fresh breeze blew softly across the water, leaving the waves unruffled. As I picked up the wine jar and poured a drink for my friends, I hummed a poem to the moon and sang a phrase on its strange beauty.

In a little while, the moon rose from the eastern hills and wandered across the sky between the Archer and the Goat. White dew settled over the river, and its shining surface reached to the sky. Letting the boat go where it pleased, we drifted over the immeasurable fields of water. I felt a boundless exhilaration, as though I were sailing on the void or riding the wind and didn't know where to stop. I was filled with a lightness, as though I had left the world and were standing alone, or had sprouted wings and were flying up to join the immortals. As I drank the wine, my delight increased and, thumping the edge of the boat, I composed a song that went:

With cassia sweep and
Oars of orchid wood,
Strike the empty moon,
Row through its drifting light.
Thoughts fly far away—
I long for my loved one
In a corner of the sky.

One friend began to play on an open flute, following my song and harmonizing with it. The flute made a wailing sound, as though the player were filled with resentment or longing, or were lamenting or protesting. Long notes trailed though the night like endless threads of silk, a sound to make dragons dance in hidden caves, or to set the widow weeping in her lonely boat.

Saddened by his playing, I straightened my robe, bowed and asked "What makes you play this way?"

He replied,

"'The moon is bright, stars grow few,
Crows and magpies fly to the south.'

That's how Cao Cao's [Ts'ao Ts'ao's] poem goes, doesn't it? There you can see Hsia-k'ou [Xiakou] to the west, Wu-ch'ang [Wuchang] to the east. A dense tangle of dark green, bounded by mountains and river—this is the very spot where the young

Chou Yu [Zhou Yu] swooped down on Cao Cao, isn't it? After Ts'ao Ts'ao had conquered Ching [Jing] and taken Chiang-ling [Jianling] he sailed down the Yangtze to the east. The stems and terns of his ships touched for a thousand miles, and his flags and pennants blocked out the sky. He drank wine overlooking the river, laid his lance across the saddle, and wrote his poems. Surely he was the greatest hero of his time—yet where is he now?

"What then of you and me? Fishermen and wood gatherers by the banks of streams, companions to fish and crayfish, friends of deer and elk, riding this leaf of a boat, dipping gourds into the wine jar and pouring for each other—we are no more than summer flies between heaven and earth, a grain of millet on the waste of the sea! It grieves me that life is so short, and I envy the long river that never stops. If we could only link arms with the flying immortals and wander where we please, embrace the moon and grow old with it. . . . But I know that such hopes cannot quickly be fulfilled, and so I confide these lingering notes to the sad air."

I asked, "Do you know how it is with the water and the moon? 'The water flows on and on like this,' but somehow it never flows away. The moon waxes and wanes, and yet in the end it's the same moon. If we look at things through the eyes of change, then there's not an instant of stillness in all creation. But if we observe the changelessness of things, then we and all beings alike have no end. What is there to be envious about?

"Moreover, everything in the world has its owner, and if a thing doesn't belong to us, we don't dare take a hair of it. Only the clear breeze over the river, or the bright moon between the hills, which our ears hear as music, our eyes see beauty in—these we may take without prohibition, these may we make free with and they will never be used up. These are the endless treasurers of the Creator, here for you and me to enjoy together!"

My friend was pleased and, laughing, washed the wine cups and filled them up again. But the fruit and other things we had brought to eat were all gone and so, among the litter of cups and bowls, we lay down in a heap in the bottom of the boat, unaware that the east was already growing light.[61]

The *First Red Cliff Ode* is a lyrical description of a particular time and place which inspired a conversation that seems "philosophical" in the popular sense: deeply felt and full of profound thoughts, or at least thoughts that sound profound, inspired by moonlight, the river, and wine.[62] It reminded one reader of the sort of conversation American college students might have late at night after a sufficient amount of drinking. Americans would probably not quote Chinese poetry and refer to ancient Chinese history, but many of them would understand Su's assurances to his friend and might quote Nietzsche, if not Zhuangzi. If this were all there were to it, one might be inclined to say that this is philosophical poetry, but not "really philosophy," but the *Ode* deserves a closer look.

Su lived in an age of philosophical turmoil and innovation. After centuries of being overshadowed by Buddhist philosophy, Chinese Confucianism was reviving and defending itself against the "foreign influence" of Buddhism. A sophisticated Neo-Confucian metaphysics and moral epistemology was emerging amid serious philosophical debates centered on traditional concepts of human nature and morality. Su was part of these debates and his poetic reflections on the effects of time and change, the frustrations of exile, and the appeal of Buddhist and Daoist monks who were "indifferent to life and death" took place in the context of these philosophical developments. Thus, the *First Red Cliff Ode* is a reasoned philosophical resolution to the Su's personal problems and those of his age.

Su's poetry generally makes use of a substantial number of quotations from earlier Chinese poets and this work is no exception.[63] He began the trip chanting poetry from the *Book of Songs*[64] and claimed to feel as though he were "sailing on the void or riding the wind," echoing Zhuangzi's description of the Daoist philosopher Lieh Tzu who "could ride the wind and go soaring around with cool and breezy skill."[65] Su then composed his own lines borrowing phrases from Qu Yuan's *Nine Hymns* and *Li Sao* of the *Chu Ci* (楚辭, *Songs of the South* or *Songs of Chu*).[66]

Su was exhilarated and delighted, but his companion was in a very different mood, playing mournful music that turned Su's joy into sadness.[67] His friend explained that he had been reflecting on the passing of time and quoted two lines from a poem written by Cao Cao about the shortness of life and the futility of human ambitions. Su's companion imagined the conquering general, Cao Cao, surveying the same mountains surrounding them now, the same river on which they are floating; he used a number of Daoist images

> fishermen and wood gatherers by the banks of streams, companions to fish and crayfish, friends of deer and elk, riding this leaf of a boat, dipping gourds into the wine jar and pouring for each other—we are no more than summer flies between heaven and earth, a grain of millet on the waste of the sea!

to note that the two friends on the river would soon suffer Cao Cao's doom and disappear into the past. Su's friend wanted to escape this fate by becoming a Daoist Immortal, a "flying transcendent" but concluded with another quotation from *Nine Hymns* of the *Chu Ci*: ". . . I know that such hopes cannot quickly be fulfilled, and so I confide these lingering notes to the sad air."[68]

These lines repeat the sentiments of the first Red Cliff poem "Battle of Red Cliff" but from a different point of view. The earlier poem considers the eve of the Battle from the perspective of the victorious young general Zhou Yu. The *First Ode* focusses on Cao Cao, the famous warrior whose optimism on the eve of his momentous defeat makes the moment even more poignant. Both poems evoke nostalgia for the lost past and mourn the disappearance of famous heroes, not to mention the poet's failed ambitions.

This time, however, Su refused to give in to sorrow. He gave his companion metaphysical solace by asking "Do you know how it is with the water and the moon? 'The water flows on and on like this,'" recalling the only passage in the *Analects* where Confucius makes a metaphysical point: "The Master was standing on the riverbank, and observed, 'Isn't life's passing just like this, never ceasing day or night!'" (*Analects* 9:26).

Classical Confucianism, with its focus on practical politics and the duty to serve, however, would be very little help to an exiled official, and a reference to the *Analects* would remind Su of his ruined career, and so the poet turned from Confucius to some complex metaphysical arguments about the nature of time.

> The moon waxes and wanes, and yet in the end it's the same moon. If we look at things through the eyes of change, then there's not an instant of stillness in all creation. But if we observe the changelessness of things, then we and all beings alike have no end.

Not only is the reflection of the moon on the river a traditional Chinese symbol for the ephemerality of human life, the many reflections and phases of the one moon was a standard Buddhist metaphor for the relationship between the phenomenal world of illusion and the one unchanging reality. While the "Battle of Red Cliff" ended by taking the moon reflecting on the river as a symbol of impermanence, Su's use of the image in this *Ode* suggests a complex Buddhist metaphysics of time. The phrase "there's not an instant of stillness in all creation" evokes a view of reality consistent with the logically rigorous monism of the *Vimalakīrti Sutra*, which views the phenomenal world as a drifting cloud "characterized by turbulence and dissolution."

The phenomenal "now" is that present time in which a set of relatively enduring objects—people, houses, trees, books, buildings, etc.—undergo a series of happenings, or events, causally connected to events involving those same objects in the past and future. On the theory of the nature of time known in contemporary philosophy of as Presentism, only the present exists, past and future are simply present mental states. The past exists "in the present" as memory; the future is present in our expectation or intentions. The view has a certain intuitive plausibility. A little reflection on Augustine's remark that if the past and future are real, they must exist "in a secret place," subverts the belief that the past and future are "as real" as the present; and several philosophers have advocated a way of life founded on a form of Presentism. Zhuangzi's "True Man" lives only in the present and Wittgenstein follows his remarks about death in the *Tractatus* by noting: "If we take eternity to mean not infinite temporal duration but timelessness, then eternal life belongs to those who live in the present."[69]

There are philosophical difficulties with Presentism, however. It leaves the ontological status of past and future mysterious, and makes causal relations between the three times difficult to explain because only one of them is real. Moreover, while "the present" seems to be a certain, albeit relatively short, period of time, it can be divided into the "actual present, the "very recent past" and the "very near future." Since the last two are not present, neither one of which is real, the "present" shrinks into the "point instant" between past and future. Although the logic of this move seems unassailable, understanding "the present" as a "point instant" undermines the initial plausibility of Presentism because the phenomenal "now" we experience is certainly not a point instant. [70]

Jeffrey Grupp argues that Indian Buddhism provides a sophisticated and convincing theory of Presentism that not only avoids most of these difficulties, but may be the most plausible theory of the nature of time there is.[71] According to Grupp, Indian Buddhism claims that viewing the empirical world as a group of enduring objects interacting and influencing each other in a chain of causality is an illusion. In reality only the present moment exists, each moment ceaselessly being destroyed and replaced by another one and the phenomenal "now" is just as much an illusion as the past and future are. On such a view nothing permanent exists, only a cosmic "bubble of froth" of point instants which is "characterized by turbulence and dissolution."[72] Thus, as Su Shi observes, there is "not an instant of stillness in all creation." There are no causal relations between succeeding moments because nothing lasts long enough to produce anything else. Grupp remarks, "[t]he effect follows upon the cause, but it is not produced by it. It springs up, so to speak, out of nothing. . . ."[73] Since nothing permanent exists, hope, fear, and desire are illusory: none of us is going to exist in the next moment. People who believe in relatively permanent empirical objects, Grupp continues, are "unaware of the fiery, boiling nature of reality . . . unaware that they will not exist beyond this present instant, and that any volition or hope is unneeded and illusory, and is based on the misery of unreality."[74] There is no reason to fear death since we won't be there to experience it.

Su Shi was familiar with the *Vimalakīrti Sutra*, and may have found something like Presentism appealing. He had written a poem recounting three visits to a Buddhist monk.

> Three times I have come to his door,
> First he had aged, second he had grown ill,
> and third he had died.
> The snap of a finger contains it all—
> Past, Future, and what is called Now.
> Accustomed now to the sight of both living and dead,
> I found myself unable to shed a tear.
> But the villages of home are hard to forget,
> And I feel my heart still moved.
> I long to go to the River Ch'ien-t'ang,
> Pay a visit to the monk Yüan-tse,
> And from the bank of the River Ko-hung,
> Await the deepening of autumn.[75]

Although the lines "The snap of a finger contains it all—Past, Future, and what is called Now"—hints at some kind of Presentism, the rest of the poem is not only nostalgic for the poet's past but refers to a story in which the monk Yüan-tse is reincarnated as a young ox herder.[76] Moreover, the second sentence of Su's remarks on time in the *First Red Cliff Ode*—"But if we observe the changelessness of things, then we and all beings alike have no end"—suggests a dualism of the changing world and the changeless one in which the Buddhas do not exist in time but rather transcend past, present, and future.[77]

While the view that the "boiling froth" is all there is, is more consistent with the Buddhist insistence on nondualism, many Song Dynasty Buddhist sects appeared to posit an unchanging, eternal essence, substance, or structure existing over and above the illusionary phenomenal world.[78] Moreover, the doctrines of various Buddhist sects were relatively fluid in the Song Dynasty, with vigorous debates between Huayan Buddhism, Chan and Tientai, as well as internal debates within the schools about the nature of reality and mind. Su was familiar with both the thoroughly monistic *Vimalakīrti Sūtra* and the relatively dualistic metaphysics of the *Śūramgama Sūtra*, and was almost certainly aware of the debates.

In the *First Red Cliff Ode* Su shores up his comforting metaphysics of time by turning to the Daoist philosopher Liezi [Lieh-tzu]. Since nothing in heaven and earth is separate from everything else, Liezi argued no one can legitimately claim to possess anything at all, hence everything we use is stolen. Although if we steal things other men have collected, things like precious metals and jewels and things people have produced, we will be punished.[79] If we steal the seasonal benefits from heaven and earth, "crops and seed, clay and wood, birds and animals, fish and turtles,"[80] or take the *yin* and *yang* energies we need to sustain our lives, we are stealing from heaven and earth, we will not be punished. In either case, Liezi claimed, we are stealing.[81]

Glossing over the question of whether both kinds of "stealing" really are stealing, Su uses Liezi's point to convince his friend to laugh and enjoy the "endless treasures of the Creator." Finishing the food and wine the two of them lie down in the boat, forgetting their sorrow over the passage of time, unaware that the night was ending. Ronald Egan claims: "It is this evocation of human continuity, in the face of which individual possessiveness is meaningless, that makes the ending of the rhapsody so immensely satisfying."[82] The *Ode* may be satisfying aesthetically, logically it is less so. The many themes Su blends together in this work probably do not hold together in a philosophically coherent position.

After all his flights into Buddhist and Daoist metaphysics about the nature of time and the universe, Su ended the *Ode* with a Confucian point—that human relations, people, and friendship are what let us survive the devastations of time and life. Rather than accept the implications of Buddhism (emptiness or a "bubbling froth") and Daoism (that when life ends we are transformed into a rat's liver) Su insisted that pleasures—eating roast port, drinking wine, enjoying the moonlight, writing poetry—make life worth living. Moreover, he continued to be nostalgic for the past, a past he believed teaches important lessons for contemporary leaders. Finally, he never lost the desire to serve in office. Su's exile in Huangzhou lasted only until he was asked to return to service in 1085. He was exiled a second time in 1094 and died on his way to return to service in 1101.[83]

Abstract Buddhist philosophy could provide emotional comfort, at a time when Su's hopes for the future seemed to have been ruined or drastically curtailed. He seemed only able to make a name for himself by planting trees. Su was looking for a philosophical view that was cheerful and optimistic about the world in which he was living.

This is the use of "philosophy" that promises to reconcile us to the vicissitudes of life, to make us feel as we do at the end of the *Ode*, that everything really is all right, optimistic, cheerful, happily drifting down the river. This view is more Daoist than Buddhist, since it does not argue that phenomenal world is "unreal" or illusion, simply that it is all there is. Like the "Battle of Red Cliff" the *First Red Cliff Ode* ends with wine drinking, although the first poem ends in resignation: "Pour out a cup then, to the river, and the moon"—while the *First Ode* ends in a mood of relaxation and reconciliation "washing the wine cups and fill them up again." The "happy ending" of the *First Red Cliff Ode* is followed, however, by the *Second Red Cliff Ode*. The "Battle of Red Cliff" is sorrowfully nostalgic and the *First Ode* is happily optimistic, but the *Second Red Cliff Ode* is deeply disturbing.

Second Red Cliff Ode

> The same year, on the fifteenth day of the tenth month, I was walking back from Snow Hall to my home at Lin-Kao. Two friends were with me, and we went by way of Yellow Mud

Slope. Frost had already fallen and the trees were bare of leaves. Our shadows appeared on the ground, and looking up, we saw that the moon had risen. Glancing around to enjoy the sight, we walked along singing songs back and forth.

After a while, I sighed and said, "Here I have guests and there's no wine! And even if I had some wine, there's nothing to eat with it. A clear moon, a fresh breeze—what will we do with such a fine night?"

"Today at sundown," said one of my friends, "I put out a net and caught some fish with big mouths and delicate scales, like the perch of Pine River. And there must be somewhere we can get some wine . . ."

As soon as I got home, I consulted my wife. "I have a gallon of wine that's been put away for a long time," she said. "I was saving it for some occasion when you might suddenly need it."

So we took the wine and fish and went for another trip to the foot of the Red Cliff. The river raced along noisily, its sheer banks rising a thousand feet. The mountains were very high, the moon small. The level of the water had fallen, leaving boulders sticking out. How much time had passed since my last visit? I couldn't recognize them as the same river and hills!

Tucking up my robe, I began to climb, picking my way along the steep embankment, pushing through tangled grass, straddling rocks the shape of tigers, clambering over roots twisted like dragons. I pulled my way up to the eagle's precarious nest, and looked down into the hidden halls of the river god. My two friends couldn't keep up.

I gave a long, shrill whoop. Trees and grass shook and swayed, the mountains rang, the valley echoed. A wind came up, roiling the water, and I felt a chill of sadness, a shrinking fear. I knew with a shudder that I couldn't stay there any longer.

I went back to my friends and got into the boat, and we turned it loose to drift with the current, content to let it stop wherever it chose. The night was half over and all around was deserted and still, when a lone crane appeared, cutting across the river from the east. Its wings looked like cart wheels, and it wore a black robe and a coat of white silk. With a long, grating cry, it swooped over our boat and went off to the west.

> Soon afterwards, I left my friends and went to bed. I dreamed I saw a Taoist immortal in a feather robe come bouncing down the road past the foot of Lin-kao. He bowed to me and said, "Did you enjoy your outing to the Red Cliff?" I asked him his name, but he looked down and didn't answer.
>
> "Ah, wait—of course—now I know! Last evening, flying over our boat and crying—that was you, wasn't it?"
>
> He turned his head and laughed, and I woke up with a start. I opened the door and peered out, but I could see no sign of him.[84]

The mood of this poem is more somber than that of the *First Ode*. The weather is colder. Su's poverty is more obvious, and the landscape itself has changed almost beyond recognition. Rather than an idyllic evening on a river with "unruffled" waves and the "strange beauty" of the moon, the river is racing nosily and the moon is simply "small." Rather than spending a companionable evening singing and playing music, reciting poetry and philosophizing, Su leaves his friends and struggles past strange and eerie shapes to reach the top of the cliff, "the eagle's precarious nest." This is the sort of place from which a Daoist immortal might soar into infinity;[85] but instead of sharing an immortal's experience, Su is badly frightened. Looking down at the river from the height he gazes into "the hidden halls of the river god," a sight long associated with death: the river god used to demand yearly sacrifices of young women. Qu Yuan committed suicide by leaping into the Miluo River. Suddenly Su lets out a "long, shrill whoop," "a whistling sound, long drawn and shrill."[86] These whistles or shouts were part of the Daoist exercises for longevity that Su had been practicing. Su may have hoped for a sympathetic reply from nature itself, but the natural world refused to accept his request, greeting him instead with a rising wind and "a chill of sadness, a shrinking fear," forcing the poet to retreat down the mountain to rejoin his friends. Su's terror made him realize that his efforts to follow the Daoist immortals in abandoning the human world were doomed to failure. To emphasize this failure a crane startles the group by flying down over the boat, its long coarse cry echoing Su's drawn out whistle. The crane, the strange rocks and trees, and the wind at the top of the cliff, are unmistakably unfriendly. The bird may even be punishing Su for assuming that he had a Daoist relationship to nature.[87] When the poet returned home after an evening of aimless drifting he dreamed of a Daoist immortal who mocked him with an ironic question. Su had clearly *not* enjoyed his visit to the Red Cliffs. Ever the social being, the poet tried to begin a conversation, but the immortal simply laughed and disappeared. In contrast to the friendly laughter at the end of the *First Ode* when Su's philosophizing had dispelled the melancholy mood, the laughter at the end of the *Second Ode* increases the sense of eeriness, despair, and mystery.

The Immortal's reply is as unsettling as Zarathustra's scornful response to the old man in the forest who has not heard that God is dead.[88] Zarathustra's laughter is a weapon in his battle against traditional hypocrisies, mocking people who do not realize that Christian redemption—the promised joy and peace of immortality—is an illusion and a lie. There is nothing more than the eternal return; everything, birth and struggle and death will happen over and over again, "world without end reprieve or rest."[89] Recognizing this fact, one can be overcome by anger and resentment, or laugh, sometimes light-heartedly embracing whatever the world of illusion can offer, sometimes harshly cynical, careening toward hysterical dementia.[90]

Like the targets of Zarathustra's laughter, Su cannot bring himself to reject the conventional morality of his time: Confucian duty and the value of human relations. If he cannot serve the state he can at least enjoy the company of his family and friends. The difference between Confucian duty and Christian redemption, however, is that when Christians have been reviled and rejected they can remain secure in God's love and look forward to their reward in Heaven. Su cannot do his Confucian duty when the government sends him into exile. Confucians do not look forward to a "life in the hereafter" where they will get the rewards they are denied here on earth. The rewards of Confucian duty are to be of use, and the dead are of no use.

Although Christian redemption was not an option for Su, he had considered accepting the emptiness of Buddhist nirvana or the Daoist rejection of human society. Ultimately these alternatives are unappealing to someone for whom the sensual world, the joys of wine, friendship, moonlight, and roast pork, means so much. On the other hand, Su continued to face his fear of failure and death. When he was sent to exile the second time he wrote:

> I'm a frightened monkey who's reached the forest,
> a tired horse unharnessed at last,
> my mind a void to fill with new thoughts;
> surroundings are old to me—I see them in dreams.

River gulls flock around, growing tamer;
old Tanka men drop in to visit.
South point lotus spreads green coins;
north hill bamboo sends up purple shots.
Bring-the-jug[91] (what does he know about wine?)
inspires me with a fine idea.
The spring river had a beautiful poem
but, drunk, I dropped it somewhere far away.[92]

Apparently wine and poetry were more successful than Buddhist philosophy or Daoist meditation in reconciling Su to the vicissitudes of his life. Accepting the view that moments of beauty and pleasure are ephemeral and fleeting, Su either enjoys the moment, as he did in the end of the *First Ode*, or writes a poem to keep the memory alive. "Write a poem quick before it gets away!"

Even more than planting trees and serving the state, writing poetry gives Su's life meaning. In another poem he is clear about the importance of writing in his life.

The many-*li*-distant hills of home are like a dream;
And my son has slowly come to speak with the accent of Wu
Every time I meet this man of Shu, we talk the entire day;
And I can almost see the O-mei hues sweeping the sky.
This Master has long forgotten words, has truly found the way.
But if I gave up writing verse, I'd have nothing left at all!
If next year I go and gather herbs in the T'ien-t'ai [Tiantai]
mountains,
I'll want even more to write poems, enough to fill the east
of Chekiang [Zhejiang].[93]

The fear and sorrow Su felt at the top of the Red Cliff were the price he had to pay for his unwillingness to abandon the world—the natural world of beauty and pleasure and the social world of friendship, family, and political service. It was ultimately impossible for him to be reconciled to the disappearance of the heroes of the past, the failure of his political ambitions, and his fear of death and to be consoled by Buddhist emptiness or Daoist transcendence.

The *First Red Cliff Ode* presents the philosophical tensions between a Confucian sense of social and cosmic order, the Daoist spiritual relation with nature, and Buddhist metaphysics. These tensions bedeviled much of

Song Dynasty intellectual life, and Su's synthesis of the three traditions in the *First Red Cliff Ode* was not particularly original, nor was it philosophically sophisticated, but it seemed satisfying as far as it went. In the *Second Red Cliff Ode* Su continued to be dissatisfied with Confucianism. Although doing his duty has led him to poverty and exile, he cannot follow the heroic Confucian model of Qu Yuan by committing suicide in face of rejection of his ruler. Su was more successful at taking Tao Qian as his model and living as a reclusive farmer; but Tao Qian's exile was voluntary. Su returned to office every time he was asked. At the end of the *Second Ode* his fear and despair remained. Look as he might "there was no sign" of the Daoist immortal, and his "this worldly" Confucianism of practical politics and attachment to the phenomenal world could give him no lasting sense of peace and meaning, no escape from the sorrowful nostalgia of the *First Red Cliff* poem and the terror he felt in prison, at the top of the Red Cliff, and at the start of his second exile.

Su's search for emotional comfort in philosophy echoes the view that philosophy should control and discipline the emotions, allowing us to "remain detached" and take refuge in lofty abstractions. Certainly not all philosophers believe this, but those who do have contributed to the presumption that there is an important distinction between philosophy and poetry. The founders of the Neo-Confucian synthesis, Cheng Yi and Zhu Xi, were deeply skeptical about the role of emotions in the good life and were deeply suspicious of Su's philosophical poetry. The Shu School (Su Shi, his brother Su Zhe, and his father Su Xun) participated in the Confucian revival of the Song Dynasty, but the Shu School was never considered part of the tradition that ultimately became Cheng-Zhu Neo-Confucianism.[94] On the other hand, many Song Dynasty thinkers who contributed to the Neo-Confucian synthesis but did not agree with the Cheng-Zhu version of it were not included in the tradition by the men, Zhu Xi in particular, responsible for writing its history. Zhu was so influential that his view of the tradition overwhelmed and obscured the complexity of Song Dynasty thought for many centuries.[95]

Su Shi and the Neo-Confucian Synthesis: The Failure of Philosophy

Su Shi and Cheng Yi

Although Cheng Yi and Su Shi were initially allies in the fight against Wang Anshi's reforms, their alliance was short-lived. Cheng opposed the whole program of reform and responded to the political turmoil of the Wang Anshi era by withdrawing to Loyang to teach and study. Su, on the other hand, believed that some reform was necessary and left active political life only when he was forced into exile. Although the two men seldom commented directly on each other's philosophical views, they disagreed fundamentally about the character of human nature, the importance of emotions in human life, and the method of self-cultivation—the life one was supposed to live.

Isolated from the political struggles in the capital, Cheng Yi and his brother Cheng Hao began to develop the Neo-Confucian metaphysical system to defend Confucianism against the influence of Buddhism; to do so they had to resolve the ancient Confucian debates about whether human nature was "good" (Mencius), "evil" (Xunzi), a mixture of good and evil, or morally neutral. Neo-Confucians argued that from birth human nature contained both *li* 理 and *qi* 氣.[96] *Li*, often translated "principle," is unchanging and permanent;[97] while *qi* is self-moving and changing. The Cheng brothers replaced the traditional Confucian notion of *tian* (天 Heaven) with that of *li*, making *tian*, as well as *dao* (道 the Way), aspects of *li*.[98] Like *tian* and *dao*, *li* is morally good, while *qi* may be good or evil.

Although the Cheng brothers never actually defined *li*, they accepted the traditional interpretation that *li* was associated with veins in jade because it was written with the "jade" radical.[99] *Li* was relatively abstract but still objectively real; moreover although there were many things in the world, *li*, principle, was basically the same in all of them. Thus by understanding the *li* in one thing, we can infer the *li* in everything else by analogy.[100] Graham proposes a metaphor which while helpful is not entirely satisfactory:

> Li may be compared to a network of roads, and things to the counties through which they run. One can take the system as a whole, or distinguish five main roads, or go on making distinctions down to the smallest lane or footpath. The roads in different counties look different, but when 'extended' always prove to belong to the same system.[101]

Qi is difficult to translate; some alternatives are "ether," "psychophysical energy," "breath" or "air." Like *li*, *qi* is inborn and part of human nature; but unlike *li, qi* is concrete, i.e., not abstract, and may be more or less pure. Graham describes pure *qi* as the "source of life, dispersing into the air at death; we breathe it in and out, and feel it rising and ebbing in our bodies as physical energy."[102] When *qi* becomes dense and inert, it condenses into solid matter, and differences in one's *qi* account for different personal traits and abilities, including the ability to understand and follow *li*.[103] The more "polluted" our *qi* is, the less able we understand and follow *li*. Because animals are born with permanently impure *qi*, they have only a vague understanding of *li*. We, on the other hand, can refine our *qi* through moral education, making it easier to understand *li* and follow it.

The dualism of *li* and *qi* is radically different from the Western dualism of mind and body/material substance.[104] As a "life force" or "energy," pure *qi* might sound like a "soul" or "will" associated with "mind" in the West, but matter is condensed *qi*, and some Song Dynasty Confucians thought the heart-mind was also *qi* because it is moved and changed by the passions. Cheng Yi, however, distinguished between the "Way-mind" (*daoxin* 道心) which is *li*, principle, and hence unchanging; and the human-mind (*ren xin* 人心) which is moved/altered by thoughts, emotions, and intentions.[105] Cheng is not always clear whether passions are good, because they are natural, and hence *li*; or whether they may be good or bad depending on the purity of one's *qi*.[106] On the other hand, he is quite suspicious of desires and emotions in general, believing that passions and desires are not uniquely human. We share them with animals; moreover following our emotions and desires diverts us from the task of purifying our *qi* and understanding *li*.

Because human nature contained *li*, Cheng Yi acknowledged one could find *li* by introspection, but he argued this method was fraught with danger because of the relationship between *li* and *qi*. Most of us are sufficiently polluted by impure *qi* that introspection is likely to deceive us into believing that Buddhist and Daoist doctrines were found in human nature, *li*.[107] Thus, Cheng recommended that we eschew introspection and discover the *li* by other methods.

According to the *Great Learning* the proper way to live is to work toward the Confucian goal of bringing peace and harmony to the whole world.

> The men of old who wished to make bright virtue plain to the world first put their countries in order, for which they had first to regulate their families, and for that to improve themselves as individuals, and for that to correct their hearts, and for that to give integrity to their intentions, and for that

> to extend their knowledge. The extension of knowledge lies in the investigation of things (*ke-wu* [*gewu*] 格物).[108]

In Song Dynasty thought the "investigation of things" meant discovering *li*. Cheng Yi advised us to follow the *Great Learning*, "correct the heart" and "give integrity to the intentions" by studying the moral principles found in the classic Confucian texts and the lives of prominent men, and by engaging in practical affairs in an appropriate manner.[109] Not only did Cheng seem to believe that the appropriate way to deal with practical affairs of his day was to withdraw from active political life, his focus on the importance of study and reflection to control human desires and emotions made him actively hostile to literature which he saw as a force that will lead us away from the Way (*tianli*). Cheng Yi insisted that people who devoted themselves to literary works were clearly attached to the outer world rather than to inner moral principles.[110]

Su and Cheng Yi agreed that human nature contained *li* from birth. The discovery of *li*, i.e., of the Way, and of its cultivation in one's life, was a major theme in the work of both men. However, Su Shi resisted any attempt to describe "human nature" aside from insisting that emotions—joy, anger, sorrow, and happiness—are a vital part of it. Thus he followed Confucius's refusal to talk about human nature, (*xing* 性).

> Zigong said, "We can learn from the Master's cultural refinements, but do not hear him discourse on subjects such as our 'natural disposition (*xing* 性)' and "the way of tian (*tiandao* 天道)." (*Analects* 5.13)

Finally Su also believed that human nature was beyond labels like "good" or "bad."[111] Thus, Su's conception of *li* was so different from that of Cheng Yi that scholars studying Su's work translate *li* as "pattern" or "inherent pattern" rather than "principle."[112] Although the Cheng brothers, and later Zhu Xi, thought of *li* as abstract, but part of part of reality itself, Su's conception of *li* was heavily influenced by Daoism and Buddhism. The Daoist philosopher Zhuangzi ("Master Zhuang") argued that discriminations between the forms of things, "this" and "that," "good" and "bad," were merely linguistic, having no basis in nonhuman (objective) reality.[113] In Buddhist thought, principles, *li*, describe how we know the world, not what the world itself is like.[114] Su's conception of *li* was neither wholly objective, mind-independent reality in the world, nor simply a subjective response, imposition, on the world. In his commentary on the *Book of Changes* Su explained that our knowledge of *li* is never complete. He wrote:

> To be unaware of transformation and thus take [the patterns of good and bad fortune] as one, and to view [the patterns] as indefinite and thus take them as two [distinct phenomena]: these are both errors. The inherent patterns of the world are always one, but the one cannot be grasped tightly. To know that they are always one but also not grasp them tightly is just about [to achieve sagehood].[115]

We come to understand something by thoroughly immersing ourselves into it. Writing about Wen Tong, a famous painter of bamboo, Su described how the painter seemed to merge with the bamboo he was painting.

> When [Wen Tong] paints bamboo,
> He sees the bamboo and does not notice people
> Oblivious, he leaves behind his corporeal self.
> His body transforms into the bamboo
> Inexhaustibly bringing forth pure and new forms.
> There is no Master Zhuang in our generation:
> Who, then, understands that these bamboo resemble the spirit?[116]

Su's conception of how to proceed with the "investigation of things" included studying ancient texts, but also, like Wen Tong, becoming totally involved in what he was doing whether it was participating in political life, becoming a farmer, or writing poetry.

Su generally wrote about *li* in terms of its relationship to writing, painting, and calligraphy. In painting he distinguished between things like people, animals, and buildings which have a constant shape, and "mountains, rocks, bamboo, trees, water, waves, mists, and clouds" which have a "constant inherent pattern," *li*, but no invariant shape. Although the phenomena of the world undergo many changes in form and shape, the *li* remains constant and is what the best painters and writers understand and express. In discussions of *li* in poetry Su frequently associates it with water. In *The Yanyu Rock Ode* he explains, "The most trustworthy thing under heaven is water. Now the size of rivers and the depth of the ocean can be estimated. It is only that [water] has no form and follows things in taking shape. Therefore through ten thousand transformations it has a necessary inherent pattern (*li*)."[117] Su also describes his own work in terms of water, suggesting that his poetry is an expression of *li*:

> [M]y writing is like a spring of ten thousand gallons; it does not choose its path as it goes out. On level land it flows smoothly and quickly, and a thousand miles a day is not difficult. When it comes to turns and breaks over mountains and stones, it follows the object to describe the form, and it cannot be known. That which can be known is that is always travels where it ought to travel, and it always stops where it ought to stop. It is like this, and for all else I too cannot know.[118]

This last remark raises a question of the how painters and poets convey the *li* of their subjects. While their work should be spontaneous and unstudied, "it does not choose its path," Su did not think artists unreflectively expressed their emotional responses to phenomena. Artists had to thoroughly understand a phenomenon, control the emotions roused by their experience, and know how to use words and the brush to express their understanding before artistic creation could become unself-conscious and spontaneous.[119]

Finally, rather than denigrate human desires and emotions as Cheng Yi did, Su Shi believed emotional sensitivity was central to human nature. Our emotional responses to the world around us must be understood and controlled if we are not to be completely at the mercy of that world; on the other hand, if we ignore our emotional responses to the world, refusing to acknowledge their importance, we would be in danger of losing our natural humanness and becoming a cold and oppressive tyrant like Jie, the evil ruler at the end of the Xia dynasty. Su's experience in political engagement and exile made him value his emotional connections to his family and friends. His love of natural beauty and his nostalgia for the events and heroes of the past reinforced his opposition to the "self-righteousness, doctrinaire inflexibility, and excessive severity" characteristic of the scholars at Loyang.[120]

Given their views it was not surprising that Su and Cheng Yi clashed dramatically when, after the overthrow of Wang Anshi's New Laws party in 1085, they were recalled to court and appointed to tutor the nine-year-old Emperor Zhezong. Cheng Yi was a puritanical moralist who lectured the young emperor on the dangers of being charmed by women. Su Shi, on the other hand, was as fond of dinners with courtesans as he was of wine and took every opportunity to ridicule the pompous scholar who soon returned to his students in Loyang.[121]

Su Shi and Zhu Xi

The Neo-Confucian scholar Zhu Xi took Cheng Yi's work as the foundation for his own systematic version of the Confucian tradition. Zhu Xi argued that after Confucius and Mencius the Confucian tradition had been lost because it had been polluted beyond recognition by additions from Daoism and Buddhism. Zhu believed that any synthesis of Daoism and Buddhism with Confucian thought was an unacceptable adulteration of the Confucian tradition, and that only his own immediate precursors, Zhou Dunyi (1017–1073 CE) and the Cheng brothers were free of this contamination. During the centuries that Buddhism had dominated Chinese thought, however, Buddhist vocabulary, Buddhist metaphysics, and Buddhist moral psychology permeated Chinese philosophy to the extent that even the fundamental Neo-Confucian conceptions of *li* and *qi* were influenced by Buddhist metaphysics.[122] Thus, despite his mission to rid Confucian thought of Buddhist and Daoist influences, Zhu's Confucianism (or Cheng-Zhu Confucianism) can be described as the "Neo-Confucian synthesis of Buddhism, Daoism and Confucianism."

Zhu believed that because the ancient sages had discovered the *Dao* and preserved it in the Classics, reading ancient texts and scholarly commentaries was the most effective way of learning and teaching the Way.[123] Su Shi, on the other hand, did not believe that the Way, *li*, could be found by moving to a level of abstraction that was somehow "beyond" emotional experience. Because Su and his brother avoided abstract speculation and talked of the Dao in terms of literary theory, moral values, and politics, Zhu Xi complained "People like the two Su brothers just wanted to talk about the Way. But how can one reject the annotations and commentaries!"[124]

Zhu Xi acknowledged that Su was an extraordinary poet, but was highly critical of him for being a dilettante who would rather drink than study seriously. Zhu Xi also shared Cheng Yi's distrust of women noting "because Su Shi epitomized self-indulgence and lack of restraint, naturally Su could not abide Cheng Yi's notion of the importance of mental discipline."[125] In addition, Zhu believed that Su's lack of intellectual rigor meant that not only did he fail to understand Buddhism, he also took it far too seriously.[126] Because he believed that Su's ideas were philosophically unsound, Zhu argued that Su's talent in presenting them made him particularly dangerous. Zhu argued that Su treated writing as equal to the Way rather than recognizing that while writing may express the Way, it is always subordinate to it. Zhu explained:

> East Slope [Su Dungpo] said, "What I consider writing coexists with the Way." In that case, writing stands on its own and so does the Way. When he writes, he goes off in search of the Way to insert it into his writings. This is his great error. His writing is always ornate and marvelous. He wraps it up and carries it off with him as he goes, not realizing that it is empty inside. If one were to identify his fundamental error, it is simply that he begins with writing and seeks thereby to gradually work up the Way. He does not try to understand the Way before he proceeds to write. This is why he is wrong from the start.[127]

Zhu went on to fault Su's writing for never going beyond present experiences with all their emotional disturbances to get to the meaning, or *li*, which lies behind them: "Su's talent is of heroic proportions, but he lets everything out all at once so that there is not the least overtone of meaning."[128]

As we have seen, however, the claim that Su tried to find the Way by writing is not strictly true.[129] Su was clear that an artist had to understand *li* thoroughly before he could express it. On the other hand, Su's understanding of *li* was far more subjective than that of Zhu and Cheng Yi. Zhu Xi argued that since objective reality and the Patterns of the Way, *tianli*, were one and the same, writers who devoted themselves to discovering the Way should immerse themselves in history and the Confucian classics, abstracting the *li* (principle, the Way) from reality, making it objective, and explaining it in as straightforward a manner as possible.[130] Su on the contrary thought that understanding of *li*, *Dao*, the Way, comes indirectly though emotional experience and action, which may include writing and reading, as well drinking wine on the river.

Cheng Yi and Zhu Xi were brilliant intellectuals who created an ingenious and sophisticated metaphysical system; but even a defender of Cheng Yi like Agnus Graham admits that "a clearer recognition that the same raw material of experience can be schematized in quite different ways, is perhaps the chief benefit that one can gain from a study of Yi-ch'uan's [Cheng Yi's] philosophy which . . . does not reflect any very rich or interesting view of life."[131]

One begins to wonder whether Cheng Yi and Zhu Xi, with their suspicion of women, their rejection of emotion as a source of understanding the reality of the Way, their preference for moralizing over beautiful calligraphy and poetry, and their contempt for wine drinking, were really very nice people. Su was a very different kind of man. He completely immersed in the world, politically active, enjoying wine and nature, loving his family–parents, brother, children, wives and concubines—but too Confucian to be a Daoist or Buddhist, and too emotionally sensitive to accept Cheng Yi and Zhu Xi's abstract understanding of the Way. Someone like Su would probably prefer to have his philosophical search for meaning and peace dismissed by the Daoist immortal's scornful laughter than by the Neo-Confucians' not-so-subtle contempt.

Philosophy and Poetry

There are times when you want philosophy, when you need philosophy, and it laughs at you. You open the door, look, and it is not there. At those times poetry is not an enemy of philosophy, but a necessary alternative at least to the kind of philosophy that cannot, does not, will not, take account of the importance of emotion and beauty (poetry, painting, music) in a good life. Such a philosophy looks for peace and meaning outside of the phenomenal world: sometimes in the eternal, objective *li*, sometimes in Heaven, or emptiness, or the mathematical laws of science. Searching for meaning in the phenomenal world may be more difficult, since everyone, great heroes and poor farmers alike, dies. Even well-governed empires disappear. Aesthetic experiences may be life transforming, but they are ephemeral. Su's poetry reflected sorrow at the lost glories of history and, at least a few times, his personal fear of death. Su occasionally suggested that his inability to stop writing about these experiences was a character flaw or a limitation, one of the reasons he could never become a Buddhist. Yet the creation of these experiences, sharing them in poetry that expresses one's understanding of the *li*, can give life meaning. It is the reason Li Zehou claims that aesthetic experiences are the highest, most meaningful experiences of life.[132] These experiences are not eternal. They do not give us transcendent permanent meaning, but if one looks for *that* one is always in danger of hearing the Immortal's scornful laughter, opening the door, and finding nothing there.

Epilogue

The world seems to have changed a great deal in the decades since I was first charmed by Han Gan's *Night-Shining White*. Although the human contribution to climate change is still contested, albeit in progressively marginal circles, the effects of new weather patterns, rising sea levels, and the loss of species are all too obvious.

At the same time the gap between the world's wealthiest and poorest peoples is increasing. In 1979 the top 1% of American households enjoyed 8% of national income; their portion rose to 17% in 2007, and 20% in 2012. The share of the lowest 5% declined from 7% in 1979 to 5% in 2007.[1] In 1965 the CEO's of the largest U.S. companies earned 20 times more than their workers did. In 1978 they earned 120 times more; and in 2013 the CEO to worker earning rate was 300-to-1.[2] Although income inequality is higher, and has risen faster in the United States than in other advanced industrial countries, the increase has occurred globally. Oxfam reported that the wealthiest 1% of the world's population increased its share of the world's wealth from 44% in 2009, to 48% in 2014, and predicted that by 2016 the wealthiest 1% would increase their share of the world's wealth to more than 50%.[3]

The United Nations Food and Agriculture Organization estimates that about 795 million people of the 7.3 billion people in the world were suffering from chronic undernourishment in 2014 through 2016. Almost all these people, 780 million, live in developing countries, where 12.9 percent, or one in eight, of the population is undernourished. Nevertheless, there are 11 million undernourished people in developed countries, and more than 15 million American children live in households that struggle to get enough to eat.[4] Some of the statistics on world hunger are improving, but the World Health Organization has become alarmed about a global obesity epidemic due primarily to inadequate access to healthy foods. [5]

Instead of working together to resolve these problems, vast numbers of the world's peoples are turning to violent ways to destroy each other. Traditional warfare has been supplemented by drone strikes, sectarian violence, and terrorist attacks. The destruction of buildings, modern cities, and ancient ruins pales beside the devastation of whole societies which has led to unprecedented refugee crises in many parts of the world. What makes this violence particularly appalling is that it is often driven by extremist religious movements whose messages of hate all too often seem to overwhelm the traditional religious messages of peace and love.

While Karl Marx got many things wrong, his understanding of the relationship between contemporary social injustice and capitalism seems almost exactly right. Within the limits of a capitalist system few, if any, of the problems of our society can be addressed. Indeed the rapacious postindustrial global capitalism of the last fifty years has made these problems more severe and more intractable.[6] The scale of the social changes that seem to be required may make us feel overwhelmed and hopeless, or so outraged we are tempted to join the calls for a revolution—unless we remember that in most revolutions the "best" people are killed first.[7]

Faced with this all too familiar catalogue of dismal facts, Li Zehou's Confucian faith that science, technology, and material progress will make for a better world seems grossly misplaced. The unintentional results of more science and more material wealth, if only for a fraction of the world's population, seems destined only to make things worse. Asked how he can maintain his optimism, Li responds that is the only reasonable thing to do.

> This is simply my belief. Because the Chinese have no real faith in a god, they believe in the potential of the human being and the ability of humans to help themselves. The history of humankind shows that it is possible to overcome many difficult obstacles and to avoid big disasters such as the nuclear danger in the cold war period. We must remember that the human being is a rational animal . . . If one is a pessimist, one still has to live (not commit suicide). Therefore, it is better to believe and live optimistically and confidently, for by doing so, a person has a more positive outlook on life, more energy, and works more constructively, leisurely, and cheerfully.[8]

Li's faith shares much with that of the great anarchist philosopher Emma Goldman who responded when she was censured for dancing: "I insisted that our Cause could not expect me to become a nun and that the movement should not be turned into a cloister. If it meant that, I did not want it. 'I want freedom, the right to self-expression, everybody's right to beautiful, radiant things.'"[9] Goldman was later credited with the apocryphal summary of these remarks: "If I can't dance, it's not my revolution."

The insistence that any struggle worth undertaking must involve dancing and beauty recalls the importance of dancing in Li Zehou's theory of the evolution of human cognition, aesthetics, and morality.[10] The Confucian aesthetic theory underlying this book insists that genuine aesthetic experience, the sense of beauty that pleases the will and spirit (*yue zhi yue shen*: 悦 志悦神) involves all our senses, and is ultimately one of great pleasure and a source of moral insight. Aesthetic experience, like religious and mystical experience, is transforming—one feels part of a greater harmony, a larger community, in a way that is anything but joyless.

The chapters in this book began with my own immediate response (aesthetic attention, pleasures of the ear and eye, *yue er yue mu* 悦耳悦目) to a particular aesthetic object. The discussion the focused on the second level of aesthetic experience, aesthetic attention (pleasures of the heart-mind and mood [*yue xin yue yi* 悦 心悦意]).

The graceful and modest robes of the Northern Wei Buddhas led to a consideration of the relationship between religion, aesthetics, and ethics. The world of Northern Wei was a brief interlude in a time of horrific cruelty and violence. These Buddhas remind us that the artist and saint both teach us to feel compassion, to recognize that bad as this life can be, it is also full of beauty and pleasure, and to acknowledge Li's version of the categorical imperative: to contribute whatever we can to human thriving.

The Chinese tradition of horse painting, focused on the relationship between aesthetics and political engagement. Attention to the *Emaciated Horse* by Gong Kai, the *Lean Horse* by Ren Renfa, the *Galloping Horse* by Xu Beihong, and Wang Huaiqing's *The Picture of Bole* demonstrates that art with a political meaning is not necessarily "bad art" or "merely propaganda," but that careful aesthetic attention will always involve understanding the social context and political meaning of the art work.[11] The aesthetic meaning of a work of art cannot be separated from its political one without a severe loss to both aesthetics and politics. *Night-Shining White* reminds us to celebrate those rare times of peace in human history, to strive for a political ideal, to refuse to accept corruption, and to smile at the self-importance of officials—and horses.

Su Shi's life and work illustrate the relationships between philosophy, politics, and poetry. Although the previous chapter may have suggested that we have to choose between poetry and philosophy, Li Zehou has defined philosophy as "science plus poetry." The Western philosophical tradition would agree that there is no conflict between philosophy and science. Much of this tradition would even accept Quine's claim that "philosophy of science is philosophy enough;" and for a lot of the twentieth-century traditional Analytic philosophy departments, at least in the United States, habitually dismissed other philosophical traditions for "writing poetry" instead of "doing philosophy." In extreme cases this attitude has led to the development of a "scientific morality" of self-interested utility maximizers, a morality that has not only been used as a club against traditional religious concerns but may seem completely devoid of any "soft" unscientific concerns for compassion and love.

Li's redefinition of philosophy suggests that philosophy is severely impoverished if it either abandons the insistence on rigor, precision, and some (albeit increasingly vague) notion of "getting it right" typical of science; or ignores the aesthetic and emotional depths of the arts—including poetry. Philosophy's traditional concern with categorical imperatives of various kinds, that is, with the question of "how we ought to live," cannot do its job if it neglects the moral and aesthetic resources of aesthetic experience.

Notes

Chapter 1

1. David L. Hall and Roger T. Ames, *Thinking Through Confucius* (Albany, NY: State University of New York Press, 1987), 135–36. Ames notes that the distinction originates with John Dewey.

2. Willard Van Orman Quine, "Mr. Strawson on Logical Theory," *Mind* 62, no. 248 (Oct. 1953), 446.

3. This way of conceiving of opposites is related to a fundamental feature of most logical orders: the law of the excluded middle. This law states that if something has the property A, it cannot also have or be not-A. If a sentence is true it cannot (at the same time) be false.

4. A. C. Graham, "Reflections and Replies," in *Chinese Texts and Philosophical Contexts*, ed. Henry Rosemont, Jr. (La Salle, IL: Open Court, 1991); David L. Hall and Roger T. Ames, *Thinking from the Han: Self, Truth and Transcendence in Chinese and Western Culture* (Albany, NY: State University of New York Press, 1998), 127; LI Chenyang, "The Confucian Ideal of Harmony," *Philosophy East and West* 56 no. 4 (2006); Tian Chenshan, "Tongbian in the Chinese Reading of Dialectical Materialism," *Philosophy East and West* 52 no. 1 (2002).

5. Hall and Ames, *Thinking Through Confucius,* 136.

6. The first part of the *Shujing* is divided into two chapters, the *Canon of Yao* and the *Canon of Shun*. The dates of composition of these texts are controversial. They may have been written as early as the eighth century BCE during the transition between Western and Eastern Zhou, and as late as the end of the Warring States period in the third century BCE. Cai Zong-qi, ed. *A Chinese Literary Mind: Culture, Creativity, and Rhetoric in* Wenxin Diaolong (Redwood City, CA: Stanford University Press, 2001), 239.

7. Cai Zong-qi, *Configurations of Comparative Poetry: Three Perspectives on Western and Chinese Literary Criticism* (Honolulu: University of Hawai'i Press, 2002), 35.

8. This assumption is known in philosophy and social science as "methodological individualism."

9. This discussion clearly oversimplifies two long and complex traditions. See the work of Chad Hansen: *A Daoist Theory of Chinese Thought* (New York: Oxford University Press, 1992); "Qing (Emotions) 情 in Pre-Buddhist Chinese Thought," in *Emotions in Asian Thought: A Dialogue in Comparative Philosophy,* ed. Joel Marks and Roger T. Ames (Albany, NY: State University of New York Press, 1995); and "Philosophy of Mind in China," in *Encyclopedia of Chinese Philosophy*, ed. Antonio S. Cua (New York: Garland Publishing, 2012), for discussion of some of the issues involved. The sharp distinction between "inner" and "outer" has been challenged by a number of philosophers, including Wittgenstein's discussion of private languages and Putnam's argument that "meaning ain't in the head." See Hilary Putnam, "The Meaning of 'Meaning'" in *The Twin Earth Chronicles*, ed. Andrew Pessin and Sanford Goldberg (Armonk, NY: M. E. Sharpe, 1996). Putnam's argument will be discussed in chapter 4.

In another vocabulary the discussion would be in terms of the relationship between signs, signifiers, and signified.

10. Interestingly, Felix Mendelssohn turned this claim on its head by arguing that only music can express thoughts and feelings directly and unambiguously. Leo Treitler, "Language and the Interpretation of Music," in *Music and Meaning*, ed. Jenefer Robinson (Ithaca, NY: Cornell University Press, 1997), 26–27.

11. See also *Analects* 16.13. Quotations from the *Analects* will be from Roger T. Ames, and Henry Rosemont, Jr., trans., *The Analects: A Philosophical Translation* (New York: Ballantine Books, 1998) unless otherwise noted.

12. Cai, *Configurations*, 39. Vincent Yu-chung Shih, trans., *The Literary Mind and the Carving of Dragons* by Liu Xie. Taipei (Taiwan, Republic of China: Chung Hwa Book Company, Ltd., 1975), translates "*zhi*" as "sentiment" or "emotion."

13. James Legge, trans., *The She King* [*Shijing*], 2nd ed. vol. 4 of *The Chinese Classics* (Hong Kong: Hong Kong University Press, 1960), 34.

14. Stephen Owen, *Readings in Chinese Literary Thought* (Cambridge, MA: Harvard University Press, 1992), 26.

15. Cai, *A Chinese Literary Mind*, 239.

16. Owen, *Readings in Chinese*, 29.

17. Mencius, *Mencius*, trans. D. C. Lau (New York: Penguin Books, 1970), 3B.2.

18. This is clearly not a problem for the quotations from Confucius and Mencius.

19. Li Zehou, *The Chinese Aesthetic Tradition*, trans. Maija Bell Samei (Honolulu: University of Hawai'i Press, 2010), 32.

20. Li Zehou, *The Chinese Aesthetic*, 20.

21. Sandra T. Francis, "The Origins of Dance: The Perspectives of Primate Evolution," *Dance Chronicle* 14, no. 2/3 (1991), 212.

22. The importance of totemic dances in Neolithic communities will be discussed in chapter 2.

23. "The Great Preface" was composed either in the late Western Han, or in the early Eastern Han, i.e., about first century CE. Victor H. Mair, ed., *The Columbia Anthology of Traditional Chinese Literature* (New York: Columbia University Press, 1994), 121.

24. *Shi zhe zhi zhi suo zhi ye* (詩者志之所之也).

25. Cai, *Configurations of Comparative,* 44–46. Cai notes that the last two paragraphs are quotations from the "Record of Music" (*Yue Ji*). Legge translates the passage as "(1) Poetry is the product of earnest thought. Thought [cherished] in the mind becomes earnest; exhibited in words, it becomes poetry. (2) The feelings (*qing* 情) move inwardly, and are embodied in words. . . ." Legge, 34. Owen, *Readings in Chinese*, 27, discusses some of the "uncommon assumptions" in Legge's translation.

26. Owen, *Readings in Chinese*, 41–42; Tang Yijie, "Emotion in Pre-Qin Ruist moral theory: An Explanation of 'Dao begins in Qing,'" *Philosophy East and West* 53, no. 2 (2003), 271–81; Robert C. Solomon, "Some Notes on Emotion, 'East and West,'" *Philosophy East and West* 45 no. 2 (1995): 171–202; and Hansen, "Qing (Emotions) 情 in Pre-Buddhist" for more detailed discussion.

Roger T. Ames, "The Mencian conception of *Ren Xing* 人性: Does it Mean 'Human Nature'?" in *Chinese Texts and Philosophical Contexts*, ed. Henry Rosemont, Jr. (LaSalle, IL: Open Court Press, 1991), 143–75; and Irene Bloom, "Mencian Arguments on Human Nature (*Renxing*)," *Philosophy East and West* 44, no. 1 (1994), 19–53 and "Human Nature and Biological Nature in Mencius," *Philosophy East and West* 47, no. 1 (1997), 21–32, engage in a spirited debate on the nature of *ren xing* (human nature)

27. *Mencius* 2A:6. Chad Hansen argues that ancient Chinese epistemology may also posit other dispositions: for example to notice or perceive things; to make distinctions The disposition is to only make distinctions; the particular distinctions we make, how we make them and how we evaluate them may be socially conditioned or conventional.

28. Owen, *Readings in Chinese*, 41–42. In the same vein Hansen, "*Qing* (Emotions) 情 in Pre-Buddhist," notes that *qing* has a double meaning: both inner "emotions" and outwardly may be a situation or circumstance. Thus Hansen wants to translate *qing* as "reality inputs"—emotional responses to external situations.

29. Tang, "Emotion in Pre-Qin," 275.

30. *Xuanxue* is often referred to as Neo-Daoism, although the label may be misleading. *Xuanxue* developed in response to the increasing decline of confidence in Confucian thought as an interpretation of the *Yijing*, *Laozi* and *Zhuangzi* that attempts to fathom the mysteries of the Dao. The movement influenced the development of Chinese Buddhism and faded when Buddhist thought became dominate in Chinese thought. See Alan Chan, "Neo-Taoism," *The Stanford Encyclopedia of Philosophy (Winter 2009 edition)*, ed. Edward N. Zalta, http://plato.stanford.edu/archives/win2009/entries/neo-taoism/, accessed January 29, 2013; and Ronnie

Littlejohn, "Daoist Philosophy," Internet Encyclopedia of Philosophy, http://www.iep.utm.edu/daoism/, accessed January 29, 2013.

31. Li Zehou, *The Chinese Aesthetic,* 35. The view that lyric poetry originates in emotion (*qing*) is said to have originated with the Han dynasty writer Lu Ji (261–303 CE) in his *Wen fu* (Exposition on Literature). Li notes, however, that it was not until the Wei-Jin period that "*shi yan zhi*" and "*shi yuan qing*" were interpreted as referring to individual aspirations and emotions.

32. Yang Guobin, "Introduction" to Liu Xie, *Dragon-Carving and the Literary Mind* (Beijing: Foreign Language and Research Press, 2003), 47. Liu Xie, *Dragon-Carving and the Literary Mind,* trans. Yang Guobin (Beijing: Foreign Language and Research Press, 2003), 711 and 758. Chapters 1–5 of the *Wenxin Diaolong* present Liu's literary theory. Chapters 6–25 describe various genres of literature. The second part begins with chapter 26 on Imagination. Chapters 27–49 discuss "style, rhetoric, literary history [and] literary appreciation. The final chapter (50) explains the title and his reasons for writing the book.

33. How much, or even whether at all, Liu Xie's *Wenxin Diaolong* was influenced by Buddhism is controversial. Victor H. Mair, "Buddhism in *The Literary Mind and Ornate Rhetoric,*" in *A Chinese Literary Mind: Culture, Creativity, and Rhetoric in* Wenxin Diaolong, ed. Cai Zong-qi (Redwood City, CA: Stanford University Press, 2001) discusses the controversy. Cai, *A Chinese Literary Mind,* 46, notes that the lack of didactic emphasis is often interpreted to mean that Liu Xie was not in the *shi yan zhi* tradition.

34. Liu Xie may not have been the first to believe this but his views are relatively well worked out. See discussions by Owen, *Readings in Chinese;* Lin Shuen-fu, "Liu Xie on Imagination" in *A Chinese Literary Mind: Culture, Creativity, and Rhetoric in* Wenxin Diaolong, ed. Cai Zong-qi (Redwood City, CA: Stanford University Press, 2001); and Cai, *A Chinese Literary Mind.*

35. Liu Xie, *Dragon-Carving,* chapter 1.2, 5.

36. Liu Xie, *Dragon-Carving,* chapter 1.1, 3 and Owen, *Readings in Chinese,* 187.

37. Liu Xie, *Dragon-Carving,* chapter 1.2, 5.

38. Owen, *Readings in Chinese,* 189.

39. Although this is my translation of 心生而言立, 言立而文明, it owes much to Owen, *Readings in Chinese,* 189; and Liu Xie, *Dragon-Carving,* chapter 1.3. 8.

40. Owen, *Readings in Chinese,* 49–50

41. Liu Xie, *Dragon-Carving,* chapter 1.4, 9. Chapter 6 of the *Wenxin Diaolong* begins by quoting both King Shun and the *Great Preface.*

42. Liu Xie, *Dragon-Carving,* chapter 1.4, 9.

43. Liu Xie, *Dragon-Carving,* chapter 5.2, 53.

44. Liu Xie, *Dragon-Carving,* chapter 29.4. 415

45. Li Wai-yee, "Between 'Literary Mind' and 'Carving Dragons'" Order and Excess in *Wenxin Diaolong,*" in *A Chinese Literary Mind: Culture, Creativity,*

and Rhetoric in Wenxin Diaolong, ed., Cai Zong-qi (Redwood City, CA: Stanford University Press, 2001), 203

46. Liu Xie, *Dragon-Carving*, 5.3, 55.

47. Liu Xie, *Dragon-Carving*, 5.5, 59. Much more evidence for the non-political use of "*zhi*" is in 48.5.

48. Li Wai-yee, "Between 'Literary Mind,'" 205.

49. Cai, *A Chinese Literary Mind*, 51.

50. Owen, *Readings in Chinese*, 20.

51. Lin, "Liu Xie on Imagination," and Ronald Egan, "Poet, Mind, and World: A Reconsideration of the '*Shensi*' Chapter of *Wenxin Diaolong*," in *A Chinese Literary Mind: Culture, Creativity, and Rhetoric in* Wenxin Diaolong, ed. Cai Zong-qi (Redwood City, CA: Stanford University Press, 2001). Although "imagination" is usually translated as "*xiangxiang*" 想像, Lin argues that while *xiangxiang* has taken on much of the meaning of the English word "imagination," originally *xiangxiang* meant only "visualizing an image of someone or something" (Lin, "Liu Xie on Imagination," 128). Lin's essay presents a detailed comparison of the "artistic imagination" of Coleridge and Kant and Liu Xie's understanding of *shensi*.

52. Lin, "Liu Xie on Imagination," 134–36.

53. Owen, *Readings in Chinese*, 202 (ch. 26.1). The reference to Zhuangzi is from chapter 28: "The Chung-shan Prince Mou said to Chang-tzu: 'My body is hereby the river and the sea, but my heart lingers on under the city gate-towers of Wei. What is to be done?'" A. C. Graham, trans. *Chuang-Tzu: The Inner Chapters* (Indianapolis, IN: Hackett Publishing Company, Inc., 2001), 229.

Owen, *Readings in Chinese*; Lin, "Liu Xie on Imagination," and Cai, *A Chinese Literary Mind* have wondered whether this actually is a "definition" of *shensi*, since the context in which this remark originally occurred makes it quite inappropriate in this context. There is however a tradition of using quotations in ways quite differently from their original context. The use of a number of the quotations from the *Book of Songs* in the *Analects* seems to be an example of this tradition.

54. Not *xin* (心), but *xiongyi* (chest, mind, heart, subjectivity 胸臆).

55. Cai, *A Chinese Literary Mind*, 52–55; Lin, "Liu Xie on Imagination." 144–45; Owen *Reading in Chinese*, 202–05.

56. Owen, *Readings in Chinese*, 202.

57. "[T]here is a Holy Man living on faraway Ku-she Mountain, with skin like ice or snow, and gentle and shy like a young girl. He doesn't eat the five grains, but sucks the wind, drinks the dew, climbs up on the clouds and mists, rides a flying dragon and wanders beyond the four seas." Zhuangzi. *Chuang Tzu: Basic Writings*, trans. Burton Watson (New York: Columbia University Press, 1964, 1996), 27.

58. Liu Xie, *Dragon-Carving*, chapter 26.3, 379.

59. My translation following Owen, *Readings in Chinese*, 204; and Lin, "Liu Xie on Imagination," 154.

60. Egan, "Poet, Mind, and World," 111.

61. My translation, following Egan, "Poet, Mind, and World," 110; and Liu Xie, *Dragon-Carving*, chapter 26.3, 379.

62. Cai, *A Chinese Literary Mind*, 47.

63. Shih, *The Literary Mind*, 372

64. Cai, *A Chinese Literary Mind*, 47.

65. M. H. Abrams, *The Mirror and the Lamp: Romantic Theory and the Critical Tradition* (New York: W. W. Norton & Company, 1958), 22.

66. Abrams, *The Mirror*, 23 and 21. Abrams notes that Mill's aesthetic theory followed Wordsworth quite closely.

67. *Analects* 15.11, although not perhaps with Confucius's experience "When the Master was in the state of Qi he heard the *shao* music and for several months he did not know the taste of meat. He said, 'I had no idea that music could achieve such heights!'" (*Analects* 17.14).

68. Lin, "Liu Xie on Imagination," makes a strong case for the similarities between Liu and Coleridge. I find them less alike than she does.

69. Samuel Taylor Coleridge, *Biographia Literaria* (Project Gutenberg's *Biographia Literaria*, by Samuel Taylor Coleridge. Release Date: July, 2004 [eBook #6081]), accessed July 23, 2014, http://www.gutenberg.org/files/6081/6081-h/6081-h.htm. This theory of fancy is a version of seventeenth-century atomism with the "law of association" playing the part in psychology that gravity played in the physical universe.

70. Coleridge, *Biographia*.

71. Abrams, *The Mirror,* 174.

72. Andrew Brook, "Kant's View of the Mind and Consciousness of Self," *The Stanford Encyclopedia of Philosophy* (Fall 2013 edition), ed. Edward N. Zalta, http://plato.stanford.edu/archives/fall2013/entries/kant-mind/. In Kant's *First Critique* Imagination is "a blind but indispensable function of the soul, without which we should have no knowledge whatsoever, but of which we are scarcely ever conscious" (A 78). Imagination is the indispensable link between sensible intuition and intellectual understanding/recognition (A 125). Sense provides intuitions which imagination synthesizes/associates into images that understanding recognizes with concepts (A 101). The faculty of imagination synthesizes various empirical intuitions given by sense into images that we can perceive (A 120).

73. Coleridge, *Biographia*.

74. Coleridge, *Biographia*.

Oxford English Dictionary (online). *Morphosis* is "the formation or development of an organ, esp. as marked by structural change; the manner in which this occurs." *Poiaesis* [poisesis, or posey], is "creative production, esp. of a work of art; an instance of this."

75. Coleridge, *Biographia.* Coleridge may be following Kant at this point. In some sections of *The Critique of Judgment* Kant seems to suggest a relationship

between imagination, artistic creation, and God's purpose in creating the universe. Kant's argument, however, is cautious and not entirely clear.

76. Egan, "Poet, Mind, and World," 103.

77. Egan, "Poet, Mind, and World," 103. Kant's argument that imagination is essential to sense perception is an unusual use of the term.

78. Egan, "Poet, Mind, and World," 103.

79. Liu Xie, *Dragon-Carving*, chapters 42, 47, and 48.

80. Abrams, *The Mirror*, 25–26.

81. Li Zehou, *The Chinese Aesthetic*, 207.

82. Li Zehou, *The Chinese Aesthetic*, 211.

83. Li Zehou and Jane Cauvel, *Four Essays On Aesthetics: Toward a Global View* (Lanham, MD: Lexington Books: A Division of Roman & Littlefield, Publishers, Inc., 2006), 120.

84. Wang Keping, "Appreciating nature in view of practical aesthetics," *Frontiers of Philosophy in China* 2 no. 1 (2007): 141.

85. The experience is usually pleasant but it may also be disturbing—ugly or jarring. Li Zehou's theory has little to say about experiences that are unpleasantly disturbing but he makes some interesting suggestions (Li and Cauvel, *Four Essays*, 121–22; and Li, *The Chinese Aesthetic*, 58).

86. Li and Cauvel, *Four Essays*, 98 and 109.

87. Li and Cauvel, *Four Essays*, 121.

88. Li Zehou, *The Path of Beauty: A Study of Chinese Aesthetics*, trans. Gong Lizeng (Oxford University Press: Hong Kong, Oxford, and New York, 1994), 236.

Chapter 2

1. James Wood, "Is That All There Is? Secularism and its discontents," *The New Yorker* (August 15, 2011), http://www.newyorker.com/magazine/2011/08/15/is-that-all-there-is.

2. Henry Rosemont, Jr., *Rationality and Religious Experience* (Peru, IL: Open Court Publishing Company, 2001), 10.

3. Li Zehou, "Some Thoughts on Neo-Confucianism," trans. Gou Da, *Social Sciences in China* 3, no. 4 (1982), 186.

4. Kant's theory is complex and subtle; moreover there is a great deal of disagreement about what precisely his arguments are and whether they should be convincing. I have presented a generally accepted sketch of his views, although I may have oversimplified some of them.

5. Or as Kant put it, "How is the synthetic *a priori* possible?"

6. The forms of space and time are the most fundamental structures of experience. All experience takes place in space and time. Kant argued that we

cannot have learned this fact from experience because experience is only possible if it is in space and time.

7. Immanuel Kant, *Critique of Practical Reason*, trans. Lewis White Beck (Indianapolis, IN, and New York: The Bobbs-Merrill Company, Inc., 1956), 30.

8. Kant, *Critique of Practical Reason*, 50.

9. Immanuel Kant, *Critique of Judgement*, trans. J. H. Bernard (New York: Hafner Press, 1951), 32.

10. Kant's use of the term "imagination" differs significantly from the ordinary understanding of the term. For discussion of some of the problems of interpretation see Nick Zangwill, "Aesthetic Judgment," *The Stanford Encyclopedia of Philosophy* (Summer 2013), ed. Edward N. Zalta, http://plato.stanford.edu/archives/sum 2013/entries/aesthetic-judgment/; Paul Guyer, "Kant, Immanuel," *Routledge Encyclopedia of Philosophy*. London: Routledge (1998, 2004), http://www.rep.routledge.com/article/DB047SECT12; Hannah Ginsborg, "Lawfulness without a Law: Kant on the Free Play of Imagination and Understanding," *Philosophical Topics* 25, no. 1 (Spring 1997): 37–81; and Hannah Ginsborg, "Kant's Aesthetics and Teleology," *The Stanford Encyclopedia of Philosophy* (Summer 2014), ed. Edward N. Zalta, http://plato.stanford.edu/archives/sum2014/entries/kant-aesthetics/.

11. Paul Guyer, *Kant* (London and New York: Routledge, 2006), 309. In the *First Critique* Kant argued that our knowledge of the empirical world is presented in the form of judgments which always have a particular logical structure. In the *Third Critique* he distinguished between the "determinate" judgments of the *First Critique* and "reflective judgments" in aesthetics and teleology.

12. Kant, *Critique of Pure Reason*, A 101, 132.

13. Kant, *Critique of Judgment*, 56 and 71–73.

14. Kant is talking here about what he calls "pure beauty." Beautiful objects that are also useful are only "dependently beautiful." See Paul Guyer, "Free and Adherent Beauty: A Modest Proposal" in *Values of Beauty: Historical Essays in Aesthetics*, ed. Paul Guyer (Cambridge: Cambridge University Press, 2005), 129–40; and Ginsborg, "Kant's Aesthetics," for discussion of free and dependent beauty.

15. Kant, *Critique of Judgment*, 149

16. Kant, *Critique of Judgment*, 80–81. Kant's claim is obviously controversial and his argument is subject to differing interpretations. See Ted Cohen, Ted. "Why Beauty is a Symbol of Morality," in *Essays in Kant's Aesthetics*, ed. by Ted Cohen and Paul Guyer (Chicago and London: The University of Chicago Press, 1982), 232–34.

17. Kant's language is not always consistent in the three *Critiques*.

18. More properly perhaps, moral motivation; but a full discussion of the *Second Critique* is beyond the scope of the current project.

19. Kant, *Critique of Judgment*, 200.

20. Chong Woei Lien, "Combining Marx with Kant: The Philosophical Anthropology of Li Zehou," *Philosophy East and West* 49, no. 2 (1999), 122.

21. Li Zehou, *Study On Marxism in China* (Hong Kong: Joint Publishing (H.K.) Co., Ltd., 1993); and Chong, "Combing Marx," 135. Chenshan Tian objects to the characterization of Mao's views as "volunteerism" because it neglects Mao's concern for continuity through change. Tian Chenshan, *Chinese Dialectics: From Yijing to Marxism* (Lanham, MD: Lexington Books, 2005), 67.

22. Li Zehou, *A Study on Marxism*, 59–64, 175–76. Li argues that after victory of the PRC Mao continued to think of politics almost exclusively in terms of an ideological struggle between two opposing forces. Once the Japanese and Kuomintang had been defeated, Mao recast the opposition in terms of the class struggle of the proletariat against bourgeois, "capitalist roaders," and "reactionary academic authorities." In addition, Li claims that because Mao believed politics, ideology, and mass movements were the driving forces of society, he failed to construct an economic base for a socialist society, ignoring both the science and technology required by modern industry, and the large class of educated professionals required to manage that industry. Li argues that Mao moved with precipitous haste to transform the small-scale agricultural society of China to a full socialist economy with large-scale cooperative agriculture and modern industry.

23. Li Zehou, "The Philosophy of Kant and a Theory of Subjectivity," *Analecta Husserliana*, 21 (1986): 141; and Li Zehou, *A Study on Marxism*, 62–72. Li does not claim that these events were only the result of the beliefs and actions of one man, or even of a small group of people. *A Study on Marxism* provides a detailed and nuanced account of how sinified Marxism closely resembled traditional, feudal, Confucian ideology and played into the psychological and cultural systems of the Chinese population as a whole.

24. Li Zehou, "The Philosophy of Kant," 140.

25. Li Zehou, "A Re-evaluation of Confucius," trans. Liu Qizhong, *Social Sciences in China* 2, no. 1 (1980), 119; and Sylvia Chan, "Li Zehou and New Confucianism," in *New Confucianism: A Critical Examination*, ed. John Makeham (New York: Palgrave Macmillan, 2003), 105. Li explicitly distances himself from the "New Confucianism" of Xiong Shili, Mou Zongsan, and their followers who often blame Marxism and Communism for destroying the Confucian tradition. Nevertheless, Sylvia Chan argues that there are reasons to consider Li a New Confucian.

26. Li Zehou, *A Study of Marxism*, 30.

27. One of the serious problems for this tradition is how to explain "weakness of the will" in which one understands the relevant syllogism and accepts the conclusion, and yet fails to do Y. Chinese practical rationality avoids this logical conundrum by focusing on what someone does rather than on what she says or thinks. As *Analects* 4.24 notes, "The exemplary person (*junzi* 君子) wants to be slow to speak yet quick to act." *Analects* 5.5 says, "Someone said, 'As for Yong, he is an authoritative person (*ren* 仁) but is not eloquent.' The Master said, 'What is the use of eloquence? A person who disputes with a ready wit often earns the

enmity of others.'" One is reminded of the generations of scholars who have found the relentless logic of Socrates and the *Critique of Practical Reason* more than a little annoying, and not at all helpful in practical life.

28. Angus C. Graham, *Yin-Yang and the Nature of Correlative Thinking* (Singapore: Institute of East Asian Philosophies. Monograph Series no. 6, 1986), 1–5; and David L. Hall and Roger T. Ames, *Anticipating China: Thinking Through the Narratives of Chinese and Western Culture* (Albany, NY: State University of New York Press, 1995), xvii–xviii, 116, 272. Both sorts of thinking are present in both China and the West, and it has been argued that the correlative, analogical system predates the causal one and serves as a necessary prerequisite or foundation for it.

29. The conclusion of a practical syllogism is an action—"Therefore I should do Y." Theoretical syllogisms have the form "S is P; A is an S; therefore A is P."

30. One approach—taken by scientific materialists and Berkeleyan idealists—has been to argue that only one realm "really exists," the other is simply an illusion. One of the most sophisticated attempts at bridging the "gulf" between the two realms was Kant's attempted reconciliation of David Hume's empiricism with Descartes' rationalism and Newton's physics; but, as we have seen, even Kant's attempt to explain the relationship between noumena and phenomena was not entirely convincing.

31. Angus C. Graham, "Reflections and Replies," in *Chinese Texts and Philosophical Contexts*, ed. Henry Rosemont, Jr. (La Salle, IL: Open Court, 1991), 286.

32. Hall and Ames, *Anticipating China,* 261. A particularly nuanced and clear explanation of this relationship is Li Chenyang, "The Confucian Ideal of Harmony," *Philosophy East and West* 56 no. 4 (2006): 583–603.

33. David L. Hall and Roger T. Ames, *Thinking from the Han: Self, Truth and Transcendence in Chinese and Western Culture* (Albany, NY: State University of New York Press, 1998), 127.

34. Roger T. Ames, and David L. Hall, trans., *Daodejing: "Making This Life Significant": A Philosophical Translation* (New York: Random House, Inc. Ballantine Books, 2003), 28.

35. Li Zehou, "A Re-evaluation," 119–20.

36. For example Mou Zongsan (1909–1995) translated all three of Kant's Critiques, and used Kantian vocabulary in his efforts to modernize Confucianism. Tu Xiaofei, "Dare to Compare: The Comparative Philosophy of Mou Zongsan," *Kritike* 1 no. 2 (December 2007), 26, http://www.kritike.org/volume-1-2.html. See Stephan Schmidt, "Mou Zongsan, Hegel, and Kant: The Quest for Confucian Modernity," *Philosophy East and West* 61, no. 2 (2011), 260–302, for a perceptive and detailed discussion of Mou Zongsan and Kant.

37. Thus, in traditional Christianity the incarnation is one of the deepest mysteries, although there are alternative traditions in Christian and Buddhist philosophical theology which attempt to reconcile the transcendent and immanent.

38. Li Zehou, *The Chinese Aesthetic Tradition*, 84.

39. Li Zehou and Jane Cauvel, *Four Essays,* 40.

40. Mou Zongsan generally translated "noumenon" as *wuzishen* 物自身, which also can be translated as "Thing-in-itself." Mou Zongsan's vocabulary of *Xianxiang Yu Wuzishen* (現象與物自身, Phenomena and Noumenon, or Phenomenon and Things-in-themselves) is far more compatible with a "two level ontology" than Li's insistence on non-dualistic, historical, biological metaphysics. See Jason Clower, "Mou Zongsan (Mou Tsung-san) (1909–1995)," *The Internet Encyclopedia of Philosophy*, http://www.iep.utm.edu/. Not only is the issue complicated in ways that translations often are, but the problems are not confined to translations between English and Chinese, see Marthe Chandler, "Philosophy of Gravity: Intuitions of Four-Dimensional Curved Spacetime," *Science & Education* 3, no. 2 (1994): 155–76.

41. Hall and Ames, *Thinking Through Confucius*, 7.

42. G. H. Mead and John Dewey also attempt to reconcile Kant and Darwin.

43. Li and Cauvel, *Four Essays*, 174.

44. "Subjectivity" may be translated two ways in Chinese: *zhuguanxing* 主觀性 and *zhutixing* 主體性. In the first translation the character *guan* 觀 has to do with ideas or concepts and hence the phrase means human consciousness. In the second translation *ti* 體 refers to material substance, the human body. Li notes that while Western philosophy from Descartes to Kant has been a philosophy of consciousness, in the Chinese tradition the distinction between subject (consciousness) and object (body) has often been unclear and has often been completely ignored. Li generally uses *zhuguanxing* to mean "subjectivity" but argues that the basis of human nature/existence is neither consciousness nor language but tool using and making. Therefore he coins a new English word, "subjectality," to translate *zhutixing*, claiming that "*subjectality* is the foundation of subjectivity." Li Zehou, "Subjectivity and 'Subjectality': A Response." *Philosophy East and West* 49, no. 2 (1999), 174–75.

45. Li Zehou, "The Philosophy of Kant," 137.

46. Li and Cauvel, *Four Essays*, 90.

47. "Men make their own history, but they do not make it as they please; they do not make it under self-selected circumstances, but under circumstances existing already, given and transmitted from the past." Karl Marx, *The Eighteenth Brumaire of Louis Bonaparte*, in *The Marx-Engels Reader* 2nd ed., ed. Robert C. Tucker (New York and London: W. W. Norton & Company, 1978), 595.

48. Marx, *The German Ideology,* in *The Marx-Engels Reader*, 2nd ed., ed. Robert C. Tucker (New York and London: W. W. Norton & Company, 1978), 150. Marx's labor theory of value grows out of his analysis of relatively complex economic systems.

49. Li Zehou, "Subjectivity," 177.

50. Although critics of Marx claim that other animals do in fact make tools, they do not do so on the scale of the Oldowan and Acheulean stone tool industries. "Oldowan and Acheulean Stone Tools," Museum of Anthropology, University of Missouri. http://anthromuseum.missouri.edu/minigalleries/handaxes/intro.shtml.

51. "Oldowan and Acheulean Stone Tools."

52. *Homo habilis, Homo erectus,* and *Homo sapiens* are standard names of different species of the genus *Homo.* Philosophers and social theorists have coined the term "*Homo faber*" as an alternative to *Homo sapiens* to emphasize that working and tool making are more significant characteristics of our species than the capacity for abstract thought.

Debates continue as to how directly related *Homo habilis* is to *Homo sapiens*; and whether *Homo sapiens* evolved in Africa and spread to other parts of the world, or evolved from populations of *Homo erectus* living in many parts of the world. Nevertheless, about 2.6 to 1.2 million years ago *Homo habilis* (perhaps an ancestor of *Homo sapiens*) developed the first stone tool industry. "Oldowan and Acheulean Stone Tools."

53. Clifford Geertz, *The Interpretation of Cultures* (New York: Basic Books, Inc., 1973), 48; Robert N. Bellah, *Religion in Human Evolution* (Cambridge, MA: Harvard University Press, 2011), 82–83; and P. Thomas Schoenemann, "Research on the Evolution of Brain and Language" (lecture, DePauw University, Greencastle, IN, November 16, 2011).

54. Donald Johanson, "Origins of Modern Humans: Multiregional or Out of Africa?" An ActionBioscience.org original article, http://www.actionbioscience.org/evolution/johanson.html.

55. Michael Tomasello, *The Cultural Origins of Human Cognition* (Cambridge, MA: Harvard University Press, 1999), 16–17. Tomasello's work builds on the research of a number of primatologists, anthropologists, linguists, and child development psychologists.

56. Tomasello, *Cultural Origins*, 7, 33–34. Although Tomasello avoids calling the relevant skill "empathy," other writers including Habermas and G. H. Mead have noticed the importance of empathy in the development of human cognitive skills. Jürgen Habermas, *Between Naturalism and Religion*, trans. Ciaran Cronin (Malden, MA: Polity Press, 2008), 171–73.

57. Tomasello, *Cultural Origins*, 216–17.

58. Despite Tomasello's insistence on the social dimensions of human cognition his discussion makes many of the assumptions of a belief-desire folk psychology, namely that there is a clear distinction between beliefs and desires, and between an inner mental world and an outer objective one. A (Chinese) folk psychology in which actions are described in terms of *zhi* (chapter 1) and *xin* (the heart-mind that is the source of both beliefs and desires) would describe things differently. See Chad Hansen, *A Daoist Theory of Chinese Thought* (New

York: Oxford University Press, 1992) and Chad Hansen, "Philosophy of Mind in China," in *Encyclopedia of Chinese Philosophy*, ed. Antonio S. Cua (New York: Garland Publishing, 2012) for discussion of these issues.

59. Li Zehou, "The Philosohy of Kant," 136.

60. Li Zehou, "Subjectivity," 175.

61. In his later works Li Zehou has completely rejected "noumenon" as a translation of *benti.*

62. Li and Cauvel, *Four Essays*, 94.

63. Li Zehou, "The Philosophy of Kant," 136.

64. Li Zehou, "The Philosophy of Kant," 136.

65. Li and Cauvel, *Four Essays*, 94.

66. Li and Cauvel, *Four Essays*, 88, 166; Gu Xin, "Subjectivity, Modernity, and Chinese Hegelian Marxism: A Study of Li Zehou's Philosophical Ideas from a Comparative Perspective," *Philosophy East and West* 46 no. 2 (1996), 215.

67. Wittgenstein actually writes about "mythology" and talks about it in terms of the rules of a language game, but the difference is unimportant in this context.

68. Ludwig Wittgenstein, *On Certainty*, trans. Denis Paul and G. E. M. Anscombe, ed. G. E. M. Anscombe and G. H. von Wright (New York: Harper & Row Publishers, 1969), 15e.

69. Li often indicates that he would prefer to call these "structures" "formations" in order to indicate that they are historical and dynamic, constantly being "formed" rather than static and eternal. Li Zehou "Subjectivity," 177; also: Roger T. Ames, "New Confucianism: A Native Response to Western Philosophy" in *Chinese Political Culture: 1989–2000*, ed. Shiping Hua (Armonk, NY: M. E. Sharpe, 2001), 86; and Li and Cauvel, *Four Essays*, 6.

70. Li and Cauvel, *Four Essays*, 134.

71. Li Zehou, "The Philosophy of Kant," 138.

72. Marx, *Economic and Philosophic*, 88–89.

73. Li and Cauvel, *Four Essays*, 92–101, and 135.

74. David Hockney, "A Day on the Grand Canal with the Emperor of China, or, Surface is Illusion but so is Depth," [VHS] (1988, 1991), directed by Philip Hass, Program for Art on Film. New York: New York, and Wen C. Fong, "Why Chinese Painting Is History" *The Art Bulletin* 85, no. 2 (June, 2003): 258–80, discuss the way Chinese painters treated perspective.

75. Li and Cauvel, *Four Essays*, 90.

76. Li Zehou, "The Philosophy of Kant," 136–41; LI Zehou, "An Outline of the Origin of Humankind," trans. Peter Wong Yih Ziun, *Contemporary Chinese Thought* 31, no. 2 (Winter 1999–2000), 23.

77. Li Zehou, *Chinese Aesthetics*, 6; Li Zehou, *The Path of Beauty*, 2–10; Li and Cauvel, *Four Essays*, 68.

78. Sandra T. Francis, "The Origins of Dance: The Perspectives of Primate Evolution," *Dance Chronicle* 14 no 2/3 (1991), 211–12.

79. Susanne K. Langer, *Philosophy in a New Key* (New York: Mentor Book, 1951), 116–17, describes one such theory; as does Robert N. Bellah, *Religion in Human Evolution* (Cambridge, MA: Harvard University Press, 2011), 129.

80. Li and Cauvel, *Four Essays*, 39. Li and Cauvel suggest that Wittgenstein's theory must be supplemented by a concern for the particular practices, material production, and tool-using in primitive societies. It may be significant that Wittgenstein's paradigm case of a language game involves the coordination of labor at a construction site.

81. Li and Cauvel, *Four Essays*, 151.

82. Li Zehou, *Chinese Aesthetic*, 5–6.

83. Gu, "Subjectivity, Modernity," 209.

84. Li Zehou, "The Philosophy of Kant," 137. Recall Tomasello's claim that the human ability to empathize, to take a third-person point of view on oneself and ones' projects is the fundamental ability that makes humans unique. Tomasello appears to think this ability originates somehow in our biological, genetic makeup. However, if one feels oneself part of a social whole, one would be able to come to view other parts of that whole as "like oneself."

85. Émile Durkheim, "Religion and ritual," in *Emile Durkheim: Selected Writings*, ed. A. Giddens (New York: Cambridge University Press, 1992), 22, 232. Although Durkheim argued that the state of collective consciousness was the source of morality, he did not claim that it was more important than individual consciousness.

86. Quoted in Jonathan Haidt, *The Righteous Mind* (New York: Pantheon Books, 2012), 221.

87. Haidt, *Righteous Mind*, 222. Mary Bockover has pointed out that a similar occurrence seems to take place when groups of people watch NFL football, and in the musical phenomena known as a "rave" that began in the 1980s.

88. Although Durkheim argued that the state of collective consciousness was particularly strong in primitive totemic rituals, he did not specifically claim that it predated individual consciousness.

89. Li Zehou, "Subjectivity," 176.

90. Li Zehou, "The Philosophy of Kant," 138.

91. Li and Cauvel, *Four Essays*, 93.

92. Jane Cauvel, "The Transformative Power of Art: Li Zehou's Aesthetic Theory," *Philosophy East and West* 49 no. 2 (1999), 150.

93. See for example Benjamin Lee Whorf, "An American Indian model of the universe," in *Language, Thought and Reality: Selected Writings of Benjamin Lee Whorf*, ed. John B. Carroll (New York: The Technology Press of Massachusetts Institute of Technology and John Wiley & Sons, Inc., 1956), and Chandler, "Philosophy of Gravity."

94. See for example Mencius's analogical logic and Mohist logic.

95. Li Zehou, "A Re-evaluation," 110; Li Zehou, *The Path of Beauty*, chapter 1 "The Era of Dragons and Phoenixes;" and *The Chinese Aesthetic Tradition*, chapter 1, "The Rites and Music Tradition" contain detailed discussions of Chinese cultural sedimentation.

96. Li and Cauvel, *Four Essays*, 88 and 166. For Li social transformations may come from changes in the economic base, the means and relations of production, and from creative individuals. The remark quoted above about creative individuals, however, was in the context of aesthetic sedimentation where individual artists are particularly important, and thus does not contradict Li's view that Maoist Volunteerism, the view that economic production can be changed by "the people's will" in the absence of the relevant material conditions, was seriously flawed.

97. Li and Cauvel, *Four Essays*, 38, 86–88.

98. Eva Schaper, "Taste, Sublimity, and Genius: The Aesthetics of Nature and Art" in *The Cambridge Companion to Kant*, edited by Paul Guyer (Cambridge University Press, 1992), 376. Schaper describes Kant's argument for this point as a set of "complicated maneuvers." In other words, the argument is not be entirely convincing.

99. Li and Cauvel, *Four Essays*, 129.

100. Li and Cauvel, *Four Essays*, 150, 47.

101. Li and Cauvel, *Four Essays*, 48–49.

102. Li and Cauvel, *Four Essays*, 99.

103. Li and Cauvel, *Four Essays*, 50.

104. Li and Cauvel, *Four Essays*, 134–35.

105. Li Zehou, *Path of Beauty*, 2; Li and Cauvel, *Four Essays*, 68.

106. Li and Cauvel, *Four Essays*, 134.

107. Li and Cauvel, *Four Essays*, 147.

108. Li and Cauvel, *Four Essays*, 98.

109. Wang Keping, "Appreciating nature in view of practical aesthetics," *Frontiers of Philosophy in China* 2, no. 1 (2007), 141–44. Wang refers to Li's work: *Zhongguo Meixue Ji Gita* (A Note on Chinese Aesthetics and Other Matters) and to *Meixue Sijang* (Four Lectures on Aesthetics). Although Wang translates *xin* 心 as "mind," I prefer "heart-mind" to remind us to avoid over intellectualization.

110. Li mentions being disoriented by modern art, but his response may be conditioned by Maoist and Stalinist aesthetics. Some American responses to Socialist Realism may also be grounded on political attitudes. On the other hand, the horrible visions of Hieronymus Bosch (1450–1516), the grotesque and twisted Taihu Rocks in a Confucian scholar's garden and Bruce Nauman's video "Clown Torture" are works of art, but can only be described as ugly. The aesthetics of the ugly, however, are beyond the scope of this work.

111. Li Zehou, *The Path of Beauty*, 114

112. Li and Cauvel, *Four Essays*, 98. The distinction between aesthetic and scientific attention is analogous to Kant's distinction between determinate (scientific) and reflective (aesthetic and teleological) judgments.

113. Li and Cauvel, *Four Essays*, 109.

114. Li and Cauvel, *Four Essays*, 107.

115. Li and Cauvel, *Four Essays*, 105.

116. Li and Cauvel, *Four Essays*, 109, 104.

117. Terry Eagleton, *The Ideology of the Aesthetic* (Oxford: Basil Blackwell, 1990), 368.

118. Li Zehou, *Chinese Aesthetic*, 224.

119. For Li's views on the importance of Qu Yuan see Li Zehou, *Chinese Aesthetic*, 145–48.

120. Li and Cauvel, *Four Essays*, 57.

121. Li and Cauvel, *Four Essays*, 13, 57; Li Zehou, "Some Thoughts," 186; and Li Zehou, "Some Tentative Remarks on China's Wisdom (excerpts)," trans. Peter Wong Yih Ziun, ed. Li Zehou, *Contemporary Chinese Thought* 31, no 2 (Winter 1999–2000): 52.

122. Li and Cauvel, *Four Essays*, 13. The quotation is made in the context of a discussion of the "naturalization of humans." Daoist and Confucian sages are "naturalized humans" and the increasing naturalization of humans appears to be the goal of a post-industrialized society. Li finds contemporary interest in yoga, qi-gong and meditation part of this process. The naturalization of humans is discussed further in Li Zehou, *Chinese Aesthetic*, 88.

123. Li Zehou, *Chinese Aesthetic*, 58.

124. Li and Cauvel, *Four Essays*, 26, 121.

125. Plato, Hegel, and Kierkegaard are obvious examples, as is Kant's belief in the importance of the transcendent, noumenal world. In other traditions the doctrine of the Brahman-Atman and the Buddhist conceptions of Nirvana also appear to be "higher realities." Mark Woodhouse, "On the Possibility of Pure Consciousness," in *The Problem of Pure Consciousness: Mysticism and Philosophy*, ed. Robert K. C. Forman (New York and Oxford: Oxford University Press, 1990), 255.

126. Paul Tillich's definition of religion as an "ultimate concern" seems to cover both too little and too much. "Shielism" does not seem to be "ultimate" in any meaningful sense and a committed atheist dedicating her life to social justice would, rightly object to being called "religious." Thus "religion" appears to be what is called in another vocabulary an "empty signifier."

127. Anna Su, *Confucianism as a World Religion: Contested Histories and Contemporary Realities* (Princeton, NJ: Princeton University Press, 2013); and Henry Rosemont, "On the 'New Confucians,'" in *The Analects (Norton Critical Editions,* Michael Nylan, ed. (New York: W. W. Norton & Company, 2014), 259, 260, and 269.

128. A religious experience may be anything with a religious content, context or "flavor," including many "mystical experiences, religious visions and auditions, non-mystical Zen experiences, and various religious feelings, such as religious awe and sublimity . . . [and] the "feeling of 'absolute dependence.'" Jerome Gellman, "Mysticism," *The Stanford Encyclopedia of Philosophy* (Spring 2014), ed. Edward N. Zalta, http://plato.stanford.edu/archives/spr2014/entries/mysticism/.

129. John Dewey, *A Common Faith,* 2nd ed. (New Haven, CT: Yale University Press. 2013), 12–13.

130. Dewey, *Common Faith, 13.*

131. Rosemont, *Rationality*, 31.

132. Rosemont, *Rationality*, 31–33.

133. Rosemont, *Rationality*, 27–28.

134. Kant, *Critique of Practical Reason*, 166.

135. Steven Weinberg, *The First Three Minutes* (New York: Basic Books, 1993), 154–55.

136. Rosemont, *Rationality*, 40.

137. The notion of a "transcendent reality" and its relation to *sunyata* in Buddhism is extremely complex. Various forms of Buddhism make different metaphysical claims and the role of transcendent reality in the Buddhist tradition seems to differ at different times, schools, and places. Discussion of these issues is beyond the scope of this discussion.

138. Bertrand Russell, "Mysticism," in *Religion and Science* (London: Oxford University Press, 1935). Russell is writing about mystical experiences rather than spiritual ones; but as I will argue mystical experiences seem to be an extreme form of spiritual or religious experience.

139. Rosemont, *Rationality*, 31.

140. Mary Bockover made this claim in discussion at the annual meeting of the Society for Asian and Comparative Philosophy, July 2013.

141. These traditions include those grounded in a "correlative cosmology" such as much of Chinese thought, as well as certain strains of theology in the Abrahamic tradition. Hall and Ames argue that the Kantian notion of transcendence, which they identify as "strict transcendence" does not appear in Asian thought (Hall and Ames, *Thinking from the Han*, 190–93). Other writers, notably Robert Cummings Neville, disagree.

142. The difference between literal and metaphorical language, however, is not always as clear as one might think. See Donald Davidson, "What Metaphors Mean," in *The Philosophy of Language*, ed. A. P. Martinich (New York: Oxford University Press, 1996), 415–26.

143. Attempts to avoid discussing these troublesome facts by distinguishing "real Christians" or "real Moslems" from "crazy fundamentalists" tend to be circular.

144. William James, *The Varieties of Religious Experience* (New York: Longmans, Green & Co., 1902), lectures 16 and 17. Released by Project Gutenberg, 1996. http://www.gutenberg.org/cache/epub/621/pg621.html; W. T. Stace, *Mysticism and Philosophy* (Philadelphia and New York: J. B. Lippincott Company, 1960); Douglas W. Shrader, "Seven Characteristics of Mystical Experiences," in *Proceedings of the 6th Annual Hawaii International Conference on Arts and Humanities* (Honolulu, HI, 2008); and Harold D. Roth, "Bimodal mystical experience in the 'Qiwulun' 齊物論 chapter of Zhuangzi," *Journal of Chinese Religions* 28 (2009): 31–50. Although James thought mystical experiences had to be transitory, and could only last a short time, later writers noticed some mystical experiences may last quite a long time, a whole day or parts of it (Gellman, "Mysticism") and in some cases may even be permanent (Stace, *Mysticism and Philosophy*, 61).

145. Ludwig Wittgenstein, *Tractatus Logico-Philosophicus,* trans. C. K. Ogden and Frank P. Ramsey (London: Kegan Paul, 1922), Proposition 7.

146. Sam Hamill, trans. *Crossing the Yellow River: Three Hundred Poems from the Chinese* (Rochester, NY: BOA Editions, Ltd., 2000), 179.

147. See Robert K. S. Forman, "Introduction," to *The Problem of Pure Consciousness: Mysticism and Philosophy*, ed. Robert K. S. Forman (Oxford and New York: Oxford University Press, 1990); Michael A Sells, *Mystical Languages of Unsaying* (Chicago: University of Chicago Press, 1994). With respect to Wittgenstein and the ineffability of the mystical see B. F. McGinness, "The Mysticism of the 'Tractatus,'" *Philosophical Review* 75, no. 3 (July 1966): 305–28; and Cora Diamond, "'We Can't Whistle It Either': Legend and Reality," *European Journal of Philosophy* 19, no. 3 (2012):335–56.

148. Stace, *Mysticism and Philosophy*, 60–61.

149. Stace, *Mysticism and Philosophy*, 80–81.

150. Stace, *Mysticism and Philosophy*, 4, 63. Stace provides a detailed hierarchical typology of mystical experiences which culminates in the union with the infinite One. Stace himself notes that it is not always possible to tell into which of his categories a particular experience falls. Moreover, the categories often merge and overlap, and there are cases where an experience has some but not all of the characteristics of a particular category. Indeed, Stace, chapter 2, uses Wittgenstein's vocabulary of "borderline cases" and "family resemblances."

151. Zhuangzi, *Chuang-Tzu: The Basic Writings*, trans. Burton Watson (New York: Columbia University Press (1996), 31, 79, 86–87. The essays in Forman, ed. *The Problem of Pure Consciousness*, also describe a "subtracting away" of the contents of one's consciousness.

152. An insight I owe to Henry Rosemont. Moreover, considering Russell's view of mystical experiences, as analogous to seeing snakes, and the claim that certain drugs induce mystical experiences, descriptions of a "bad trip" on drugs sound like a more than unpleasant loss of ego.

153. Stace, *Mysticism and Philosophy*, 81.

154. Li and Cauvel, *Four Essays*, 121; Li, *Chinese Aesthetic*, 189.

155. Translation following Ronald Egan "Poet, Mind, and World," 110; and Liu Xie, *Dragon-Carving and the Literary Mind*, trans. Yang Guobin (Beijing: Foreign Language and Research Press, 2003), 379.

156. Li and Cauvel, *Four Essays*, 38. The phrase *yan wei zhi* resonates with Zhuangzi's desire to find someone who has forgotten words (Zhuangzi, *Chuang-Tzu*, 140), and with Wang Bi's *xuanxue* metaphysics. Tang Yijie, *Confucianism, Buddhism, Daoism, Christianity and Chinese Culture* (Peking: Council for Research in Values and Philosophy, 1991), http://books.goooble.com/books?id=ZnNveOjlJ8YC&pg.

157. Li and Cauvel, *Four Essays*, 121.

158. Rosemont, *Rationality*, 31.

159. Eliot Deutsch, *Essays on the Nature of Art* (Albany, NY: State University of New York Press, 1996), 99. Socrates's description in the *Symposium* of how one moves from appreciation of a beautiful object to a sense of being in the presence of Beauty itself, may be an early statement of this kind of religious experience.

160. Li Zehou, "Some Tentative Remarks," 51–52.

161. Li and Cauvel, *Four Essays*, 121. It might appear that the goal of Daoist meditation, described as the process of "sitting and forgetting" sensations, feelings, concepts, morality, even one's own body, making "the body like a withered tree and the mind like dead ashes" (Zhuangzi, *Chuang-Tzu*, 31) seems to be such a life denying process. Li insists, however, that while Zhuangzi's sage, or true man, is free of arbitrary social conventions and moral rules, he is still part of the natural world (Li Zehou, *Chinese Aesthetic*, chapter 3, "The Daoist-Confucian Synthesis"). Zhuangzi knows the fish are enjoying themselves because he and they are part of the same situation, the natural world and the beautiful day on the river Hao.

162. Li Zehou, *Chinese Aesthetic*, 42, 50.

163. Li and Cauvel *Four Essays,* 121–122.

164. Li Zehou, *Chinese Aesthetic*, 188. The difference may not be all that great since Li calls aesthetic experiences "quasi-religions" and restricts his understanding of religious experiences to the narrow sense—i.e., as making an ontological claim about the existence of transcendent realm.

165. Li Zehou, "Some Tentative Remarks," 52, 60.

166. Li Zehou, "Some Tentative Remarks," 59–62. China began to modernize in the Ming Dynasty (1368–1644), but the very conservative Qing Dynasty (1644–1912) hindered the process until the encounter with Western military and economic power made modernization necessary for China's survival. Li argues that the assimilation of Marx's conception of the humanization of nature changed the understanding of *tian ren he yi* from a quietist acceptance of the will of heaven into the active, energy required for a modern industry.

Chapter 3

1. Michael Tanner, "Sentimentality," in *Art and Morality,* ed. José Luis Bermúdez and Sebastian Gardner (Routledge: London and New York, 2003), 109.

2. A. B. Griswold, "Prolegomena to the Study of the Buddha's Dress in Chinese Sculpture: With Particular Reference to the Rietberg Museum's Collection,"*Artibus Asiae* 26, no. 2 (1963): 85, 98–99.

3. Katherine Tsiang, "Changing patterns of divinity and reform in the late Northern Wei," *The Art Bulletin* 84, no. 2 (June, 2002): 222.

4. Tsiang, "Changing patterns," 226. This similarity attests to the regular contacts between northern and southern monasteries and imperial courts.

5. Li Zehou, *The Path of Beauty*, 114.

6. Li Zehou, *The Path of Beauty*, 114.

7. Finbarr Barry Flood, "Between Cult and Culture: Bamiyan, Islamic Iconoclasm, and the Museum," *The Art Bulletin* 84, no. 4 (December 2002): 653, quoting Alfred Gell.

8. Eliot Deutsch, *Essays on the Nature of Art* (Albany, NY: State University of New York Press, 1996), 98. Mystical experiences are the only religious experience Deutsch identifies. The relationship between mystical, religious, spiritual, and aesthetic experiences is discussed in detail in chapter 2.

9. Deutsch, *Essays*, 91.

10. Deutsch, *Essays*, 99.

11. Deutsch, *Essays*, 91. (Italics in the original.)

12. The most famous of these caves are the Yungang caves in Datong, Shanxi Province; the Binglingsi caves near Lanzhou in Gansu Province; the Longmen caves south of Luoyang, Henan Province; and the Mogao Caves near Dunhuang in Gansu Province.

13. Li Zehou, *The Path of Beauty*, 129.

14. Li considered "Confucianism" to be a practical attitude, reflecting what Hall and Ames call a correlative cosmology, rather than a commitment to any particular set of Confucian virtues. See chapter 2 for details.

15. Li Zehou, *The Path of Beauty*, 107.

16. Mao Zedong, "Yenan Forum on Literature and Art" in *Selected Works of Mao Tse-tung*, vol. 3 (Peking: Foreign Languages Press, 1967), 69–98. Marx tried to distinguish genuinely socialist art from "poster and slogan" pastiches; but in practice official Chinese art often degenerated into ham fisted and boring didactics.

17. What of the occasions when we appreciate an artwork that is still playing a role in a religious ritual? Being a tourist in a church or temple during the celebration of a religious rite probably *should* make us uneasy. Our human concern for the practitioners whose ceremonies we are observing is in conflict with the attempt to observe the art work as "art for art's sake."

18. The story of the Elgin marbles may be the most famous case; but Peter Hopkirk, *Foreign Devils on the Silk Road* (Amherst: The University of Massachusetts Press, 1983) and James Clifford, "Four Northwest Coast Museums: Travel Reflections" in *Exhibiting Cultures: The Poetics and Politics of Museum Display*, ed. Ivan Karp and Steven D. Lavine (Washington, DC: Smithsonian Institution Press, 1991) tell similar stories. Chapter 4, "The Meaning of 'Horse'" will explore the relationship between art, politics, war and conquest.

19. By the Tang dynasty, cave paintings were peaceful, colorful depictions of Buddhist heavens and ordinary life in China. Roderick Whitfield, *Dunhuang: Caves of the Singing Sands: Buddhist Art from the Silk Road* (London: Textile & Art Publications, 1995) contains photographs of the Dunhuang murals depicting the sacrifice of the prince.

20. An excellent place to begin a study of Buddhism is Stephen J. Laumakis, *An Introduction to Buddhist Philosophy* (Cambridge: Cambridge University Press, 2008) and Peter D. Hershock, *Chan Buddhism* (Honolulu: University of Hawai'i Press, 2005). The classic source for the story of the impact of Buddhism on China is Erik Zürcher, *The Buddhist Conquest of China* (Leiden: E. J. Brill. 1959).

21. The appearance of this particular style of Buddhist statue in both northern and southern China at almost the same time has been taken by some scholars to indicate that the "barbarian" Wei must have borrowed it from the Han southerners. This belief probably reflects the prejudice of the Han elite against "foreign barbarians." Other scholars think it indicates continuing communication between Buddhist monasteries and sites throughout the period. Statues and murals in northern caves and grottos were also probably far better preserved from destruction by war, erosion, and theft by looters than they were in more accessible sites.

22. Philippe Koutouzis, "Introduction," to *Body & Nature: Two Chinese Artists*, ed. Wang Kęping, and Jeng Jundian (New York: Marlborough Chelsea, 2004), 2.

23. Michael Loewe, *Ways to Paradise: The Chinese Quest for Immortality* (London: George Allen & Unwin, 1979); Maurice Cotterell, *The Terracotta Warriors: The Secret Codes of the Emperor's Army* (Rochester, VT: Bear & Company, 2004); Suzanne E. Cahill, *Transcendence & Divine Passion: The Queen Mother of the West in Medieval China* (Redwood City, CA: Stanford University Press, 1993); and Wu Hung, "Where are they going? Where did they come from: Hearse and 'Soul-carriage' in Han Dynasty Tomb Art," *Orientation* 29, no. 6 (1998). The idea that Shi Huangdi was trying to escape his enemies was suggested by Steve Goldberg in an informal lecture given to the China Field Trip: On the Silk Road (sponsored by the East-West Center, in Xian, Shaanxi Province, China, July 1997).

24. Ning Qiang, "The Emergence of the 'Dunhuang Style' in the Northern Wei Dynasty," *Orientations* 23, no 5 (May, 1992): 47. Material accompanying slides of these statues purchased in China in 1997 point out the Han influence. Essays published in the West focus on the Indian and Gandharan influences.

25. Du Jiwen, "The Multi-ethnic Character of Chinese Buddhism," in *Buddhist Studies in the People's Republic of China*, trans. and ed. Michael R. Saso (Tendai Educational Foundation: Honolulu,1992); and David A. Utz, "Aršak, Parthian Buddhists, and 'Iranian' Buddhism" in *Buddhism Across Boundaries—Chinese Buddhism and the Western Regions*, ed. John R. McRae and Jan Nattier (Fo Guang Shan Foundation for Buddhist and Culture Education, 1999). The earliest Chinese versions of Buddhist texts are hundreds of years earlier than the Indian Siddham Sanskrit versions, suggesting that they were formulated in Central Asia or near the Gandharan kingdom with its close ties to Greek civilization and philosophy

26. Rajeshwari Ghose, "The Meeting of Minds: Buddhism as a Cross-Cultural Discourse," in *In the Footsteps of the Buddha: An Iconic Journey from India to China*, ed. Rajeswari Ghose (Hong Kong: University Museum and Art Gallery of the University of Hong Kong, 1998), 12.

27. The Ming dynasty novel *Journey to the West* by Wu Cheng'en describes these dangers in great detail, albeit in a fictional fantasy form. Hopkirk, *Foreign Devils* describes the dangers faced centuries later by Western explorers.

28. Du, "The Multi-ethnic," 23.

29. Zenryu Tsukamoto, *A History of Early Chinese Buddhism from Its Introduction to the Death of Hui-yüan*, trans. Leon Hurvitz (Tokyo, New York, San Franscso: Kodansha International Ltd., 1985), 42.

30. Tsukamoto, *A History*, 47.

31. Richard B. Mather, "Chinese and Indian Perceptions of Each Other between the First and Seventh Centuries," *Journal of the American Oriental Society* 112, no. 1 (1992).

32. Tsukamoto, *A History*, 60, quoting from the *Hou Han shu* (*History of the Later Han*).

33. Zürcher, *The Buddhist Conquest*, 39–40. Given the practical cast to Chinese thought described in chapter 2, it is not surprising that the first translations of the languages of Central Asia into Chinese were undertaken for political and military reasons. When the Han empire expanded into Central Asia in the last decades of the second century BCE, its Department of Foreign Relations developed a phonetic translation system that broke foreign words apart, often at random, into syllabic units and assigned little used Chinese characters to syllables solely on the basis of phonetic values, with no regard at all to the semantic content of the characters.

34. Robert Hans van Gulik, *Siddham: An Essay on the History of Sanskrit Studies in China and Japan* (Nagpur: International Academy of Indian Culture, 1956), 11.

35. Zürcher, *The Buddhist Conquest*, 33. The earliest important missionary translator was An Shigao. Tradition tells us he was a prince from Parthia, in northeast Iran, who abandoned his title for the religious life. An Shigao arrived in Luoyang, the capital of the Eastern Han Dynasty (25–220), in 148 CE and

worked for more than twenty years at Loyang where he organized one of the first translation teams.

36. Zürcher, *The Buddhist Conquest*, 31.

37. Zürcher, *The Buddhist Conquest*, 58–59.

38. Arthur F. Wright, "Buddhism and Chinese Culture," in *Studies in Chinese Buddhism*, ed. Robert M. Sommers (New Haven, CT, and London: Yale University Press, 1990), 8. Wright presents a particularly intelligible comparison of the two.

39. Zürcher, *The Buddhist Conquest*, 203.

40. Zürcher, *The Buddhist Conquest*, 33.

41. Tang Yung-tung, "On 'Ko-yi,' The Earliest Method by which Indian Buddhism and Chinese Thought Were Synthesized" in *Radhakrishnan: Comparative Studies in Philosophy* (New York: Harper, 1951), 280.

42. Zürcher, *The Buddhist Conquest*, 1984; See Victor H. Mair, "What is *Geyi*, After All?" in *Philosophy and Religion in Early Medieval China*, ed. Alan K. L. Chan (Albany, NY: State University of New York Press, 2010), 227–29. Mair argues that "matching concepts" is a bad translation of "*geyi*," one that has mislead generations of scholars into irrelevant philosophical speculations about translation. Mair claims that *geyi* has nothing to do with translation. While "concepts" or "meanings" are adequate translations of *yi*, Mair argues that *ge* means nothing at all like "matching" or "pairing." Instead he notes: "Perhaps the easiest way to think of how these fundamental [philological] facets of *ge* relate to the problem of *geyi* is to visualize a set of pigeonholes and contemplate its function as a device for the classification of discrete items. From classifications, it is only a short step to categorizations, which is precisely what the *ge* of *geyi* signifies." This history of Western understandings of *geyi* demonstrates how translation issues continue to bedevil understanding.

43. For example, see Anna Sun, *Confucianism as a World Religion: Contested Histories and Contemporary Realities* (Princeton, NJ: Princeton University Press, 2013).

44. In 304 the Northern tribes rebelled and the fragmentation of northern China known as the Era of Sixteen Kingdoms began (304–439). See David A. Graff, *Medieval Chinese Warfare, 300–900* (London and New York: Routledge, 2002); Thomas J Barfield, *The Perilous Frontier: Nomadic Empires and China* (Cambridge, MA: Blackwell, 1989); and Marylin Martin Rhie, *Early Buddhist Art of China & Central Asia.* Volume 2 (London, Boston, Lieden, Köln: Brill, 2002) for details about Chinese-nomad relations in this fascinating period.

45. Lao-Tzu [Laozi], *Tao Te Ching* [*Daodejing*], trans. Stephen Addiss and Stanley Lombardo (Indianapolis, IN: Hackett Publishing Company, 1993).

46. Zürcher, *The Buddhist Conquest*, 90.

47. Tang Yung-tung, "On 'Ko-yi,'" 286.

48. Tanag Yung-tung, "On 'Ko-yi,'" 284–85

49. Zürcher, *The Buddhist Conquest*, 191, 200–03.

50. Tsukamoto, *A History*, 770.

51. Tang Yijie. *Confucianism, Buddhism, Daoism, Christianity and Chinese Culture* (Peking: Council for Research in Values and Philosophy, 1991), 115, http://books.google.com/books?id=ZnNveOjlJ8YC&pg.

52. Yang Lu, "Narrative and Historicity in the Buddhist Biographies of Early Medieval China: The Case of Kumarajiva," accessed December 20, 2013, http://www2.ihp.sinica.edu.tw/file/1464kwiaSfk.pdf. Despite Kumārajīva's reputation as a translator, his translations have been criticized for having been abbreviated to the extent of distorting the originals. He may have been appealing to a Chinese sense of literary style, but he may also have been working from texts that were less elaborate than the ones his critics were using.

53. Zürcher, *The Buddhist Conquest,* 207, 229; Du, "The Multi-ethnic," 26, 41. Zürcher (*The Buddhist Conquest,* 227–29) provides an insightful summary of the fascinating correspondence and debate between Huiyuan and Kumārajīva.

54. Arthur F. Wright, "Fo-t'u-teng: A Biography," *Harvard Journal of Asiatic Studies* 11, no. 3/4 (December, 1948): 336.

55. Zürcher sees no evidence that Fotudeng had any particular skills as a translator or exegete nor do any of his close disciples suggest that he was a particularly great teacher (*The Buddhist Conquest*, 183).

56. Zürcher, *The Buddhist Conquest*, 146.

57. Arthur F. Wright, *Buddhism in Chinese History* (Redwood City, CA: Stanford University Press, 1959), 59.

58. Graff, *Medieval Chinese*, 60.

59. Charles Holcombe, *A History of East Asia: From the Origins of Civilization to the Twenty-First Century* (New York: Cambridge University Press, 2011), 65.

60. Tsukamoto, *A History*, 41.

61. Tsukamoto, *A History*, 90.

62. Wright, *Buddhism in Chinese*, 60; Tsukamoto, *A History*, 76; and Daniel L. Overmyer, *Folk Buddhist Religion: Dissenting Sects in Late Traditional China* (Cambridge, MA: Harvard University Press, 1976), 19.

63. Jacques Gernet, *Buddhism in Chinese Society: An Economic History from the Fifth to the Tenth Centuries*, trans. Franciscus Verellen (New York: Columbia University Press, 1995). Provides details of the often troubled relationship between the increasingly powerful and wealthy Buddhist monasteries and the imperial government. Wright, *Buddhism in Chinese*; Tsukamoto, *A History*; and Amy McNair, *Donors of Longmen: Faith, Politics, and Patronage in Medieval Chinese Buddhist Sculpture* (Honolulu: University of Hawai'i Press, 2007) describe Taiwu's persecutions.

64. Although the east wall was thoroughly destroyed by looters, it has been reconstructed and parts of it are housed in the Nelson Atkins Museum in Kansas City, Missouri, and the Metropolitan Museum of Art in New York City. Details of how the museums obtained sections of the wall provide a fascinating account of the relationships between looters and museum curators. McNair, *Donors of Long-*

men, 42–43, describes the process by which the museums obtained their sections of the wall and calls the New York case, with some justification, "premeditated international art theft."

65. McNair, *Donors of Longmen*, 50.

66. This famous debate is discussed in chapter 5.

67. Which particular Empress and Emperor are being honored, however, are matters of some debate. McNair, *Donors of Longmen*, 43–44.

68. McNair, *Donors of Longmen*, 40–48.

69. Graff, *Medieval Chinese*, 101.

70. Li and Cauvel, *Four Essays*, 104. The precise nature of aesthetic pleasure is complex and Li's discussions of it may not always be consistent, although he does say it is impossible to describe it in words.

71. Li and Cauvel, *Four Essays*, 104–05; 110–12.

72. Religious experiences in the narrow sense identified in chapter 2 entail this commitment. If religious experiences are described without referring to, or making ontological claims about, a Transcendent realm of the Sacred (or God), they are indistinguishable from those Rosemont (*Rationality and Religious Experience*) calls spiritual experiences. The relationship between religious, spiritual, and aesthetic experiences is discussed in chapter 2.

73. See chapter 2 for details of Li's theory of historical sedimentation.

74. Li and Cauvel, *Four Essays*, 162.

75. Li and Cauvel, *Four Essays*, 121.

76. Li and Cauvel, *Four Essays,* 163.

77. There are, however, many people who do not find the idea of immortality at all comforting. The sentiment is expressed in Swinburne's poem "From too much love of living . . ." and in Jan Łukasiewicz's hope that the effects of a particular cause may someday be overcome and disappear into mere possibility (Jan Łukasiewicz, *Z Zagadnien Logiki I Filozofi* [Problems of Logic and Philosophy]), 126. Passage translated by Peter Geach and quoted by Arthur Prior, *Past, Present and Future*, Oxford at the Clarendon Press, 1967, p. 28.). The hope that "in the end" everyone I love and everything I care about will be safe and at peace—because they will be completely gone, and Socrates's thought that death might be a great dreamless sleep, expresses something close to a rejection of the comfort of immortality.

78. Another function of religious institutions is to provide intellectual pleasure for elites interested in theology.

79. Lillian Daniel, "Spiritual But Not Religious? Please Stop Boring Me." *Huffpost Religion Blog.* Posted September 13, 2011. Updated November 13, 2011. http://www.huffingtonpost.com/lillian-daniel/spiritual-but-not-religio_b_959216.html.

The contemporary phenomenon known as "Spiritual but Not Religious" is quite complicated. See Mark Oppenheimer, "Examining the Growth of the

'Spiritual but Not Religious,'" *New York Times* July 18, 2014, http://www.nytimes.com/2014/07/19/us/examining-the-growth-of-the-spiritual-but-not-religious, for a relatively balanced introduction to the topic.

80. Quoted in chapter 2.

81. Li and Cauvel, *Four Essays*, 75. The authors seem quite heartened by the appearance of these practices in contemporary American life.

Chapter 4

1. Maxwell K. Hearn, *How to Read Chinese Painting* (New Haven, CT, and London: The Metropolitan Museum of Art, 2008), 5.

2. Li Chu-Tsing, "The Freer *Sheep and Goat* and Chao Meng-Fu's Horse Paintings," *Artibus Asiae* 30, no. 4 (1968), 300; Suzanne Cahill, "Night Shining White," *Tang Studies* 4 (1986), 93. Cahill argues that Night-Shining White was being trained as one of the emperor's famous dancing horses.

3. Chang Willow Weilan Hai, Yang Renkai, and David Ake Sensabaugh, *The Last Emperor's Collection: Masterpieces of Painting and Calligraphy from the Liaoning Provincial Museum* (New York: China Institute, 2008), 2; Metropolitan Museum of Art's website, "Night Shining White," *The Collection On line,* http://www.metmuseum.org/collection/the-collection-online/search/3990; and Hearn, *How to Read,* 3–7. These texts present details of the painting's history and provenance.

4. Hillary Putnam, "The Meaning of 'Meaning,'" in *The Twin Earth Chronicles*, ed. Andrew Pessin and Sanford Goldberg (Armonk, NY: M. E. Sharpe, 1996), 3–52.

5. As abstract entities, cognitive contents are related conceptually and historically to Plato's Ideas (*eidos*) or Forms. Catherine Fruhan points out that art historians generally discuss these topics using the alternative vocabulary of semiotics.

6. This view appears in the writings of Frege and the Wittgenstein of the *Tractatus;* it also has much in common with structuralism in linguistics.

7. The distinction between cognitive and emotive contents is close to (if not identical with) the distinction between denotation and connotation.

8. Putnam, "The Meaning," 25.

9. Putnam, "The Meaning," 49.

10. Putnam's argument relies, roughly, on the intuition that no matter what other people call it; water is, was, and always will be H_2O. Putnam's philosophy is obviously more complex and sophisticated than my remarks indicate.

11. Eliot Deutsch, *Essays on the Nature of Art* (Albany, NY: State University of New York Press, 1996), 84–85. Deutsch believes that works of art have an aesthetic content, although he acknowledges that the definition of art is always culture bound.

12. Arthur Danto, *The Philosophical Disenfranchisement of Art* (New York: Columbia University Press, 1986), ix. Danto argues, however, that this image must be abandoned since there is no such timeless power.

13. Deutsch, *Essays*, 84.

14. Deutsch, *Essays*, 82.

15. Maureen Mullarkey, "Mullarkey Replies," *The Nation* March 6, 1989, 320. Mullarkey's views are often considered extreme and controversial.

16. Deutsch, *Essays*, 84.

17. Arthur Danto, "The Artworld," *Journal of Philosophy* 61 (1964), 581 originally described the art world as made up of people who know a great deal of art theory and history. Danto, *The Philosophical Disenfranchisement,* xxvi–xxvii and 108–09, later suggested that the most important members of this world were the collectors, critics and curators active in the "art scene" located in Paris in the first half of the twentieth century; and in New York after the Second World War.

Robert J. Yanal, "The Institutional Theory of Art," in *The Encyclopedia of Aesthetics*, ed. Michael Kelly (Oxford University Press, 1998) describes the development of the Institutional View of Art by George Dickie from remarks by Danto. Yanal also discusses the relationship between Dickie's theory and Danto's work, and the evolving understanding of the membership of the art world.

18. John Dewey, *Art as Experience* (New York: Penguin Putnam Inc., 1934), 6, noted this phenomena.

19. Mullarkey, "Mullarkey," 320.

20. The vast amounts of money provided for scientific research by large pharmaceutical companies may tend to erode popular faith in science.

21. In what follows I will use the phrases "aesthetic content," "aesthetic meaning," and "meaning of a work of art" interchangeably with the understanding that while the "representational content" and "emotive content" may contribute to the meaning of a work of art, this meaning cannot be identified or reduced to its representational or emotive content.

22. Michael D. Gunther, "Old Old Stones: The Monuments of Art History." www.art-and-archaeology.com. This article contains an image of the funeral banner; see "Funeral Banner of Lady Dai," http://www.art-and-archaeology.com/china/hunan/pm02.html.

23. James Cahill, "Confucian Elements in the Theory of Painting," in *The Confucian Persuasion*, ed. Arthur F. Wright (Redwood City, CA: Stanford University Press, 1960), 117.

24. Interpretations of the Six Laws will be discussed below.

25. *I Ching* [*Yijing*], trans. Richard Wilhelm; rendered into English by Cary F. Baynes, 3rd ed. (Princeton, NJ: Princeton University Press 1967), 273.

26. *I Ching* [*Yijing*], 275.

27. *Book of Songs: Shijing*, trans. Arthur Waley (New York: Grove Press, 1996).

28. Arthur Waley, "The Heavenly Horses of Ferghana: A New View." *History Today* 5, no. 2 (February, 1955), 97.

29. Robert E. Harrist, Jr., "The Legacy of Bole: Physiognomy and Horses in Chinese Painting," *Artibus Asiae* 57, no. 1/2 (1997), 136.

30. Madeline K. Spring, *Animal Allegories in T'ang China* (New Haven, CT: American Oriental Society, 1993), 107–08.

31. Harrist, "The Legacy," 139, 150.

32. This tomb is described in chapter 3.

33. One could accuse Goldberg of "bad faith," of confusing/reducing his aesthetic conscience with his social conscience, but it would be more appropriate to interpret his remark as the sort of immediate response: "That's not beautiful," of the aesthetic attitude, which begins the process of forming an aesthetic judgment. On the other hand, Goldberg's judgment is consistent with Kant's theory of "aesthetic judgments" in which the utility of this chariot would mean that it was not an example of "pure beauty," but only "dependently" beautiful. See chapter 2 for discussion of these issues.

34. Sima Qian, *Records of the Grand Historian: Han Dynasty Volume II.* Rev, ed, trans. Burton Watson (Hong Kong and New York: Columbia University Press, 1992), 63.

35. Lin Ying, *Celestial Horses: The Apogee of Chinese Art and Civilization* (Beijing: Foreign Language Press 2002), 35, 49.

36. Homer H. Dubs, trans., *The History of the Former Han Dynasty by Pan Ku (Ban Gu): A Critical Translation with Annotation*, vol. 2 (Baltimore: Waverly, 1938–55), 132–33.

37. Thomas J. Barfield, *The Perilous Frontier: Nomadic Empires and China* (Cambridge, MA: Blackwell, 1989), 139–42. The older son of Li Shimin, the second Tang emperor, showed a decided preference for Turkish music, lifestyle, and customs. One of those customs, that of terrorizing his citizens and murdering people who offended him, so outraged the Confucian Chinese that they insisted he was unfit to rule. When he plotted to overthrow his father, Li Shimin agreed and sent him into exile.

38. Lin, *Celestial Horses*, 116–18; and Bill Cooke, ed., *Imperial China: The Art of the Horse in Chinese History* (Lexington, KY: Exhibition Catalogue, Kentucky Horse Park, 2000), 52–53, tell the tragic story of the dancing horses.

39. Cooke, *Imperial China*, 48; and Beckwith, Christopher I., "The Impact of the Horse and Silk Trade on the Economies of T'ang China and the Uighur Empire," *Journal of the Economic and Social History of the Orient* 34, no. 2 (1991): 185–90 discuss the Tang horses and the Dynasty's relationship with the nomads who supplied most of them.

40. Edwin G. Pulleyblank, "Liu K'o, a Forgotten Rival of Han Yu," in *Essays on Tang and pre-Tang China* (Burlington, VT, Singapore, Sidney: Ashgate, 2001), 160.

41. Du Fu, "Song of a Painting," in *An Anthology of Chinese Literature: Beginning to 1911,* trans. and ed. Stephen Owen (New York: W. W. Norton & Company, 1996), 429–31.

42. Joseph J. Lee, "Tu Fu's Art Criticism and Han Kan's Horse painting," *Journal of the American Oriental Society* 90 no. 3 (July–Sept. 1970), 455–57.

43. Du Fu, "On Seeing a Horse-painting by Ts'ao Pa in the House of Recorder Wei Feng" and "A Song of Painting: To General Ts'ao Pa," in *A Little Primer of Tu Fu*, trans. and ed. David Hawkes (Oxford: Clarendon Press, 1967), 138–55.

44. Li Chu-Tsing, "The Freer *Sheep and Goat*," 300. Zhao Mengfu wrote this poem about the painting *Five Horses* by Li Gonglin (ca. 1040–1106) who continued the tradition of Han Gan.

45. I do not mean to suggest that all, or even most of the Renaissance artists and scientists held the same conscious and coherent philosophical theory. Leonardo da Vinci, for example, was far more concerned with scientific accuracy than with any Platonic Ideal of beauty. It is also significant that the scientific revolution began the conquest of nature, including the conquest of the Amerindians—another site of conflict between empires and nomads on horseback.

46. Richard M. Barnhardt, et al., *Three Thousand Years of Chinese Painting* (New Haven, CT, and London: Yale University Press, 1977), 79.

47. Arthur Danto, *The Philosophical disenfranchisement of Art* (New York: Columbia University Press, 1986), 206. Danto admits that this is only one way of telling the story of the history of (Western) art. Walter Benjamin, "The Work of Art in the Age of Mechanical Reproduction," Marxist Internet Archive (Feb. 2006). http://www.marxists.org/reference/subject/philosophy/works/ge/benjamin.htm. (First published in 1936) also discusses the impact of cinema on the development of art.

48. Danto, *The Philosophical*, 180.

49. Danto, *The Philosophical*, 209. Danto's views are controversial but have been quite influential.

50. Wen C. Fong, "Why Chinese Painting is History," *The Art Bulletin* 85, no. 2 (June 2003), 259.

51. Jerome Silbergeld, "Commentary on James Cahill's 'Chinese Art and Authenticity,'" *American Academy of Arts and Sciences Bulletin* 55, no. 1 (Fall 2001), 35.

52. Fong, "Why Chinese Painting," 259.

53. Danto, *The Philosophical*, 180.

54. Fong, "Why Chinese Painting," 259.

55. Wen C. Fong, "The Modern Chinese Art Debate," *Artibus Asiae* 53, no. 1/2 (1993): 290–305 and *Between Two Cultures: Late-Nineteenth and Twentieth-Century Chinese Paintings from the Robert H. Ellsworth Collection in the Metropolitan Museum of Art* (New York: Metropolitan Museum of Art. 2001).

56. Gao Jianping, *The Expressive Act in Chinese Art: From Calligraphy to Painting* (Stockholm, Uppsala, Sweden: Uppsala University, 1996), 120–21.

57. Gao, *The Expressive Act*, 125.

58. Susan Bush and Hsio-yen Shih, ed. *Early Chinese Texts on Painting* (Cambridge, MA: Harvard University Pres, 1985), 110.

59. Chen Jiang Hong, *The Magic Horse of Han Gan*, trans. Claudia Zoe Bedrick (Brooklyn, NY: Enchanted Lion Books, 2006).

60. This aspect of the critical tradition explains some of the controversies in the interpretation of Xie He's "Six Laws of Painting." There are a number of scholarly articles about these laws including W. R. B. Acker, *Some T'ang and Pre-Tang texts on Chinese painting* (Leiden: E. J. Brill, 1954); James Cahill, "The Six Laws and How to Read Them." *Ars Orientalis* 4 (1961), 372–81; James Cahill, "Good Grief, Not the Six Laws Again! (*Ching Yuan Chai So-shih 4*)," *The Writings of James Cahill*, http://jamescahill.info/; Alexander Soper, "The First Two Laws of Hsieh Ho," *Far Eastern Quarterly* 8 (1949), 412–23; Victor H. Mair, "Xie He's 'Six Laws' of Painting and Their Indian Parallels," in *Chinese Aesthetics: The Ordering of Literature, the Arts, and the Universe in the Six Dynasties*, ed. Cai Zong-qi (Honolulu: University of Hawai'i Press, 2004), 81–122.

61. Lee, "Tu Fu's Art Criticism," 452.

62. This is the first of Xie He's "Six Laws of Painting."

63. Cai Zong-qi, *Configurations of Comparative Poetics: Three Perspectives on Western and Chinese Literary Criticism* (Honolulu: University of Hawai'i Press, 2001), 39.

64. Franklin Perkins, "Motivation and the Heart in the Xing Zi Chu" *Dao: A Journal of Comparative Philosophy* 8 (June 2009): 117–31; Tang Yijie. "Emotion in pre-Qin Ruist Moral Theory: An Explanation of "Dao Begins in Qing,"" trans. Brian Bruya and Hai-ming Wen, *Philosophy East and West* 53, no. 2 (April 2003): 271–81; Cai, *Configurations of Comparative Poetics;* Roger T. Ames and David L. Hall, *Focusing the Familiar: A Translation and Philosophical Interpretation of the "Zhongyong"* (Honolulu: University of Hawai'i Press, 2001); and Chad Hansen, "Qing (Emotions) 情 in Pre-Buddhist Chinese Thought," in *Emotions in Asian Thought: A Dialogue in Comparative Philosophy*, eds. Joel Marks and Roger T. Ames (Albany, NY: State University of New York Press, 1995): 181–203. The historical development and metaphysical implications of the relationship between *zhi* and *qing* are complex and often contested. Some of the issues involved are discussed in the texts cited above and in chapter 1.

65. Bush and Shih, ed., *Early Chinese Text*, 203.

66. Bush and Shih, ed., *Early Chinese Texts*, 207.

67. Bush and Shih, ed., *Early Chinese Texts*, 224.

68. Bush and Shih, ed., *Early Chinese Texts*, 225.

69. Ames and Hall, *Focusing the Familiar*, 89–90.

70. Bush and Shih, ed., *Early Chinese Texts*, 208.

71. Bush and Shih, ed., *Early Chinese Texts*, 201.

72. "Gong Kai," *Wikipedia, The Free Encyclopedia*, http://en.wikipedia.org/wiki/Gong_Kai (3 November 2014).

73. Li Chu-Tsing, "The Freer *Sheep and Goat*," 306

74. Soper, "The First Two Laws," 422. The phrase "*qi yun*" is part of the First Law of Painting.

75. Li Chu-Tsing, "The Freer *Sheep and Goat*," 312–313.

76. In yet another chapter in the history of the relationship between China and foreign invaders, two of these stone horses now belong to and are displayed in the Pennsylvania Museum of Art in Philadelphia. This Chinese government would like them to be returned.

77. Lin Ying, *Celestial Horses*, 165.

78. Jonathan Hay, "Kubilai's Grooms," *Res: A Journal of Anthropology and Aesthetics* 17 & 18 (Spring, Autumn 1989), 133.

79. Hay, "Kubilai's Grooms," 119.

80. Hay, "Kubilai's Grooms," 120.

81. Hay, "Kubilai's Grooms," 120–21. To support his claim Hay provides a copy of the painting with the relevant circles drawn over the figures.

82. Hay, "Kubilai's Grooms," 123, 128.

83. Ames and Hall, *Focusing the Familiar*, 114.

84. Lao-Tzu [Laozi], *Tao Te Ching* [*Daodejing*], trans. Stephen Addiss and Stanley Lombardo (Indianapolis, IN: Hackett Publishing Company, 1993), 35. (Translation slightly modified.)

85. Li Zehou, *Chinese Aesthetic*, xiv.

86. Li Zehou, *Chinese Aesthetic*, 177.

87. LI Zehou, *Chinese Aesthetic*, 178.

88. LI Zehou, *Chinese Aesthetic*, 174–75.

89. Li Zehou, *Chinese Aesthetics*, xiv.

90. Hay, "Kubilai's Grooms," 138.

91. Hay, "Kubilai's Grooms," 138.

92. *Lean Horse and Fat Horse* by Ren Renfa is in the collection of The Palace Museum in Beijing. The website Art History Sisters (blog), "Attribution Problem Assessment," May 14, 2013, http://arthistorygeeks.tumblr.com/post/50419776636/attribution-problem-assessment-when-first, contains an excellent image of this painting.

93. Sung Hou-mei, *Decoded Messages: The Symbolic Language of Chinese Animal Painting* (New Haven, CT: Yale University Press, 2009), 187.

94. Barnhardt, et al., *Three Thousand Years*, 141.

95. Barnhardt, et al., *Three Thousand* Years, 172.

96. Li Zehou, *The Path of Beauty*, 210. Whether and how China actually began to "modernize" in the Ming is somewhat controversial involving the relationship between "modernization" and capitalism.

97. Ray Huang, *China: A Macro History.* Rev. ed. (Armonk, NY: M. E. Sharpe, Inc., 1997), 202–05

98. Li Zehou, *The Path of Beauty*, 221.

99. Marshall P. S. Wu, *The Orchid Pavilion Gathering: Chinese Painting from the University of Michigan Museum of Art*, vol. 1 (Ann Arbor, University of Michigan, 2000), 243.

100. Wu, *The Orchid Pavilion*, vol. 1, 243–44.

101. Wu, *The Orchid Pavilion*, vol. 1, 245, 310. See Wu, vol. 2, 148 for more on Jin Nong's attitude.

102. Wu, *The Orchid Pavilion*, vol. 2, 144.

103. Wu, *The Orchid Pavilion*, vol. 1, 310.

104. Li Zehou, *The Chinese Aesthetic*, 202.

105. Barnhardt, et al., *Three Thousand Years*, 191; National Palace Museum Staff (*Guo li gu gong bo wu yuan*), *Special Exhibition of Horse Painting* (Taibei: Government publication, 1990). These texts present a number of traditional horse paintings including several titled *One Hundred Horses.* The use of perspective in Chinese painting, and Western misunderstanding of it, is discussed in Fong, "Why Chinese Painting," and David Hockney, "A Day on the Grand Canal."

106. One critic has argued, however, that the placement of the human guardians of the horses in *One Hundred Horses* at either end of the scroll, as well as the way the one or two aged horses in the picture are being "invited" to join the herd, is an attempt to flatter the emperor by portraying him as caring for his citizens.

107. Michael Sullivan, *The Arts of China*, 5th ed. (Berkeley: Ahmanson Murphy Fine Arts Imprint, University of California Press, 2008), 262–63; Barnhardt, et al., *Three Thousand Years*, 190.

108. Sullivan, *The Arts*, 262–63.

109. Barnhardt, et al., *Three Thousand Years*, 203.

110. Michael Sullivan, *Art and Artists of Twentieth Century China* (Berkeley: University of California Press, 1996), 68.

111. Wen C. Fong, *Between Two Cultures: Late-Nineteenth- and Twentieth-Century Chinese Paintings from the Robert H. Ellsworth Collection in the Metropolitan Museum of Art* (New York: Metropolitan Museum of Art, 2001), 89.

112. Sullivan, *Art and Artists*, 72.

113. Sullivan, *Art and Artists*, 71; Shao Yiyang, "Why Realism? From Social Realism to Neo-Realism in Modern Chinese Art (Part I)," CAFA Art Info 25 (October 2011), http://en.cafa.com.cn/why-realism-from-social-realism-to-neo-realism-in-modern-chinese-art-part-i.html. The story of how Chinese artists adopted Socialist Realism is complicated and owed at least as much to the wood cuts of Lu Xun as it did to the influence of Soviet Russia.

114. Sullivan, *The Arts*, 398–99.

115. Sullivan, *Art and Artists*, 71.

116. Sullivan, *Art and Artists*, 68, 72.

117. Fong, *Between Two Cultures*, 97.

118. Barnhardt, et al., *Three Thousand Years*, 321.

119. Sullivan, *Art and Artists*, 68.

120. Mao Zedong, "Yenan Forum on Literature and Art," in *Selected Works of Mao Tse-tung* [Mao Zedong], vol. 3 (Peking: Foreign Languages Press, 1967). 85.

121. Mao, "Yenan Forum," 89–90.

122. Holland Cotter, "Artists, Toe the Party Line," review of "Art and China's Revolution," *New York Times*, September 4, 2008; Gao Jianping, "Chinese Aesthetics in the Past Two decades," *Acta Orientalia Vilnius* (2002) 130–33. Gao describes the "aesthetic debates" in China in the 1950s and 1960s, and the "aesthetics craze" of 1979–1984.

123. Ralph Croizer, "Art and Society in Modern China—a Review Article," *The Journal of Asian Studies* (1990), 597.

124. Croizer, "Art and Society," 589.

125. Joan Ledolb Cohen, *The New Chinese Painting: 1949–1986* (New York: Harry N. Abrams, Inc., 1987), and Michael Sullivan, "Some Thoughts about Wang Huaiqing," 2002, http://wanghuaiqing.artron.net/news_2.php?newid=28135&aid=A0000050.

126. *The Picture of Bole* by Wang Huaiqing is in the collection of the National Art Museum of China. Their website <http://www.namoc.org/en/collections/fineart/> contains an excellent image of this painting.

127. Joan Cohen, *The New* Chinese, 78.

128. Chapter 2 discusses the phrase *tian ren he yi* and Li Zehou's interpretation of it.

129. Stephen Little, *New Songs on Ancient Tunes: 19th–20th Century Chinese paintings and Calligraphy from the Richard Fabian Collection* (Honolulu: Honolulu Academy of Arts. 2007), 33; Amy McNair, "Texts of Taoism and Buddhism and the Power of Calligraphic Style," in *The Embodied Image: Chinese Calligraphy from the John B. Elliott Collection*, ed. Robert E. Harrist, Jr. and Wen C. Fong (Princeton, NJ: The Art Museum, Princeton University, 1999) 232, 230; and Gordon S. Barrass, *The Art of Callligraphy in Modern China* (Berkeley: The University of California Press, 2002) 204–06 and 240–42. These texts discuss the Bronze and Stone Studies (*jinshixue* 金石學) that began in the Song Dynasty.

130. Hsingyuan Tsao, "Reading and Misreading: Double Entendre in Locally Oriented Logos," in *Xu Bing and Contemporary Chinese Art*, ed. Hsingyuan Tsao and Roger T. Ames (Albany, NY: State University of New York Press, 2011), 15–16.

131. Artnet, "New Art Records January–June 2008," http://www.artnet.com/magazineus/news/artmarketwatch/new_art_records_2008.pdf.

132. Xiao Changyan, "Lots of bargains but few buyers in store," *China Daily*, November 11, 2008, http://www.chinadaily.com.cn/cndy/2008-11/20/content_7222162.htm.

133. Exploring the relationship between contemporary Chinese art (the work of Xu Bing, Gu Wenda, Wu Shanzhuan, and the movement known as "political pop" to name just a few) and the current government of China is complex and beyond the scope of this chapter.

134. Deutsch, *Essays*, 84. The art historian Catherine Fruhan disagrees, noting that "free speech" arguments frequently indicate that both sides are highly invested in, or afraid of, the power of art.

135. Deutsch, *Essays*, 88.

136. References to John Winthrop's "Shining City on a Hill" serve a similar purpose for Americans when used by politicians like John F. Kennedy and Ronald Reagan to inspire us to revitalize national ideals.

137. The uniqueness of the Holocaust—that the representatives of the highest values of the European Enlightenment used the achievements of that age to perpetrate genocide—may make such a comparison unacceptable; but, given the Chinese tradition of respect for learning and the past, the fact that the Cultural Revolution used the weapons of the state in an attempt to eliminate the educated elite, there are similarities.

139. Donatella Lorch, "The A-Team: On Patrol with the Special Forces." *Newsweek*. January 14, 2002: 20–25. Doug Stanton, *Horse Soldiers* (New York: Scribner, 2009) tells the story of the U.S. soldiers and the Afghan horses.

140. For example, see the previous discussion of Castiglione's work, and Hockney, "A Day on the Grand Canal."

Chapter 5

1. The examination system was abolished briefly during the Yuan Dynasty (1206–1368). In the fourteenth-century study of the Five Classics: the *Yijing* (*Book of Changes*), *Shijing* (*Book of Songs* or *Classic of Poetry*), *Shujing* (*Classic of History*), *Chunqiu* (*Spring and Autumn Annals*) and a collection of books on the rituals and ceremonies of the Western Zhou dynasty (1027–771 BCE), were replaced by the Four Books: *Da Xue* (the *Great Learning*), *Zhong yong* (the *Doctrine of the Mean*), the *Analects of Confucius*, and the *Mencius*.

2. Lin Tongqi and Li Minghua, "Subjectivity: Marxism and 'The Spiritual' in China since Mao," *Philosophy East and West* 44 no. 4 (October 1994), 609.

3. Ronald C. Egan, *Word, Image, and Deed in the life of Su Shi* (Cambridge, MA: Harvard-Yenching Institute, Harvard University Press, 1994), 358–59.

4. Burton Watson, introduction to *Selected Poems of Su Tung-Po* (Port Townsend, WA: Copper Canyon Press, 1994), 4; Beata Grant. *Mount Lu Revisited: Buddhism in the Life and Writing of Su Shi* (Honolulu: University of Hawaii Press, 1994), 9.

5. James T. C. Liu, *Reform in Sung China: Wang An-shih (1021–1086) and his New Policies* (Cambridge, MA: Harvard University Press, 1959), 1–7.

6. Wang Anshi, "*From Ten-Thousand-Word Memorial* 1058." http://classroom.kleinisd.net/webs/tbonar/upload/memoria3.pdf. (March 9, 2011).

7. Lin Yutang, *The Gay Genius: The Life and Times of Su Tung Po* (Westport, CT: Greenwood Press, 1971), 94.

8. Conrad Schirokauer, "Chu Hsi and Hu Hung," in *Chu Hsi and Neo-Confucianism*, ed. Wing-tsit Chan (Honolulu: University of Hawai'i Press, 1986), 480; and Liu, *Reform*, 32.

9. Amy Gordanier, "The 'New Laws' of Wang Anshi," http://academic.reed.edu/chinese/chin-hum/claypools09/Hum%20230%20Project/new_laws.html (March 9, 2011).

10. Liu, *Reform*, 27–28.

11. Liu, *Reform*, 28–29. The School was named for the areas of Szechwan from which the Su family came and traced much of its politics to Ouyang Xiu.

12. Egan, *Word, Image, and Deed*, 60.

13. Fu Yunlong, trans. *The Great Learning and the Doctrine of the Mean*, ed. Cai Xiqin (Beijing: Sinolingua, 1996), 5–6.

14. A. C. Graham, *Two Chinese Philosophers: Ch'êng Ming-tao and Ch'êng Yi-ch'uan* (London: Lund Humphries, 1958), 76.

15. Michael A. Fuller, *The Road to East Slope: The Development of Su Shi's Poetic Voice* (Redwood City, CA: Stanford University Press,. 1990), 44, 86.

16. Fuller, *The Road to East Slope*, 166.

17. Fuller, *The Road to East Slope*, 121.

18. Su Shi, *Selected Poems of Su Tung-Po*, trans. Burton Watson (Port Townsend, WA: Copper Canyon Press, 1994), 80.

19. Su, *Selected Poems*, 81. The translator notes that another interpretation of the words "I do a dance" is "I stop to piss."

20. Fuller, *The Road to East Slope*, 254, 261; Grant, *Mount Lu,* 109; Lin Yutang, *The Gay Genius*, 234.

21. Xiaofei Tian, *Tao Yuanming & Manuscript Culture: The Record of a Dusty Table* (Seattle: University of Washington Press, 2005), 6–7.

22. Tao Qian, *The Selected Poems of T'ao Ch'ien*, trans. David Hinton (Port Townsend, WA: Copper Canyon Press, 1993), 19.

23. Tao, *Selected Poems*, 20.

24. Tao, *Selected Poems*, 21.

25. Tao, *Selected Poems*, 22.

26. Grant, *Mount Lu*, 107.

27. Fuller, *The Road to East Slope,* 271–72. It is not clear whether he took this name as a reference to Bo Juyi's poems, or simply because of the location of his land.

28. Su, *Selected Poems*, 89.

29. Su, *Selected Poems*, 90.

30. Fuller, *The Road to East Slope*, 282.

31. Fuller, *The Road to East Slope*, 281–83.

32. Fuller, *The Road to East Slope*, 284.

33. Fuller, *The Road to East Slope*, 283. Xiaofei Tian, *Tao Yuanming*, points out that Tao Qian actually makes a number of classical references, although Tao's references are more oblique than Su's.

34. See for example: Tao, 29, 43, 47.

35. Fuller, *The Road to East Slope*, 294–95, discusses Su's pride in the skill of his son Su Mai.

36. David Hawkes, trans, *The Songs of the South* [*Ch'u-tz-u*] (Oxford: Clarendon Press, 1959), 51–61.

37. Fuller, *The Road to East Slope*, 264.

38. Chapter 3 discusses *xuanxue* or Dark Learning.

39. Zhuangzi, *Chuang Tzu. Basic Writings*, trans. Burton Watson (New York: Columbia University Press, 1964, 1996), 81.

40. Zhuangzi, *Chuang Tzu*, 31.

41. Zhuangzi, *Chuang Tzu*, 74. Li Zehou, *The Chinese Aesthetic Tradition*, trans. Maija Bell Samei (Honolulu: University of Hawai'i Press. 2010), chapter 3, "The Daoist-Confucian Synthesis" describes the "True Man" as a fully "naturalized human being."

42. Or so it seemed to many ordinary practitioners. Scholars have often criticized Chinese Buddhism for misunderstanding Indian theology.

43. Egan, *Word, Image, and Deed,* 196.

44. Grant, *Mount Lu*, 78.

45. Grant, *Mount Lu*, 76.

46. Grant, *Mount Lu*, 77. Although Grant and Egan both discuss these two sutras, Grant makes slightly more of the contrast between the "dualistic" *Śūramgama Sūtra* and the "monistic" *Vimalakīrti Sūtra* than Egan does.

47. John R. McRae, trans. *The Vimalakīrti Sutra* (Berkeley, CA: Numata Center for Buddhist Translation and Research, 2004). https://www.bdkamerica.org/digital/dBET_Srimala_Vimalakirti_2004.pdf (March 25, 2011), 73.

48. McRae, *Vimalakīrti Sutra*, 77.

49. McRae, *Vimalakīrti Sutra*, 77. The text does not mean that all silence is the profound teaching. Vimalakīrti speaks great deal on many occasions. The disciples are also silent when they become confused after being questioned by Vimalakīrti or the goddess, but their silence is not profound. "'Silence' and 'speech'" are simply another dualism. "Just as speech is ultimately meaningless, so silence exists only in contrast with speech." Robert A. F. Thurman, trans., *The Holy Teaching of Vimalakīrti: A Mahāyāna Scripture* (University Park, PA: The Pennsylvania State University Press, 2006), 132.

50. Su, *Selected Poems*, 27.

51. Su, *Selected Poems*, 37.

52. Grant, *Mount Lu*, 105–06.

53. Egan, *Word, Image, and Deed*, 245.

54. Scholars are not sure precisely where this famous battle took place. Su was almost certainly aware that the site he visited was probably north and west of the actual historical site. Itakura Massaki discusses some of the issues involved in the creative and imaginative use of history in Su's poems about the Red Cliffs and in the paintings inspired by them. Itakura Massaki, "The Words and Images Surrounding The Ode on the Red Cliff—with Qiao Zhongchang's Handscroll of the Second Red Cliff Text as an Example" (paper presented at Taiwan 2002 Conference on the History of Painting in East Asia. October 4–7, 2002).

55. "Battle of Red Cliffs." *Wikepedia: The Free Encyclopedia. Wikimedia Foundation, Inc.* http://en.wikipedia.org/wiki/Battle_of_Red_Cliffs (accessed April 10, 2011). The battle of Red Cliff continues to be part of military legend. It appears in the fourteenth-century novel, *The Romance of the Three Kingdoms*, in a contemporary (2008–2009) film by John Woo, and a series of video games. The purported location of the battle is a popular tourist site.

56. Cai Zong-qi, ed. *How to Read Chinese Poetry: A Guided Anthology* (New York: Columbia University Press. 2008), 262–64. Cai discusses the development of the *manci* style, and Su Shi's use of it.

57. Su Shi (Su Dongpo), "Nien nu Chiao—Battle of Red Cliff." Translator not given. http://www.chinapage.com/poet-e/sushi2e.htm (February 20, 2011). Cai, *How to Read Chinese Poetry*, 270–71 and Egan, *Word, Image, and Deed*, 226–27 contain other translations of this poem.

58. Susan Bush and Hsio-yen Shih, eds. *Early Chinese Texts on Painting* (Cambridge, MA: Harvard University Press, 1985).

59. Bush and Shih, *Early Chinese*, 203.

60. Cai, *How to Read*, 273.

61. Su, *Selected Poems*, 94–96.

62. The *Red Cliff Odes* are written in the *fu* style of poetry. Cyril Drummond Le Gros Clark, *The Prose-poetry of Su Tung-p'o*, 2nd ed. (New York: Paragon Books Reprint Corp, 1964), 40–47; Egan, *Word, Image, and Deed*, 222; Li Zehou, *The Path of Beauty*, 69–77; and Cai, *How to Read*, 4–8 discuss the *fu* style which has been called prose-poetry, and is written in an irregular metric and occasional rhyme. The *fu* style originated the ancient State of Chu and was first used in religious spells and incantations. Qu Yuan's *Li Sao* from the *Chu Ci* (*Songs of the South*) is an early example of *fu* style poetry. In the Han dynasty *fu* were usually long narrations or descriptions, but after the Han the popularity of fu poetry declined. In the Song Dynasty poets like Ouyang Xiu and Su Shi revived the form in a more personal and flexible form. Su's *fu* poetry has a rhythm but generally avoids a particular metrical style.

63. Clark, *The Prose-poetry*, 46.

64. "Red Cliff Rhapsodies, 1 and 2," translated with notes by Richard Strassberg, in *The Columbia Anthology of Traditional Chinese Literature*, ed. Victor Maier (New York: Columbia University Press, 1994), 438; and Clark, *The Prose-poetry*, 129. The Odes Su hums are both about beautiful and unattainable or virtuous women. Arthur Waley, trans. *The Book of Songs: Shijing* (New York: Grove Press, 1996), 32 and 87 provides translations of "The Bright Moon" and "The Cry of the Osprey."

65. Zhuangzi, *Chuang Tzu*, 26; and Clark, *The Prose-poetry*, 129.

66. Clark, *The Prose-poetry*, 130; and Hawkes, *Songs of the South*, 23, 38 discuss these references. The line "With cassia sweep and oars of orchid wood," recalls the third of the *Nine Hymns* "The Princess of the Hsiang." The phrase "my loved one," or alternatively "beautiful maidens of old" is a phrase from the *Li Sao* where it is traditionally interpreted to refer to the King of Chu.

67. Many scholars believe that Su's companion on this trip was Yang Shichang [Yang Shih-ch'ang] a Daoist priest known for his flute playing. Su "Red Cliff Rhapsodies, 440; and Clark *The Prose-poems*, 130.

68. Clark, *The Prose-poems*, 134, gives the last line of Hymn 4 of the *Nine Hymns,* "The Ladies of the River Hsiang," as "Time cannot be suddenly attained." Hawkes, *Songs of the South*, 109, translates this line as "Oh, rarely, rarely the time is given," which echoes the penultimate line in Hymn 3, "For time once gone cannot be recovered."

69. Ludwig Wittgenstein, *Tractatus Logico-Philosophicus*, 2nd ed., trans. D. F. Pears and B. F. McGuinness (London and New York: Routledge & Kegan, 1971), 6.4311.

70. Jeffrey Grupp, "The R-theory of Time, or Replacement Presentism: The Buddhist Philosophy of Time," *The Indian International Journal of Buddhist Studies* (IIJBS) 6 (2005): 51–122. A number of philosophical and psychological theories explore the related phenomena of the "specious present," i.e., our consciousness of the immediate present, but their views are not as intuitively plausible as Presentism, and they may make most versions of Presentism incoherent.

71. Grupp, "The R-theory."

72. Grupp, "The R-theory," 115.

73. Grupp, "The R-theory," 65, quoting Stcherbatsky's *Buddhist Logic* (1930, 1962).

74. Grupp, "The R-theory," 117–18.

75. Grant, *Mount Lu*, 76–77.

76. Grant, *Mount Lu*, 77.

77. Grant, *Mount Lu*, 77.

78. Ari Borrell, "*Ko-wu* or *Kung-an*? Practice, Realization, and Teaching in the Thought of Chang Chiu-ch'eng," in *Buddhism in the Sung*, ed. Peter N. Gregory and Daniel A. Getz, Jr. (Honolulu: University of Hawai'i Press, 1999) describes a number of these debates and argues that the relatively rigid doctrinal

categories and classifications familiar to later historians of Chinese Buddhism may reflect the way each sect wrote its own history rather than the actual situation.

79. Graham, A. C, trans. *The Book of Lieh-tzǔ* (London: John Murray, 1960), 31.

80. Graham, *The Book of Lieh-tzǔ*, 30.

81. Graham, *The Book of Lieh-tzǔ*, 31.

82. Egan, *Word, Image, and Deed*, 224.

83. Watson, introduction to *Selected Poems*, 6.

84. Su, *Selected Poems*, 97–98.

85. Egan, *Word, Image, and Deed*, 248.

86. Clark, *The Prose-poems*, 137.

87. Egan, *Word, Image, and Deed*, 249. Egan claims that Su had been rejected by the natural world, but it seems to me that the "rejection" was mutual.

88. Friedrich Nietzsche, "Thus Spoke Zarathustra," in *The Portable Nietzsche*, ed. and trans. Walter Kaufmann (New York: Penguin Books, 1986), 124.

89. Rudyard Kipling, "The Sons of Martha," in *Rudyard Kipling's Verse* (Garden City, NY: Doubleday and Company, Inc., 1946), 380.

90. Kathleen Marie Higgins, *Nietzsche's Zarathustra* (Philadelphia, PA: Temple University Press, 1987), 232; and Henri Birault, "Beatitude in Nietzsche," in *The New Nietzsche*, ed. David B. Allison (Cambridge, MA: The MIT Press, 1986), 221.

91. Su, *Selected Poems*, 132. "Bring-the-jug" is the name of a bird whose cry is said to sound like the words "*t'i-hu*" or "bring the jug!"

92. SU, *Selected Poems*, 131,132.

93. Grant, *Mount Lu*, 67–68.

94. Hoyt Cleveland Tillman, "A New Direction in Confucian Scholarship: Approaches to Examining the Differences between Neo-Confucianism *and Tao-hsūeh*," *Philosophy East and West* 42 no. 3 (Jul. 1992). Scholars (A. C. Graham, de Bary, and Tillman) have argued that the term "Neo-Confucian" is seriously misleading. Sometimes it is taken to mean almost any Confucianism after the Song Dynasty; sometimes it is conflated with with "*daoxue*," the Study of the Way; and sometimes it is limited to the Cheng-Zhu branch of Confucianism. I will generally take "Neo-Confucianism" to mean Cheng-Zhu Confucianism. Discussion of the differences between Cheng-Zhu and Lu-Wang Neo-Confucianism schools is beyond the scope of this study.

95. Tillman, "A New Direction;" Hoyt Cleveland Tillman, *Confucian Discourse and Chu Hsi's Ascendancy* (Honolulu: University of Hawai'i Press, 1992), and the essays in John Makeham, ed., *New Confucianism: A Critical Examination* (New York: Palgrave Macmillan. 2003) discuss some of these complexities.

96. This discussion simplifies a vastly complex and sophisticated metaphysical system that integrated cosmology, ontology and moral psychology.

97. It is difficult to know how to translate "*li*." Feng Youlan (1895–1990) translated it as "universal" or "idea." Diane B. Obenchain, "Introduction to Feng Youlan: Something Exists." *Journal of Chinese Philosophy* 21 nos. 3/4 (September/

December 1994): lxxxiii; but these terms import too much Western philosophy. Although in his study of the Cheng brothers (*Two Chinese Philosophers*) A. C. Graham translated *li* as "principle," he was not satisfied with this translation noting that "'Principle' suggests a truth formulated in words in order to make deductions, while *li* suggests rather a pattern running through things, even sharing their three dimensions and variously describable in words." A. C. Graham, *Yin-Yang and the Nature of Correlative Thinking*. Singapore: Institute of East Asian Philosophies. Monograph Series no 6. 1986, 155. Graham notes a further difficulty in discussing *li* in English. It is not thought of as a collection of individual units but as a whole that can be divided in various ways depending on context. Graham, *Two Chinese Philosophers*, 1958, 58.

98. Graham, *Two Chinese Philosophers*, 10.

99. Graham, *Two Chinese Philosophers*, 8, notes that the meaning of this association may be inferred from various compounds with *li*, "twig" (*tiai-li* 條理), "path" (*dao-li* 道理), and "veins of the body" (*mo-li* 脈理).

100. Graham, *Two Chinese Philosophers*, *10.*

101. Graham, *Two Chinese Philosophers*, 58.

102. Graham, *Two Chinese Philosophers*, 31. Graham translates *qi* as "ether" because it "it means so little that it cannot be positively misleading." Graham, *Two Chinese Philosophers*, 31. Unfortunately, "ether" is definitely mythological; it is a substance that does not exist. This may only be "negatively misleading."

103. Graham, *Two Chinese Philosophers*, 48.

104. In the West, perhaps going back to Plato, but at least since Descartes, mind (subject) is sharply distinguished from matter (object) and much of the history of modern Western philosophy has been concerned with the relationship between the two. Chinese thought, on the other hand, has been criticized for failing to sharply distinguish between subjects and objects.

Graham, *Two Chinese Philosophers*, 13, notes that the vocabulary of "universal" and "particular" gives rise to problems about how the two are related, but this problem did not come up for Song philosophers. Like grain in wood, a network of veins or paths, when we "extend" them in one direction we get finer and finer distinctions; tracing them back we see they are one network. Principle, *li*, is to be understood not as a "universal" but as "unchanging." What changes is *qi*.

105. Graham, *Two Chinese Philosophers*, 64.

106. Graham, *Two Chinese Philosophers*, 53.

107. Graham, *Two Chinese Philosophers*, 6.

108. From the *Great Learning*, quoted by Graham, *Two Chinese Philosophers*, 74.

109. Graham, *Two Chinese Philosophers*, 76.

110. Egan, *Word, Image, and Deed*, 95–97.

111. Egan, *Word, Image, and Deed*, 10.

112. Fuller, *The Road to East Slope*, 84; Egan, *Word, Image, and Deed*, 387. A. C. Graham expressed some doubt about translating *li* as "principle" in his

discussion of the Cheng brothers. On the other hand "principle" is a less misleading translation of *li* in Cheng Yi and Zhu Xi writings than it is in Su Shi's.

113. Zhuangzi, *Chuang Tzu*, 34–40.

114. Fuller, *The Road to East Slope*, 91.

115. Fuller, *The Road to East Slope*, 88.

116. Fuller, *The Road to East Slope*, 87.

117. Fuller, *The Road to East Slope*, 53.

118. "Critique of My Writing," in Fuller, *The Road to East Slope*, 85.

119. Fuller, *The Road to East Slope*, 86, 90.

120. Liu, *Reform in Sung China*, 29.

121. Lin Yutang, *The Gay Genius,* 155, 262–63; and Graham, *Two Chinese Philosophers*, xvi.

122. Douglas L. Berger, "Did Buddhism Ever Go East? The Westernization of Buddhism in Chad Hansen's Daoist Historiography," *Philosophy East and West* 61 no. 1 (2011), 41; Chad Hansen, *A Daoist Theory of Chinese Thought: A Philosophical Interpretation* (New York: Oxford University Press, 1992); and Grant, *Mount Lu*, 78.

123. Richard John Lynn, "Chu Hsi a Literary Theorist and Critic," in *Chu Hsi and Neo-Confucianismm*, ed. Wing-tsit Chan (Honolulu: University of Hawaii' Press, 1986), 339.

124. Kao Ming, "Chu Hsi's Discipline of Propriety," in *Chu Hsi and Neo-Confucianismm*, ed. Wing-tsit Chan (Honolulu: University of Hawai'i Press, 1986), 320.

125. Egan, *Word, Image, and Deed*, 358.

126. Zhu's own understanding of Buddhism is subject to some controversy also (Charles Wei-Hsun Fu, "Chu Hsi on Buddhism," in *Chu Hsi and Neo-Confucianism*, ed. Wing-tsit Chan (Honolulu: University of Hawai'i Press, 1986), 381–84. Fu describes some of the controversy about Zhu's own understanding of Buddhism.

127. Egan, *Word, Image, and Deed*, 358, quoting Zhu Xi's *Classified Sayings.*

128. Lynn, "Chu Hsi," 348, quoting Chu Hsi *Chu Tzu yü-lei* [Classified Conversations of Chu Hsi].

129. Fuller *The Road to East Slope*, 81.

130. Lynn, "Chu Hsi," 339.

131. Graham, *Two Chinese Philosophers*, 5.

132. See chapter 2.

Epilogue

1. Robert Pears, "Top Earners Doubled Share of Nation's Income, Study Finds," *New York Times*, October 25, 2011, http://www.nytimes.com/2011/10/26/us/politics/top-earners-doubled-share-of-nations-income-cbo-says.html?_r=1; Drew DeSilver, "U.S. income inequality, on rise for decades, is now highest

since 1928," PEW Research Center, December 5, 2013, http://www.pew research.org/fact-tank/2013/12/05/u-s-income-inequality-on-rise-for-decades-is-now-highest-since-1928/. The PEW Research Centered estimated the 2012 data.

2. Alyssa Davis and Lawrence Mishel, "CEO Pay Continues to Rise as Typical Workers are Paid Less," Economic Policy Institute, June 12, 2012, http://fortune.com/2015/06/22/ceo-vs-worker-pay/http://fortune.com/2015/06/22/ceo-vs-worker-pay/. The ratio peaked in 2000 at 384-to-1.

3. Larry Elliott and Ed Pikington, "New Oxfam report says half of global wealth held by the 1%," *The Guardian*, January 19, 2015, http://www.theguardian.com/business/2015/jan/19/global-wealth-oxfam-inequality-davos-economic-sumit-switzerland.

4. Feeding America, "Feeding America," accessed April 7, 2016, http://www.feedingamerica.org/hunger-in-america/impact-of-hunger/hunger-and-poverty/hunger-and-poverty-fact-sheet.html.

5. WHO, "Controlling the global obesity epidemic," accessed April 7, 2016, http://www.who.int/nutrition/topics/obesity/en/.

6. Henry Rosemont, Jr. *Against Individualism* (Lanham, MD: Lexington Books, 2015); and Peter D. Hershock, *Valuing Diversity* (Albany, NY: State University of New York Press, 2012).

These two books present nuanced philosophical analyses of the ideological grounds of global injustice and inequity.

7. Li Zehou's study of, and experience of, revolutions in China have made him unwilling to call for another revolution at this time.

8. Li and Cauvel, 182–83.

9. Emma Goldman, *Living My Life* (New York: Alfred A. Knopf, Inc., 1931), https://theanarchistlibrary.org/library/emma-goldman-living-my-life.

10. See chapter 2 for Li on the importance of dancing.

11. Catherine Fruhan convinced me of this point in her class on the Italian Renaissance. Her "lecture" on September 11, 2001 was appropriate to the day, delivered a pointed history lesson, and, unfortunately, anticipated our future.

Bibliography

Abrams, M. H. *The Mirror and the Lamp: Romantic Theory and the Critical Tradition.* New York: W.W. Norton & Company, 1958.

Acker, W. R. B., *Some T'ang and Pre-Tang Texts on Chinese Painting.* Leiden: E. J. Brill, 1954.

Ames, Roger T. *Confucian Role Ethics: A Vocabulary.* Honolulu: University of Hawai'i Press, 2011.

———. "The Mencian Vonception of Ren Xing 人性: Does it Mean 'Human Nature'?" In *Chinese Texts and Philosophical Contexts,* edited by Henry Rosemont, Jr., 143–75. LaSalle, IL: Open Court Press, 1991.

———. "New Confucianism: A Native Response to Western Philosophy." In *Chinese Political Culture: 1989–2000,* edited by Shiping Hua, 70–99. Armonk, NY: M. E. Sharpe, 2001.

Ames, Roger T., and David L. Hall, trans. *Daodejing: "Making This Life Significant": A Philosophical translation.* New York: Random House, Inc. Ballantine Books, 2003.

———. *Focusing the Familiar: A Translation and Philosophical Interpretation of the* Zhongyong. Honolulu: University of Hawai'i Press, 2001.

Ames, Roger T., and Henry Rosemont, Jr. *The Analects: A Philosophical Translation.* New York: Ballantine Books, 1998.

Artnet. "New Art Records January–June 2008." http://www.artnet.com/magazineus/news/artmarketwatch/new_art_records_2008.pdf.

Barfield, Thomas J. *The Perilous Frontier: Nomadic Empires and China.* Cambridge, MA: Blackwell, 1989.

Barnhart, Richard M., Yang Xin, Nie Chongzheng, James Cahill, Lang Shaojun, and Wu Hung. *Three Thousand Years of Chinese Painting.* New Haven, CT: Yale University Press, 1977.

Barrass, Gordon S. *The Art of Callligraphy in Modern China.* Berkeley: The University of California Press, 2002.

Battle of Red Cliffs." *Wikepedia: The Free Encyclopedia. Wikimedia Foundation, Inc.* http://en.wikipedia.org/wiki/Battle_of_Red_Cliffs (accessed April 10, 2011).

Baxendall, Michael. *Painting & Experience in Fifteenth-Century Italy*. 2nd ed. New York: Oxford University Press, 1988.

Beckwith, Christopher I. "The Impact of the Horse and Silk Trade on the Economies of T'ang China and the Uighur Empire." *Journal of the Economic and Social History of the Orient* 34, no. 2 (1991): 183–98.

Bellah, Robert N. *Religion in Human Evolution*. Cambridge, MA: Harvard University Press, 2011.

Bellah, Robert N., Richard Madsen, William M. Sullivan, Ann Swidler, and Steven M. Tipton. *Habits of the Heart: Individualism and Commitment in American Life*. Berkeley, CA: University of California Press, 1985.

Benjamin, Walter. "The Work of Art in the Age of Mechanical Reproduction," Marxist Internet Archive (Feb. 2006). http://www.marxists.org/reference/subject/philosophy/works/ge/benjamin.htm.

Berger, Douglas L. "Did Buddhism Ever Go East? The Westernization of Buddhism in Chad Hansen's Daoist Historiography." *Philosophy East and West* 61 no. 1 (2011): 38–55.

Birault, Henri. "Beatitude in Nietzsche." In *The New Nietzsche*, edited by David B. Allison, 219–31. Cambridge, MA: The MIT Press, 1986.

Bloom, Irene. "Human Nature and Biological Nature in Mencius." *Philosophy East and West* 47, no. 1 (1997): 21–32.

———. "Mencian Arguments on Human Nature (Renxing)." *Philosophy East and West*, 44 no. 1 (1994): 19–53.

Book of Songs: Shijing. Translated by Arthur Waley. New York: Grove Press, 1996.

Borrell, Ari. "*Ko-wu* or *Kung-an*? Practice, Realization, and Teaching in the Thought of Chang Chiu-ch'eng." In *Buddhism in the Sung*, edited by Peter N. Gregory and Daniel A. Getz, Jr., 62–108. Honolulu: University of Hawai'i Press, 1999.

Brook, Andrew, "Kant's View of the Mind and Consciousness of Self," *The Stanford Encyclopedia of Philosophy* (Fall 2013 edition), edited by Edward N. Zalta. http://plato.stanford.edu/archives/fall2013/entries/kant-mind/.

Brooks, David. "The Other Education." *New York Times* Op-Ed column. November 26, 2009.http://www.nytimes.com/2009/11/27/opinion/27brooks.html?ref=davidbrooks.

Bush, Susan. *The Chinese Literati on Painting*. Cambridge, MA: Harvard University Press, 1971.

Bush, Susan, and Hsio-yen Shih, ed. *Early Chinese Texts on Painting*. Cambridge, MA: Harvard University Press, 1985.

Cahill, James. "Confucian Elements in the Theory of Painting." In *The Confucian Persuasion*, edited by Arthur F. Wright, 115–49. Redwood City, CA: Stanford University Press, 1960.

———. Good Grief, Not the Six Laws Again! (*Ching Yuan Chai So-shih 4*)." *The Writings of James Cahill*. http://jamescahill.info/.

———. "The Six Laws and How to Read Them." *Ars Orientalis* 4 (1961): 372–81.

Cahill, Suzanne. "Night Shining White." *Tang Studies* 4 (1986): 91–94.

———. *Transcendence & Divine Passion: The Queen Mother of the West in Medieval China.* Redwood City, CA: Stanford University Press, 1993.

Cai Zong-qi, ed. *A Chinese Literary Mind: Culture, Creativity, and Rhetoric in* Wenxin Diaolong. Redwood City, CA: Stanford University Press, 2001.

Cai Zong-qi. *Configurations of Comparative Poetry: Three Perspectives on Western and Chinese Literary Criticism.* Honolulu: University of Hawai'i Press, 2002.

———, ed. *How to Read Chinese Poetry: A Guided Anthology*. New York: Columbia University Press, 2008.

———. "The Making of a Critical System: Conceptions of Literature in Wenxin Dialong and Earlier Texts." In *A Chinese Literary Mind: Culture, Creativity, and Rhetoric in* Wenxin Diaolong, edited by Cai Zong-qi, 33–59. Redwood City, CA: Stanford University Press, 2001.

Cauvel, Jane. "The Transformative Power of Art: Li Zehou's Aesthetic Theory." *Philosophy East and West* 49, no. 2 (1999): 150–73.

Chan, Alan, "Neo-Taoism," *The Stanford Encyclopedia of Philosophy (Winter 2009 edition),* edited by Edward N. Zalta. http://plato.stanford.edu/archives/win2009/entries/neo-taoism/.

Chan, Sylvia. "Li Zehou and New Confucianism." In *New Confucianism: A Critical Examination*, edited by John Makeham, 105–28. New York: Palgrave Macmillan, 2003.

Chandler, Marthe. "Philosophy of Gravity: Intuitions of four-dimensional curved spacetime." *Science & Education* 3, no. 2 (1994): 155–76.

Chang Willow Weilan Hai, Yang Renkai, and David Ake Sensabaugh. *The Last Emperor's Collection: Masterpieces of Painting and Calligraphy from the Liaoning Provincial Museum*. New York: China Institute, 2008.

Chen Jiang Hong. *The Magic Horse of Han Gan.* Translated by Claudia Zoe Bedrick. Brooklyn, New York: Enchanted Lion Books, 2006.

Chong Woei Lien. "Combining Marx with Kant: The Philosophical Anthropology of Li Zehou." *Philosophy East and West* 49, no. 2 (1999): 120–49.

———. "History as the Realization of Beauty Li Zehou's Aesthetic Marxism." *Contemporary Chinese Thought* 31, no. 2 (Winter 1999–2000): 3–19.

Clark, Cyril Drummond Le Gros. *The Prose-poetry of Su Tung-p'o*. 2nd ed. New York: Paragon Books Reprint Corp., 1964.

Clark, Kenneth. *Leonardo da Vinci.* London: Penguin Books, 1993

Clifford, James. "Four Northwest Coast Museums: Travel Reflections." In *Exhibiting Cultures: The Poetics and Politics of Museum Display*, edited by Ivan Karp and Steven D. Lavine, 212–54. Washington, DC: Smithsonian Institution Press, 1991.

Clower, Jason. "Mou Zongsan (Mou Tsung-san) (1909–1995)," *The Internet Encyclopedia of Philosophy*, ISSN 2161-0002, http://www.iep.utm.edu/.

Cohen, Joan Lebold. *The New Chinese Painting: 1949–1986.* New York: Harry N. Abrams, Inc., 1987.

Cohen, Ted. "Why Beauty is a Symbol of Morality." In *Essays in Kant's Aesthetics.* Edited by Ted Cohen and Paul Guyer, 221–36. Chicago: The University of Chicago Press, 1982.

Coleridge, Samuel Taylor. *Biographia Literaria.* First published in 1817. Project Gutenberg's Biographia Literaria, by Samuel Taylor Coleridge. Release Date: July, 2004 [EBook #6081]. http://www.gutenberg.org/files/6081/6081-h/6081-h.htm.

Confucius. *The Analects of Confucius: A Philosophical Translation.* Translated by Roger T. Ames and Henry Rosemont, Jr. New York: The Ballantine Publishing Group, 1998.

Cooke, Bill, ed. *Imperial China: The Art of the Horse in Chinese History.* Exhibition Catalogue. Lexington, KY: Kentucky Horse Park, 2000,

Cotter, Holland. "Artists, Toe the Party Line." Review of "Art and China's Revolution." *New York Times*, September 4, 2008.

Cotterell, Maurice. *The Terracotta Warriors: The Secret Codes of the Emperor's Army.* Rochester, VT: Bear & Company, 2004.

Croizer, Ralph. "Art and Society in Modern China—a Review Article." *The Journal of Asian Studies* (1990): 578–602.

Daniel, Lillian. "Spiritual But Not Religious? Please Stop Boring Me." *Huffpost Religion Blog.* Posted September 13, 2011. Updated November 13, 2011. http://www.huffingtonpost.com/lillian-daniel/spiritual-but-not-religio_b_959216.html.

Danto, Arthur. "The Artworld." *Journal of Philosophy* 61, no. 19 (1964): 571–84.

———. *The Philosophical Disenfranchisement of Art.* New York: Columbia University Press, 1986.

———. *The Transfiguration of the Commonplace.* Cambridge, MA: Harvard University Press, 1981.

Davidson, Donald. "What Metaphors Mean." In *The Philosophy of Language*, edited by A. P. Martinich, 415–26. New York: Oxford University Press, 1996.

Davis, Alyssa, and Lawrence Mishel. "CEO Pay Continues to Rise as Typical Workers are Paid Less." Economic Policy Institute, June 12, 2012. http://fortune.com/2015/06/22/ceo-vs-worker-pay/http://fortune.com/2015/06/22/ceo-vs-worker-pay/.

DeSliver, Drew. "U.S. income inequality, on rise for decades, is now hightest since 1928." PEW Research Center, December 5, 2013. http://www.pewresearch.org/fact-tank/2013/12/05/u-s-income-inequality-on-rise-for-decades-is-now-highest-since-1928/.

Deutsch, Eliot. *Essays on the Nature of Art.* Albany, NY: State University of New York Press, 1996.

Dewey, John. *A Common Faith*. 2nd ed. New Haven. CT: Yale University Press, 2013.

DeWoskin, Kenneth J. "Echoes of Deep Antiquity: Chinese Music Archaeology." In *Asian Art*. Arthur M. Sacker Gallery, Smithsonian Institution. Spring 1990:18–41.

———. *A Song for One or Two: Music and the Concept of Art in Early China*. Ann Arbor, Center for Chinese Studies. The University of Michigan, 1982.

Diamond, Cora. "'We Can't Whistle It Either': Legend and Reality." *European Journal of Philosophy* 19, no. 3 (2012): 336–56.

Du Fu. "On Seeing a Horse-painting by Ts'ao Pa In the House of Recorder Wei Feng" and "A Song of Painting: To General Ts'ao Pa." In *A Little Primer of Tu Fu*. Translated and edited by David Hawkes, 138–55. Oxford: Clarendon Press, 1967.

———. "Song of a Painting." In *An Anthology of Chinese Literature: Beginning to 1911*. Translated and edited by Stephen Owen, 429–31. New York: W. W. Norton & Company, 1996.

Du Jiwen. "The Multi-ethnic Character of Chinese Buddhism." In *Buddhist Studies in the People's Republic of China*. Translated and edited by Michael R. Saso, 22–69. Honolulu: Tendai Educational Foundation, 1992.

Dubs, Homer H. Translator. *The History of the Former Han Dynasty by Pan Ku (Ban Gu): A Critical Translation with Annotation*. Vol. 2. Baltimore, MD: Waverly, 1938–1955: 938–55.

Durkheim, Émile. "Religion and ritual." In *Emile Durkheim: Selected Writing*. Edited by A. Giddens. 219–38. Cambridge, MA: Cambridge University Press, 1972.

Eagleton, Terry. *The Ideology of the Aesthetic*. Oxford: Basil Blackwell, 1990.

Ebrey, Patricia Buckley. "During the Period of Division." *A Visual Sourcebook of Chinese Civilization*. November 26, 001. http://depts.washington.edu/chinaciv/1xardivi.htm.07).

Egan, Ronald. "Poet, Mind, and World: A Reconsideration of the 'Shensi' Chapter of *Wenxin Diaolong*." In *A Chinese Literary Mind: Culture, Creativity, and Rhetoric in* Wenxin Diaolong, edited by Cai Zong-qi, 101–26. Redwood City, CA: Stanford University Press, 2001.

———. *Word, Image, and Deed in the life of Su Shi*. Harvard-Yenching Institute, Cambridge, MA: Harvard University Press, 1994.

Elliott, Larry, and Ed Pikington. "New Oxfam report says half of global wealth held by the 1%." *The Guardian*, January 19, 2015, http://www.theguardian.com/business/2015/jan/19/global-wealth-oxfam-inequality-davos-economic-sumit-switzerland.

Feeding America. "Feeding America." Accessed April 7, 2016. http://www.feedingamerica.org/hunger-in-america/impact-of-hunger/hunger-and-poverty/hunger-and-poverty-fact-sheet.html.

Fischer-Schreiber, Ingrid, et al. *The Encyclopedia of Eastern Philosophy and Religion*. Boulder, CO: Shambhala Publications, 1994.

Flood, Finbarr Barry. "Between Cult and Culture: Bamiyan, Islamic Iconoclasm, and the Museum." *The Art Bulletin* 84, no. 4 (December 2002): 641–59.

Fong, Wen C. *Between Two Cultures: Late-Nineteenth- and Twentieth-Century Chinese Paintings from the Robert H. Ellsworth Collection in the Metropolitan Museum of Art*. New York: Metropolitan Museum of Art, 2001.

———. "The Modern Chinese Art Debate." *Artibus Asiae*, 53 no. 1/2 (1993): 290–305.

———. "Why Chinese Painting Is History." *The Art Bulletin* 85, no. 2 (June, 2003): 258–280.

Forman, Robert K. S., ed. *The Problem of Pure Consciousness: Mysticism and Philosophy*. Oxford: Oxford University Press, 1990.

Francis, Sandra T. "The Origins of Dance: The Perspectives of Primate Evolution." *Dance Chronicle* 14 no. 2/3 (1991): 203–20.

Fu, Charles Wei-Hsun. "Chu Hsi on Buddhism." In *Chu Hsi and Neo-Confucianism*, edited by Wing-tsit Chan, 377–407. Honolulu: University of Hawaii Press, 1986.

Fu Yunlong, trans. *The Great Learning and the Doctrine of the Mean*. Edited by Cai Xiqin. Beijing: Sinolingua, 1996.

Fuller, Michael A. *The Road to East Slope: The Development of Su Shi's Poetic Voice*. Redwood City, CA: Stanford University Press, 1990.

Gao Jianping "Chinese Aesthetics in the Past Two decades" *Acta Orientalia Vilnius* 3 (2002): 129–38

———. *The Expressive Act in Chinese Art: From Calligraphy to Painting*. Stockholm, Uppsala, Sweden: Uppsala University, 1996.

Gellman, Jerome, "Mysticism," *The Stanford Encyclopedia of Philosophy* (Spring 2014 edition), edited by Edward N. Zalta. http://plato.stanford.edu/archives/spr2014/entries/mysticism/.

Geertz, Clifford. *The Interpretation of Cultures*. New York: Basic Books, Inc., 1973

Gernet, Jacques. *Buddhism in Chinese Society: An Economic History from the Fifth to the Tenth Centuries*. Translated by Franciscus Verellen. New York: Columbia University Press, 1995. (Published in French in 1956.)

Ghose, Rajeshwari, ed. *In the Footsteps of the Buddha: An Iconic Journey from India to China*. Hong Kong: University Museum and Art Gallery of the University of Hong Kong, 1998.

———. "The Meeting of Minds: Buddhism as a Cross-Cultural Discourse." In *In the Footsteps of the Buddha: An Iconic Journey from India to China*, edited by Rajeshwari Ghose, 1–16. Hong Kong: University Museum and Art Gallery of the University of Hong Kong, 1998.

Ginsbord, Hannah. "Kant's Aesthetics and Teleology." *The Stanford Encyclopedia of Philosophy*, edited by Edward N. Zalta (Summer 2014 edition). http://plato.stanford.edu/archives/sum2014/entries/kant-aesthetics/.

———. "Lawfulness without a Law: Kant on the Free Play of Imagination and Understanding." *Philosophical Topics* 25, no. 1 (Spring 1997): 37–81.

Goldberg, Stephen J. "Aesthetics, Chinese." In E. Craig (ed.), *Routledge Encyclopedia of Philosophy*, edited by E. Craig. (1998). London: Routledge, 1998. http://www.rep.routledge.com/article (10 December 2012).

———. Informal lecture given to China Field Trip: On the Silk Road. Sponsored by the East-West Center, Xian, Shaanxi Province, China. July, 1997.

Goldman, Emma. *Living My Life*. New York: Alfred A. Knopf Inc., 1931. https://theanarchistlibrary.org/library/emma-goldman-living-my-life.

Gordanier, Amy. "The 'New Laws' of Wang Anshi." http://academic.reed.edu/chinese/chin-hum/claypools09/Hum%20230%20Project/new_laws.html.

Graff, David *A. Medieval Chinese Warfare, 300–900*. London: Routledge, 2002.

Graham, A. C., trans. *The Book of Lieh-tz* . London: John Murray, 1960.

———, trans. *Chuang-Tzu: The Inner Chapters*. Indianapolis, IN: Hackett Publishing Company, Inc., 2001.

———. "Reflections and Replies." In *Chinese Texts and Philosophical Contexts*, edited by Henry Rosemont, Jr. 267–322. La Salle, IL: Open Court, 1991.

———. *Two Chinese Philosophers: Ch'êng Ming-tao and Ch'êng Yi-ch'uan*. London: Lund Humphries, 1958.

———. *Yin-Yang and the Nature of Correlative Thinking*. Singapore: Institute of East Asian Philosophies. Monograph Series No. 6, 1986.

Grant, Beata. *Mount Lu Revisited: Buddhism in the Life and Writing of Su Shi*. Honolulu: University of Hawai'i Press, 1994.

Gray, John. *Straw Dogs: Thoughts on Humans and Other Animals*. New York: Farrar, Straus and Giroux, 2007.

Gregory, Peter N., and Daniel A. Getz, Jr., eds. *Buddhism in the Sung*. Honolulu: University of Hawai'i Press, 1999.

Griswold, A. B. "Prolegomena to the Study of the Buddha's Dress in Chinese Sculpture: With Particular Reference to the Rietberg Museum's Collection." *Artibus Asiae* 26, no. 2. (1963): 85–131.

Grupp, Jeffrey "The R-theory of Time, or Replacement Presentism: The Buddhist Philosophy of Time." *The Indian International Journal of Buddhist Studies* (IIJBS) 6 (2005): 51–122.

Gu Xin. "Subjectivity, Modernity, and Chinese Hegelian Marxism: A Study of Li Zehou's Philosophical Ideas from a Comparative Perspective." *Philosophy East and West* 46, no. 2 (April 1996): 205–45.

Gunther, Michael. Website. "Old Stones: The Monuments of Art History." www.art-and-archaeology.com.

Guyer, Paul. "Free and Adherent Beauty: A Modest Proposal." In *Values of Beauty: Historical Essays in Aesthetics*, 129–40. Cambridge, MA: Cambridge University Press, 2005.

———. "Kant, Immanuel." *Routledge Encyclopedia of Philosophy*. London: Routledge, (1998, 2004). http://www.rep.routledge.com/article/DB047SECT12

———. *Kant.* London: Routledge. 2006.

Habermas, Jürgen. *Between Naturalism and Religion.* Translated by Ciaran Cronin. Malden, MA: Polity Press, 2008.

Haidt, Jonathan. *The Righteous Mind.* New York: Pantheon Books, 2012.

Hall, David L., and Roger T. Ames. *Anticipating China: Thinking Through the Narratives of Chinese and Western Culture.* Albany, NY: State University of New York Press, 1995.

———. *Thinking from the Han: Self, Truth and Transcendence in Chinese and Western Culture.* Albany, NY: State University of New York Press, 1998.

———. *Thinking Through Confucius.* Albany, NY: State University of New York Press, 1987.

Hamill, Sam, trans. *Crossing the Yellow River: Three Hundred Poems from the Chinese.* Rochester, NY: BOA Editions, Ltd., 2000.

Hansen, Chad. *A Daoist Theory of Chinese Thought.* New York: Oxford University Press, 1992.

———. "Philosophy of Mind in China." In *Encyclopedia of Chinese Philosophy* edited by Antonio S. Cua. New York: Garland Publishing, 2012.

———. "Qing (Emotions) 情 in Pre-Buddhist Chinese Thought." In *Emotions in Asian Thought: A Dialogue in Comparative Philosophy*, edited by Joel Marks and Roger T. Ames. 181–203. Albany, NY: State University of New York Press, 1995.

Harrist, Robert E., Jr. "The Legacy of Bole: Physiognomy and Horses in Chinese Painting." *Artibus Asiae* 57, no. 1/ 2 (1997): 135–56.

Hartel, Herbert, and M. Laing. *Along the Ancient Silk Routes: Central Asian Art from the West Berlin State Museum.* An exhibition lent by the Museum fur Indische Kunst, Staatliche Museen Preussischer Julturbesitz Berlin, Federal Republic of Germany. New York: Metropolitan Museum of Art, 1982.

Hawkes, David, trans. *The Songs of the South (Ch'u-tz-u).* Oxford: Clarendon Press, 1959.

Hay, Jonathan. "Kubilai's Grooms." *Res: A Journal of Anthropology and Aesthetics* 17 & 18 (Spring Autumn 1989), 117–39.

Hearn, Maxwell K. *How to Read Chinese Painting.* New York: The Metropolitan Museum of Art, 2008.

Hershock, Peter D. *Chan Buddhism.* Honolulu: University of Hawai'i Press. 2005.

———. *Valuing Diversity.* Albany, NY: State University of New York Press, 2012.

Holcombe, Charles. *A History of East Asia: From the Origins of Civilization to the Twenty-First Century.* New York: Cambridge University Press, 2011

Higgins, Kathleen Marie. *Nietzsche's Zarathustra.* Philadelphia, PA: Philadelphia University Press, 1987.

Hockney, David. "A Day on the Grand Canal with the Emperor of China, or, Surface Is Illusion but So Is Depth" [VHS] (1988, 1991). Directed by Philip Hass, Program for Art on Film. New York: New York.

Hopkirk, Peter. *Foreign Devils on the Silk Road.* Amherst: The University of Massachusetts Press, 1984.

Huang, Ray. *China: A Macro History*, rev. ed. Armonk, NY: M. E. Sharpe, Inc., 1997.

I Ching [*Yijing*]. Translated by Richard Wilhelm; rendered into English by Cary F. Baynes. 3rd ed. Princeton, NJ: Princeton University Press, 1967.

James, William. *The Varieties of Religious Experience;* lectures 16 and 17. Reprint of the 1902 New York edition. Project Gutenberg, 1996. http://www.gutenberg.org./cache/epub/621/pg621.html.

Johanson, Donald. "Origins of Modern Humans: Multiregional or Out of Africa?" An ActionBioscience.org original article. (May 2001). http://www.actionbioscience.org/evolution/johanson.html.

Kipling, Rudyard. "The Sons of Martha." In *Rudyard Kipling's Verse.* Garden City, New York: Doubleday and Company, Inc., 1946.

Kant, Immanuel. *Critique of Pure Reason.* Translated by Norman Kemp Smith. London: Macmillian & Co Ltd., 1958. (First published in 1781).

———. *Fundamental Principles of the Metaphysic of Morals.* Translated by Thomas K. Abbott. Indianapolis, IN: The Bobbs-Merrill Company, Inc., 1949. (First published in 1785.)

———. *Critique of Practical Reason.* Translated by Lewis White Beck. Indianapolis, IN, and New York: The Bobbs-Merrill Company, Inc., 1956. (First published in 1788.)

———. *Critique of Judgement.* Translated by J. H. Bernard. New York: Hafner Press, 1951. (First published in 1790.)

Kao Ming. "Chu Hsi's Discipline of Propriety." In *Chu Hsi and Neo-Confucianismm*, edited by Wing-tsit Chan, 312–36. Honolulu: University of Hawai'i Press, 1986.

Koestler, Arthur. *The Invisible Writing.* New York: Henry Holt & Co., 1984.

Koutouzis, Philippe. "Introduction" to *Body & nature: two Chinese artists*, 2–3. Edited by Wang Keping, and Jeng Jundian, 2–3. New York: Marlborough Chelsea, 2004.

Laozi [Lao-Tzu]. *Tao Te Ching* [*Daodejing*]. Translated by Stephen Addiss and Stanley Lombardo. Indianapolis, IN: Hackett Publishing Company, 1993.

Langer, Susanne K. *Philosophy in a New Key.* New York: Mentor Book, 1951.

Laumakis, Stephen J. *An Introduction to Buddhist Philosophy.* Cambridge, UK: Cambridge University Press, 2008.

Lee, Joseph J. "Tu Fu's Art Criticism and Han Kan's Horse painting." *Journal of the American Oriental Society* 90, no. 3 (July–Sept. 1970): 449–61,

Legge, James, trans., *The She King* (*Shijing*). 2nd ed. Volume 4 of *The Chinese Classics.* Hong Kong: Hong Kong University Press, 1960.

Li Chenyang. "The Confucian Ideal of Harmony." *Philosophy East and West* 56, no. 4 (2006): 583–603.

Li Chu-Tsing. "The Freer *Sheep and Goat* and Chao Meng-Fu's Horse Paintings." *Artibus Asiae* 30, no. 4, (1968): 279–332.

Li Wai-yee. "Between 'Literary Mind' and 'Carving Dragons': Order and Excess in *Wenxin Diaolong*." In *A Chinese Literary Mind: Culture, Creativity, and Rhetoric in* Wenxin Diaolong, edited by CAI Zong-qi, 193–226. Redwood City, CA: Stanford University Press, 2001.

Li Zehou. *The Chinese Aesthetic Tradition.* Translated by Maija Bell Samei. Honolulu: University of Hawai'i Press, 2010.

———. "An Outline of the Origin of Humankind." Translated by Peter Wong Yih Ziun. *Contemporary Chinese Thought* 31, no. 2 (Winter 1999–2000): 20–25. Originally published in *Li Zehou zhexue meixue wenxuan* [Collected Writings by Li Zehou on Philosophy and Aesthetics], Changsha: Hunan renmin chubanshe, 1985.

———. *The Path of Beauty: A Study of Chinese Aesthetics*. Translated by Gong Lizeng. Hong Kong: Oxford University Press, 1994.

———. "The Philosophy of Kant and a Theory of Subjectivity." *Analecta Husserliana* 21 (1986): 135–49.

———. "A Re-evaluation of Confucius." Translated by Liu Qizhong. *Social Sciences in China* 2, no. 1 (1980): 99–127.

———. *A Study on Marxism in China*. Hong Kong: Joint Publishing (H. K.) Co., Ltd., 1993.

———. "Some Thoughts on Neo-Confucianism." Translated by Gou Da. *Social Sciences in China* 3, no. 4 (1982): 155–89.

———. "Some Tentative Remarks on China's Wisdom (Excerpts)." Translated by Peter Wong Yih Ziun and edited by Professor Li Zehou. *Contemporary Chinese Thought* 31, no 2. (Winter 1999–2000): 44–61. From the Chinese text: "Shitan Zhongguo de zhihui," in *Zhongguo gudai sixiangshi lun*. Beijing: Remin chubanshe, 1985: 299–322.

———. "The Western Is the Substance, and the Chinese Is for Application." Translated by Peter Wong Yih Jiun. *Contemporary Chinese Thought* 31, no. 2 (Winter 1999–2000): 32–39. From the Chinese text: "Manshuo Xiti Zhongyoung," in *Zhongguo xiandia sixiang shi lun*. Beijing: Dongfang chubanshe, 1987).

Li Zehou, and Jane Cauvel. *Four Essays On Aesthetics: Toward a Global View*. Lanham, MD, Boulder, CO, New York, Toronto, Oxford: Lexington Books: A Division of Roman & Littlefield, Publishers, Inc., 2006.

Lin Shuen-fu. "Liu Xie on Imagination." In *A Chinese Literary Mind: Culture, Creativity, and Rhetoric in* Wenxin Diaolong, edited by Cai Zong-qi, 127–60. Redwood City, CA: Stanford University Press, 2001.

Lin Tongqi, and Li Minghua. "Subjectivity: Marxism and 'The Spiritual' in China since Mao." *Philosophy East and West* 44 no. 4 (October 1994): 609–46.

Lin Ying. *Celestial Horses: The Apogee of Chinese Art and Civilization*, bilingual ed. Beijing: Foreign Language Press, 2002.

Lin Yutang. *The Gay Genius: The Life and Times of Su Tung po*. Westport, CT: Greenwood Press, 1971.

Little, Stephen. *New Songs on Ancient Tunes: 19th–20th Century Chinese Paintings and Calligraphy from the Richard Fabian Collection*. Honolulu: Honolulu Academy of Arts, 2007.

Liu, James T. C. *Reform in Sung China: Wang An-shih (1021–1086) and his New Policies*. Cambridge, MA: Harvard University Press, 1959.

Liu Xie. *Dragon-Carving and the Literary Mind*. 2 vols., bilingual ed. Translated by Yang Guobin. Beijing: Foreign Language and Research Press, 2003.

Littlejohn, Ronnie. "Daoist Philosophy," *The Internet Encyclopedia of Philosophy*, ISSN 2161-0002, http://www.iep.utm.edu/daoism/, Januaray 29, 2013.

Loewe, Michael. *Ways to Paradise: The Chinese Quest for Immortality*. London: George Allen & Unwin, 1979.

Lorch, Donatella, "The A-Team: On Patrol with the Special Forces." *Newsweek*, January 14, 2002: 20–25.

Lynn, Richard John. "Chu Hsi a Literary Theorist and Critic." In *Chu Hsi and Neo-Confucianism* edited by Wing-tsit Chan, 337–54. Honolulu: University of Hawai'i Press, 1986.

Makeham, John, ed. *New Confucianism: A Critical Examination*. New York: Palgrave Macmillan, 2003.

Mair, Victor H. "Buddhism in *The Literary Mind and Ornate Rhetoric*." In *A Chinese Literary Mind: Culture, Creativity, and Rhetoric in* Wenxin Diaolong, edited by Cai Zong-qi, 63–81. Redwood City, CA: Stanford University Press, 2001.

———, ed. *The Columbia Anthology of Traditional Chinese Literature*. New York: Columbia University Press, 1994.

———. "What is *Geyi*, After All?" In *Philosophy and Religion in Early Medieval China*, edited by Alan K. L. Chan, 226–64. Albany, NY: State University of New York Press, 2010,

———. "Xie He's 'Six Laws' of Painting and Their Indian Parallels." In *Chinese Aesthetics: The Ordering of Literature, the Arts, and the Universe in the Six Dynasties*, edited by Cai Zong-qi. 81–122. Honolulu: University of Hawai'i Press, 2004.

Mao Zedong. "Yenan Forum on Literature and Art." In *Selected Works of Mao Tse-tung*, vol. 3, 69–98, Peking: Foreign Languages Press, 1967.

Marx, Karl. *Economic and Philosophical Manuscripts of 1844*. In *The Marx-Engels Reader*. 2nd ed. Edited by Robert C. Tucker, 66–125. New York: W. W. Norton & Company, 1978.

———. *The Eighteenth Brumaire of Louis Bonaparte*. In *The Marx-Engels Reader*, 2nd ed. Edited by Robert C. Tucker, 594–617. New York: W. W. Norton & Company, 1978.

———. *The German Ideology: Part I*. In *The Marx-Engels Reader*, 2nd ed. Edited by Robert C. Tucker, 146–200. New York: W. W. Norton & Company, 1978.

———. *Theses on Feurerbach*. In *The Marx-Engels Reader*, 2nd ed. Edited by Robert C. Tucker, 143–45. New York: W. W. Norton & Company, 1978.

Mather, Richard B. "Chinese and Indian Perceptions of Each Other between the First and Seventh Centuries." *Journal of the American Oriental Society* 112, no. 1 (1992):1–8.

Massaki, Itakura. "The Words and Images Surrounding The Ode on the Red Cliff—with Qiao Zhongchang's Handscroll of the Second Red Cliff Text as an Example." Paper presented at Taiwan 2002 Conference on the History of Painting in East Asia. October 4–7, 2002.

McGinness, B. F. "The Mysticism of the 'Tractatus.'" *Philosophical Review* 75, no. 3 (July 1966): 305–28.

McNair, Amy. *Donors of Longmen: Faith, Politics, and Patronage in Medieval Chinese Buddhist Sculpture*. Honolulu: University of Hawai'i Press, 2007.

———. "Texts of Taoism and Buddhism and the Power of Calligraphic Style." In *The Embodied Image: Chinese Calligraphy from the John B. Elliott Collection*. Edited by Robert E. Harrist, Jr. and Wen C. Fong, 224–39. Princeton, NJ: The Art Museum, Princeton University, 1999.

McRae, John R., trans. *The Vimalakīrti Sutra*. Berkeley, CA: Numata Center for Buddhist Translation and Research, 2004. https://www.bdkamerica.org/digital/dBET_Srimala_Vimalakirti_2004.pdf.

Mencius. *Mencius*. Translated by D. C. Lau Trans. New York: Penguin Books, 1970.

Metropolitan Museum of Art. "Night Shining White." *The Collection On line*. http://www.metmuseum.org/collection/the-collection-online/search/39901.

Mullarkey, Maureen. "Mullarkey Replies." *The Nation*, March 6, 1989, 290 and 320.

National Palace Museum Staff (*Guo li gu gong bo wu yuan*). *Special Exhibition of Horse Painting*. Taibei: Government publication, 1990.

Neville, Robert Cummings. *Boston Confucianism: Portable Tradition in the Late-Modern World*. Albany, NY: State University of New York Press, 2000.

Nietzsche, Friedrich. "Thus Spoke Zarathustra." In *The Portable Nietzsche*. Edited and translated by Walter Kaufmann, 103–439. New York: Penguin Books. 1986.

Ning Qiang. "The Emergence of the 'Dunhuang Style' in the Northern Wei Dynasty." *Orientations* 23, no 5 (May, 1992):45–48.

Obenchain, Diane B. "Introduction to Feng Youlan: Something Exists." *Journal of Chinese Philosophy* 21 nos. 3/4 (September/December 1994): i–cxii.

"Oldowan and Acheulean Stone Tools." Museum of Anthropology, University of Missouri. http://anthromuseum.missouri.edu/minigalleries/handaxes/intro.shtml

Oppenheimer, Mark. "Examining the Growth of the 'Spiritual but Not Religious.'" *New York Times*, July 18, 2014. http://www.nytimes.com/2014/07/19/us/examining-the-growth-of-the-spiritual-but-not-religious.

"Origin of language." Wikipedia, the free encyclopedia WEB (accessed January 19, 2012).

Overmyer, Daniel L. *Folk Buddhist Religion: Dissenting Sects in Late Traditional China.* Cambridge, MA: Harvard University Press, 1976.

Owen, Stephen, ed. and trans. *An Anthology of Chinese Literature: Beginnings to 1911*. New York: W. W. Norton & Company, 1996.

———. *Readings in Chinese Literary Thought*. Cambridge, MA: Harvard University Press, 1992.

Pears, Robert. "Top Earners Doubled Share of Nation's Income, Study Finds." *New York Times*, October 25, 2011. http://www.nytimes.com/2011/10/26/us/politics/top-earners-doubled-share-of-nations-income-cbo-says.html?_r=1.

Perkins, Franklin. "Motivation and the Heart in the Xing Zi Chu." *Dao: A Journal of Comparative Philosophy* 8 no. 2 (June 2009):117–31.

Prior, Arthur. *Past, Present and Future.* Oxford: Clarendon Press, 1967.

Pulleyblank, Edwin G. "Liu K'o, a Forgotten Rival of Han Yu." In *Essays on Tang and Pre-Tang China*, 145–60. Burlington, VT: Ashgate, 2001.

Putnam, Hillary. "The Meaning of 'Meaning.'" In *The Twin Earth Chronicles*. Edited by Andrew Pessin and Sanford Goldberg, 3–52. Armonk, NY: M. E. Sharpe, 1996.

Quine, Willard Van Orman. "Mr. Strawson on Logical Theory." *Mind* 62 no. 248. (Oct. 1953): 433–51.

Rhie, Marylin Martin. *Early Buddhist Art of China & Central Asia*. Vol. 2. Leiden: Brill, 2002.

Rosemont, Henry, Jr. *Against Individualism*. Lanham, MD: Lexington Books, 2015.

———. "On the 'New Confucians.'" In *The Analects (Norton Critical Editions)*. Edited by Michael Nylan, 259–71. New York: W. W. Norton & Company, 2013.

———. *Rationality and Religious Experience*. Peru, IL: Open Court Publishing Company, 2001.

Roth, Harold D. "Bimodal Mystical Experience in the 'Qiwulun' 齊物論 Chapter of Zhuangzi." *Journal of Chinese Religions* 28 (2009): 31–50.

Russell, Bertrand, 1935, "Mysticism" In *Religion and Science.* London: Oxford University Press.

Sagan, Carl. *Cosmos*. New York: Random House, 1980.

Saussy, Haun. *The Problem of a Chinese Aesthetic*. Redwood City, CA: Stanford University Press, 1993.

Schaper, Eva. "Taste, Sublimity, and Genius: The Aesthetics of Nature and Art." In *The Cambridge Companion to Kant*. Edited by Paul Guyer, 367–93. Cambridge, UK: Cambridge University Press, 1992.

Schirokauer, Conrad. "Chu Hsi and Hu Hung." In *Chu Hsi and Neo-Confucianism*. Edited by Chan Wing-tsit, 480–502. Honolulu: University of Hawai'i Press, 1986.

Schmidt, Stephan. "Mou Zongsan, Hegel, and Kant: The Quest for Confucian Modernity." *Philosophy East and West* 61 no. 2 (April 2011): 260–302

Schoenemann, P. Thomas "Research on the evolution of brain and language." Lecture presented at DePauw University, Greencastle, IN, November 16, 2011.

Sells, Michael A. *Mystical Languages of Unsaying.* Chicago: University of Chicago Press, 1994.

Shao Yiyang. "Why Realism? From Social Realism to Neo-Realism in Modern Chinese Art (Part I)." CAFA Art Info. 25 October 2011. http://en.cafa.com.cn/why-realism-from-social-realism-to-neo-realism-in-modern-chinese-art-part-i.html (August 22, 2012).

Shih, Vincent Yu-chung, trans. *The Literary Mind and the Carving of Dragons* by Liu Xie. Taipei: Chung Hwa Book Company, Ltd., 1975.

Shrader, Douglas W. "Seven Characteristics of Mystical Experiences." *Proceedings of the 6th Annual Hawaii International Conference on Arts and Humanities.* Honolulu, 2008.

Silbergeld, Jerome. "Commentary on James Cahill's 'Chinese Art and Authenticity.'" *American Academy of Arts and Sciences Bulletin* 55, no. 1 (Fall 2001): 31–35.

Sima Qian. *Records of the Grand Historian: Han Dynasty Volume II.* Rev. ed. Translated by Burton Watson. Hong Kong: Columbia University Press, 1992.

Solomon, Robert C. "Some Notes on Emotion, 'East and West.'" *Philosophy East and West* 45 no. 2 (1995): 171–202.

Soper, Alexander. "The First Two Laws of Hsieh Ho." *Far Eastern Quarterly* 8 (1949): 412–23.

Spring, Madeline K. *Animal Allegories in T'ang China.* New Haven, CT: American Oriental Society, 1993.

Stace, W. T. *Mysticism and Philosophy*. Philadelphia, PA: J. B. Lippincott Company, 1960.

Stanton, Doug. *Horse Soldiers*. New York: Scribner, 2009.

Su, Anna. *Confucianism as a World Religion: Contested Histories and Contemporary Realities*. Princeton, NJ: Princeton University Press, 2013

Su Shi (Su Dongpo). "Nien nu Chiao—Battle of Red Cliff." Translator not given. http://www.chinapage.com/poet-e/sushi2e.htm.

———. "Red Cliff Rhapsodies, 1 and 2." Translated with notes by Richard Strassberg. In *The Columbia Anthology of Traditional Chinese Literature*, edited by Victor Maier, 438–42. New York: Columbia University Press, 1994.

———. *Selected Poems of Su Tung-Po.* Translated by Burton Watson. Port Townsend, WA: Copper Canyon Press, 1994.

Sullivan, Michael. *Art and Artists of Twentieth Century China.* Berkeley: University of California Press, 1996.

———. *The Arts of China.* 5th ed. revised and expanded. Berkeley: University of California Press, 2008.

———. "Some Thoughts about Wang Huaiqing." 2002. http://wanghuaiqing.artron.net/news_2.php?newid=28135&aid=A0000050.

Sun, Anna. *Confucianism as a World Religion: Contested Histories and Contemporary Realities*. Princeton, NJ: Princeton University Press, 2013.

Sung Hou-mei. *Decoded Messages: The Symbolic Language of Chinese Animal Painting*. New Haven, CT: Yale University Press, 2009.

Tang Yijie. *Confucianism, Buddhism, Daoism, Christianity and Chinese Culture*. Peking: Council for Research in Values and Philosophy, 1991. http://books.goooble.com/books?id=ZnNveOjlJ8YC&pg.

———. "Emotion in Pre-Qin Ruist moral theory: An Explanation of 'Dao begins in Qing.'" Translated by Brian Bruya and Hai-ming Wen. *Philosophy East and West* 53, no. 2 (April 2003): 271–81.

Tang Yung-tung. "On 'Ko-yi,' The Earliest Method by which Indian Buddhism and Chinese Thought Were Synthesized." In *Radhakrishnan: Comparative Studies in Philosophy*. New York: Harper, 1951.

Tanner, Michael, "Sentimentality." In *Art and Morality*, edited by José Luis Bermúdez and Sebastian Gardner, 95–110. London and New York: Routledge, 2003.

Tao Qian. *The Selected Poems of T'ao Ch'ien*. Translated by David Hinton. Port Townsend, WA: Copper Canyon Press, 1993.

Temple, Robert. *The Genius of China: 3,000 Years of Science, Discovery, and Invention*. Introduction by Joseph Needham. New York: Simon and Schuster, 1986.

Thurman, Robert A. F., trans. *The Holy Teaching of Virmalakīrti: A Mahāyāna Scripture*. University Park, PA: The Pennsylvania State University Press, 2006.

Tian Chenshan. "Tongbian in the Chinese Reading of Dialectical Materialism." *Philosophy East and West* 52 no. 1 (2002): 126–44.

Tian Chenshan. *Chinese Dialectics: From Yijing to Marxism*. Lanham, MD: Lexington Books, 2005

Tian Xiaofei. *Tao Yuanming & Manuscript Culture: The Record of a Dusty Table*. Seattle: University of Washington Press, 2005.

Tillman, Hoyt Cleveland. "A New Direction in Confucian Scholarship: Approaches to Examining the Differences between Neo-Confucianism and *Tao-hsűeh*." *Philosophy East and West* 42 no. 3 (July 1992): 455–74.

Tomasello, Michael. *The Cultural Origins of Human Cognition*. Cambridge, MA: Harvard University Press, 1999.

Tsiang, Katherine. "Changing patterns of divinity and reform in the late Northern Wei." *The Art Bulletin* 84, no. 2 (June, 2002): 222–45.

Tsukamoto, Zenryu. *A History of Early Chinese Buddhism from Its Introduction to the Death of Hui-yüan*, vol. 1. Translated by Leon Hurvitz. Tokyo, New York, San Francisco: Kodansha International Ltd., 1985.

Treitler, Leo. "Language and the Interpretation of Music." In *Music and Meaning*, edited by Jenefer Robinson, 23–82, Ithaca, NY: Cornell University Press, 1997.

Tsao Hsingyuan. "Reading and Misreading: Double Entendre in Locally Oriented Logos." In *Xu Bing and Contemporary Chinese Art*. Edited by Hsingyuan Tsan and Roger T. Ames, 1–32. Albany, NY: State University of New York Press, 2011.

Tu Xiaofei. "Dare to Compare: The Comparative Philosophy of Mou Zongsan." *Kritike* 1 no. 2. December 2007: 24–35. http://www.kritike.org/volume-1-2.html.

Tucker, Robert C., ed. *The Marx-Engels Reader*, 2nd ed. New York and London: W. W. Norton & Company, 1978.

UNESCO. World Water Day 2013. Accessed April 7, 2016. http://www.unwater.org/water-cooperation-2013/water-cooperation/facts-and-figures/en/.

Utz, David A. "Aršak, Parthian Buddhists, and 'Iranian' Buddhism." In *Buddhism Across Boundaries—Chinese Buddhism and the Western Regions*, edited by John R. McRae and Jan Nattier, 421–47. Fo Guang Shan Foundation for Buddhist and Culture Education, 1999.

van Gulik, Robert Hans. *Siddham: An Essay on the History of Sanskrit Studies in China and Japan*. Nagpur: International Academy of Indian Culture, Nagpur.

Waley, Arthur. "The Heavenly Horses of Ferghana: A New View." *History Today* 5 no. 2. (February, 1955): 95–103.

WANG Anshi. "*From Ten-Thousand-Word Memorial* 1058." http://classroom.kleinisd.net/webs/tbonar/upload/memoria3.pdf (March 9, 2011).

WANG Keping. "Appreciating nature in view of practical aesthetics." *Frontiers of Philosophy in China* 2007, 2(1):140–49

Watson, Burton, trans. *Chuang-Tzu: Basic Writings*. New York: Columbia University Press, 1964.

———, trans. *Selected Poems of Su Tung-Po*. Port Townsend, WA: Copper Canyon Press, 1994.

Weinberg, Steven. *The First Three Minutes*. New Yor: Basic Books, 1993.

Whitfield, Roderick. *Dunhuang: Caves of the Dinging Sands: Buddhist Art from the Silk Road*. London: Textile & Art Publications, 1995.

WHO. "Controlling the global obesity epidemic." Accessed April 7, 2016. http://www.who.int/nutrition/topics/obesity/en/.

Whorf, Benjamin Lee. "An American Indian Model of the Universe" (ca. 1936). In *Language, Thought and Reality: Selected writings of Benjamin Lee Whorf*, edited by John B. Carroll, 57–64. New York: The Technology Press of Massachusetts Institute of Technology and John Wiley & Sons, Inc., 1956.

Wittgenstein, Ludwig. *On Certainty*. Edited by G. E. M. Anscombe and G. H. von Wright. Translated by Denis Paul and G. E. M. Anscombe. New York: Harper & Row Publishers, 1969.

———. *Tractatus Logico-Philosophicus*. Translated by C. K. Ogden and Frank P. Ramsey. First English edition published in 1922. London: Kegan Paul.

———. *Tractatus Logico-Philosophicus*, 2nd edition of this translation. Translated by D. F. Pears and B. F. McGuinness. London and New York: Routledge & Kegan, 1971.

———. *On Certainty*. Edited by G. E. M. Anscombe and G. H. von Wright. Translated by Denis Paul and G. E. M. Anscombe. New York: Harper & Row Publishers, 1969.

Wood, James. "Is That All There Is? Secularism and Its Discontents." *The New Yorker* (August 15, 2011). http://www.newyorker.com/magazine/2011/08/15/is-that-all-there-is.

Woodhouse, Mark. "On the Possibility of Pure Consciousness." In *The Problem of Pure Consciousness: Mysticism and Philosophy*, edited by Robert K. C. Forman, 254–68. New York: Oxford University Press, 1990.

Wright, Arthur F. "Buddhism and Chinese Culture." In *Studies in Chinese Buddhism*, edited by Robert M. Sommers, 1–32. New Haven, CT: Yale University Press, 1990.

———. *Buddhism in Chinese History*. Redwood City, CA: Stanford University Press, 1959.

———. "Fo-t'u-teng: A Biography." *Harvard Journal of Asiatic Studies* 11, no. 3/4 (December, 1948): 321–71.

Wu Hung "Where are they going? Where did they come from: Hearse and 'Soul-carriage' in Han Dynasty Tomb Art." *Orientations* 29 no. 6 (1998): 22–31.

Wu, Marshall P. S. *The Orchid Pavilion Gathering: Chinese Painting from the University of Michigan Museum of Art. Chinese Painting from the University of Michigan Museum of Art.* 2 vols. Ann Arbor: University of Michigan, 2000.

Xiao Changyan. "Lots of bargains but few buyers in store." *China Dail,* November 11, 2008. http://www.chinadaily.com.cn/cndy/2008-11/20/content_7222162.htm.

Yanal, Robert J. "The Institutional Theory of Art." In *The Encyclopedia of Aesthetics*, edited by Michael Kelly, 508–12. New York: Oxford University Press, 1998.

Yang, Guobin. "Introduction" to Liu Xie. *Dragon-Carving and the Literary Mind.* 2 vols., bilingual ed. Translated by Yang Guobin. Beijing: Foreign Language and Research Press, 2003.

Yang Lu. "Narrative and Historicity in the Buddhist Biographies of Early Medieval China: The Case of Kumarajiva," accessed December 20, 2013, http://www2.ihp.sinica.edu.tw/file/1464kwiaSfk.pdf.

Yang Xiaoneng, ed. *The Golden Age of Chinese Archaeology: Celebrated Discoveries from the People's Republic of China.* Washington, DC: The National Gallery of Art, 1999.

Zangwill, Nick. "Aesthetic Judgment." *The Stanford Encyclopedia of Philosophy*, edited by Edward N. Zalta (Summer 2013 edition), http://plato.stanford.edu/archives/sum2013/entries/aesthetic-judgment/.

Zhuangzi. *Chuang Tzu: Basic Writings*. Translated by Burton Watson. New York: Columbia University Press, 1964, 1996.

Zürcher, Erik. *The Buddhist Conquest of China*. Leiden: E. J. Brill, 1959.

Index

Note: Page numbers in italics indicate illustrations.

www.ingramcontent.com/pod-product-compliance
Lightning Source LLC
La Vergne TN
LVHW101547020926
846999LV00029B/258
* 9 7 8 1 4 3 8 4 6 6 5 8 3 *